MORGAN AND DEESE'S CLASSIC
HANDBOOK FOR STUDENTS

HOW TO STUDY

Third Edition revised by

James Deese
Ellin K. Deese

McGRAW-HILL BOOK COMPANY
New York St. Louis San Francisco Auckland Bogotá
Düsseldorf Johannesburg London Madrid Mexico
Montreal New Delhi Panamá Paris São Paulo
Singapore Sydney Tokyo Toronto

First McGraw-Hill Paperback edition, 1957
Second McGraw-Hill Paperback edition, 1969
Third McGraw-Hill Paperback edition, 1979

1 2 3 4 5 6 7 8 9 0M U M U7 8 3 2 1 0 9

LIBRARY OF CONGRESS CATALOGING IN PUBLICATION DATA
Morgan, Clifford Thomas.
    How to study.
    Includes index.
    1. Study, Method of.   I. Deese, James Earle,
joint author.   II. Deese, Ellin K.,
joint author.   III. Title.
LB1049.M68 1979   371.3'02812   79-12014
ISBN 0-07-043115-9

Book design by Elliot Epstein

CONTENTS

iii

PREFACE

Knowing how to study efficiently doesn't come naturally. Even students who are eager to learn and who want to do well in college don't always know what to do. They may not know how much to study or how to distribute their time wisely. Many students don't know how to read a textbook, particularly the kinds of textbooks they are likely to encounter in college. They don't know how to absorb and remember information from lectures. Indeed, they may not be prepared for the lecture style of teaching at all.

Furthermore, many potentially good students are deficient in basic skills; they may not be able to read well enough for college-level material. They may have only the vaguest notions about English grammar. And many students have trouble putting their ideas into words in such a way that other people can understand them. Large numbers of students fear and avoid mathematics and science.

Still others have sufficient preparation and are good at studying but don't know some particular things essential for success in college. They may not know, for example, how to use all of the resources of the college library.

This book is intended for all of these students. It is for students still in high school intending to go on to college, for students entering college, for older people returning to college, and even for students who aren't ready for college yet.

We have made some points by recounting brief case histories of students and their problems. These are all drawn from life, though of course the details have been altered. One or more of them may ring a bell for you. If so, we hope that you will find something that will help you over your particular difficulties.

This book is a practical guide to studying. It tells you how to plan for and use time, how to get the most out of textbooks, how to make and outline notes, and how to prepare for and take examinations. It also gives directions for dealing with foreign languages, the sciences, and mathematics. It tells you how to write papers and reports, and it tells you what you can do to improve your use of language and your ability to read.

It is never too late to improve your study skills and hardly ever too early to begin. If you are a high school student planning to continue your studies beyond high school, you should master the techniques presented here. Use the book to evaluate your study skills and to help you decide whether you have the motivation to face a difficult academic program. Your parents might want to read the book or portions of it, too. It may help them to appreciate some of the problems you are up against.

This edition, we believe, is an improvement over the previous ones. Students and colleges change, and we have altered the book to accommodate these changes. We have improved various sections as the result of advice from critics and students. We particularly wish to thank Natalie K. Moyle and Joan E. Gore, both of the University of Virginia, for critical readings of particular chapters. Several anonymous reviewers provided us with invaluable insights into weak points of the previous edition.

James Deese
Ellin K. Deese

WHY GO TO COLLEGE?

Going to college is one of the good things of American life. Turn-of-the-century books such as *Dink Stover at Yale,* Hollywood musicals of the thirties, and even TV series portray college as one of the best times of life, a time when exuberant young people come together for fun and the adventure of learning. Even though that image is now tarnished a bit by the explosive growth in colleges and by the intense competition among college students for getting into professional schools, it is still there. Many people blossom socially for the first time in college. For most Americans, it is the first time they are really challenged by ideas. It is the time of the end of growing up and the beginning of adult life. It is the time many people look back on as the most exciting, significant, and enjoyable in their lives.

Perhaps because going to college is so much a part of the American dream, many people go for no particular reason. Some go because their parents expect it, others because it is what their friends are doing. Then, there is the belief that a college degree will automatically ensure a good job and high pay.

Some students drift through four years, attending classes, or skipping them as the case may be, reading only what can't be avoided, looking for "gut" courses, and never being touched or changed in any important way. For a few of these people, college provides no satisfaction, yet because of parental or peer pressure, they cannot voluntarily leave. They stop trying in the hope that their teachers will make the decision for them by failing them.

To put it bluntly, unless you are willing to make your college years count, you might be better off doing something else. Not everyone should attend college, nor should everyone who does attend begin right after high school. Many college students profit greatly from taking a year or so off. A year out in the world helps some people to sort out their priorities and goals. If you are really going to get something out of going to college, you have to make it mean something, and to do that you must have some idea why you are there, what you hope to get out of it, and perhaps even what you hope to become.

EVALUATING YOUR PRIORITIES

Put yourself in the position of a high school student wondering whether or not he ought to go to college, or an older person trying to decide whether to return to college, or even in the fix of a college student trying to decide whether she should stick it out or not. If you think about it, you will realize that these are the kinds

CHAPTER ONE

GETTING OFF TO A GOOD START

1

of situations in which you need the most thorough self-examination.

Are you interested in ideas, books, science, or art? You don't have to have the enthusiasm of a specialist in some subject to enjoy it and profit from its study, but if you would rather be repairing machines than studying, maybe you had better give a thought to what you are doing. There are a lot of good occupations that don't require a college education. Furthermore, people often develop an interest in ideas, books, and intellectual pursuits when they have been out of school for a while.

High school is not the kind of place where many students develop intellectual interests. Take Bill. He finished high school with satisfactory grades and very high SAT scores. He would have been a good prospect for many selective colleges. Wisely, however, he saw that he wasn't at that point interested in learning from books. He liked working with his hands, and he liked being out of doors. His father was a physician, so you can imagine that he was under a lot of pressure to go to college. But he managed to weather the pressure, and he got himself a construction job. There he discovered that he had a real talent for carpentry. He began doing free-lance cabinetry work and made a success of it. After five years he found himself developing an interest in science. The kinds of books that had bored him in high school now were interesting. He went into bookstores and bought books on physics, the weather, and chemistry. It dawned on him that there were a lot of exciting occupations in which he could combine his love of doing things with his hands with intellectual pursuits. By the time he applied for college at age twenty-three, his goals were clear, and he had a strong urge to do well. The four years he spent as an undergraduate were happy and productive. He graduated with honors, and he ended up doing top-notch work in the medical school where his father had gone. For Bill and for a lot of other students, taking a break between high school and college was the right thing to do.

One of the things Bill did was to think a lot about what he was interested in during his last year of high school. Many students need to do that, but in addition, they need to take stock of their abilities. College requires abilities that are sometimes not touched at all in high school or at best are underused. A lot of studies tell us students tend to overrate themselves on those kinds of traits and skills that make for success in college. One of the most important things you can do is to make an honest appraisal of your strengths and weaknesses. You will find a table on page 3, which you can use to rate your traits and abilities. This will help you make such an appraisal.

Check where you honestly think you stand on the traits and abilities listed. Discuss your ratings with people who really know you well—your friends, counselors, teachers—people who can tell you where you might have overestimated or underestimated yourself.

Most students take standardized tests in school. If you can learn your scores, you can use them to evaluate yourself. In doing so, take into account the people who take a particular test and who establish the norms for it. You may have scored on some test, for example, at the 90th percentile for high school seniors. That means that you scored better than 90 percent of the students who took the test. Remember, however, that not all high school seniors go on to college. For those students who actually go on to college, you might have scored at only the 50th percentile. Because some colleges are more selective than others, you might find that the same score puts you only at the 30th percentile among the entering freshmen at the college of your choice. The meaning of a score is usually relative to the population in which you find yourself. When evaluating your abilities, you need to take into account what kind of college you are at, or plan to attend.

Usually, your college's counseling service or your high school counselors can help you evaluate your test scores accurately. Nearly every college has a counseling center for interviewing, testing, and counseling students about their academic and personal problems. Trained counselors know not only how to give and interpret tests but also how to put together a total picture of your academic and personal qualifications. Remember that tests by themselves are not infallible, and they always need to be interpreted. Counselors are aware of this and know how to put your test scores in their proper context.

EXAMINING ALTERNATIVES

To sum up: Going to college or staying in college once you are there are not your only alternatives. You might want to enter the job market right after high school. If you have a particular aptitude for, or you want to learn, a particular trade, you can go into a vocational training or apprenticeship program. Postponing college for a definite—or indefinite—period of years is increasingly popular among high school graduates. Even jobs that are temporary and not particularly interesting may help develop personal maturity that will make college more meaningful later on. And if you are in college and feel that you are only marking time, see your dean or advisor about the possibility of a leave of absence. Most colleges have flexible leave policies.

SELF-RATING OF TRAITS AND ABILITIES

In the spaces below, check where you honestly think you stand on the traits and abilities listed. After you have done that, discuss your ratings with some other people who know you really well—students, friends, parents, counselors—and who might show you where you have overestimated or underestimated yourself.

In my college, I think I am in the—

Upper fifth	Middle three-fifths	Lower fifth	
			in speed of reading textbooks
			in ability to understand textbooks
			in ability to take notes
			in general preparation for college
			in amount of time I study
			in not wasting time
			in work habits
			in vocabulary (words I know and use)
			in grammar and punctuation
			in spelling
			in mathematical skills

Students and parents often get upset about any departure from the traditional sequence of high school, college, and then graduate or professional school. They tend to think that this is all just preparation for life and that it should be gotten through as quickly as possible. But we don't just prepare for life, we live it. We live it from the moment we are born to the day we die. The trick is to live it well—responsibly, productively, happily, meaningfully. Everyone is different. People do not develop at the same rate. Some experiences are wasted at one stage and significant at another. If college is right for you now, fine. If not, postpone or interrupt your education, or find out what you can do to make it better. In the next few pages we will deal with some of the things that might help make it better for you.

WHAT TO EXPECT

There are more than 2,600 colleges and universities in the United States, and no two are exactly alike. Some serve mainly local students; others have national and international student bodies. Many have fewer than 1,000 students, and there are some with more than 45,000 students. Some are private, some public. Some are four-year, some two-year, and some four-year with affiliated graduate and professional schools. Some are church-related and others nonsectarian. Some are very hard to get into, while others will take any high school graduate. If you are still facing a choice of a college, you might want to consult one of the books that describes each institution. These books are available in any bookstore, and they are brought up to date each year. College counselors in high schools make frequent use of them. A decision as to which institution to attend may depend upon cost, distance from home, size, programs offered, and whether it will offer the kind of social life you want. Whatever your decision is or has been, you should remember that no institution is perfect. Problems you may have had in high school aren't going to disappear because you are in college. Furthermore, college life means a new set of demands.

LIVING ARRANGEMENTS

Living at Home. If you are attending a local college, especially one without residence halls, you will probably live at home and commute to classes. This arrangement has a lot of advantages. It is cheaper. It provides a comfortable and familiar setting, and it means you'll get the kind of home cooking you are used to instead of the monotony that characterizes even the best institutional food.

However, commuting students need to go out of their way to become involved in the life of their college and to take special steps to meet their fellow students. Often, this means seeking out those kinds of college functions designed to introduce students to one another. It means a certain amount of initiative on your part in seeking out and talking to people in your classes whom you think you might like.

One problem that commuting students sometimes face is their parents' unwillingness to recognize that they are adults. The transition from high school to college is a big one, and if you live at home you need to develop the same kind of independence you would have if you were living away. Home rules that might have been appropriate when you were in high school don't apply. If your parents are reluctant to renegotiate, you can speed the process along by letting your behavior show that you have the responsibility that goes with maturity. Parents are more willing to acknowledge their children as adults when they behave like adults. If, however, there is so much friction at home that it interferes with your academic work, you might want to consider sharing an apartment with one or more friends. Sometimes this is a happy solution when family tensions make everyone miserable.

Living in a Dormitory. If you have decided to attend a college away from home, the odds are that you will spend at least your freshman year in a dormitory. For some students, dormitory life is the greatest thing ever; others find it less to their liking. Not all dormitories are alike. Some consist of suites of four or five rooms which share a common living room, while others consist of individual rooms, usually shared by two students, opening onto a corridor. Some contain complete apartments for four to six persons, often in a high-rise building. Probably the most common arrangement is a double room, and that means a roommate. Students who have their own room at home and are used to a lot of privacy sometimes find it difficult to adapt to living with someone else. Usually college housing offices try to match people with similar interests and values, but they don't always succeed. And even when people are well matched, a certain amount of give-and-take is necessary.

Many roommates, even when randomly matched, become close friends, and most get along well enough through the year. But in a few cases, hostility springs up almost from the beginning. If you have a roommate problem, try to solve it. The first step is to make an effort to work it out between yourselves. Often the offending student doesn't know that things he or she says and does bother other people. Sometimes, just bringing grievances out in the open in as pleasant and unemotional a way as possible helps. If the problem persists, the resident staff member, typically an upperclassman or graduate student living in the dormitory, may be able to help. If things are really bad, the resident counselor can tell you what you have to do to initiate a change.

Dormitory life offers a lot of tempting distractions. Something interesting is always going on, and it is easy to postpone studying in favor of a card game, a gossip session, or even just watching TV. Learning to resist these temptations when you have work to do can be the single most important step in a successful college career.

At many colleges, students have a choice between coeducational and single-sex dormitories. Typically, the relationships between men and women in coeducational dormitories is that of being good friends. Pairing off is the exception rather than the rule, and dating is usually with persons who live elsewhere.

Most schools have rules prohibiting alcohol and drugs in the dormitories. These are often ignored by the residents. Although this book isn't meant to deal with problems of alcohol and drug abuse, we have to say something about them, for they often play a role in poor study habits. You have to make a personal decision about whether or not you are going to drink. But if you do drink or take drugs, you should know the difference between use and abuse. Students who regularly drink beyond their capacity or spend a lot of time stoned inevitably will end up in academic trouble. Disciplinary action or even arrest may be a result. If you don't drink or take drugs, don't feel socially inadequate or be tempted to do something that doesn't fit your personal values. Life styles differ, and sooner or later at any institution you will find people you can be comfortable with.

One of the best aspects of dormitory living is that it gives you a chance to get to know many different kinds of people and to form relationships that are satisfying and that enrich your life. Often students make their closest friends during their freshman year, and these are usually from among the people on their hall or in their suite.

ORIENTATION AND ADVISING

Every college or university has some kind of orientation program for entering students. Don't skip any part of this program if you can help it, even if the speakers are boring and repetitive. You may miss out on some useful information. Also, you can get to know other incoming students. Everyone is floundering around together, and it is easy to strike up conversations with the people around you, even if only to exchange gripes.

You're likely to be handed a lot of miscellaneous printed and mimeographed material. Read it through and save it, because later in the year you'll have questions that didn't occur to you at first. If you have some question that the handouts don't answer, go to official sources—resident staff, faculty advisors, deans—rather than rely on guesses or the student grapevine.

Usually orientation includes a tour of the campus. Get to know the layout and the surrounding student community. You'll feel at home sooner when you know something about the place. Check out the library. You will be spending a lot of time there; the sooner you know how it works, the more efficient your studying will be. Explore the student union, if there is one. On most campuses, this is the hub of student activities. Wander through the classroom buildings. This is a good time to find out how long it will take you to bike or walk from your dormitory to where your classes will be.

The orientation issue of the student newspaper will have a lot of useful information. Most students read the student paper daily or weekly, depending upon its publication schedule. It is the best and most up-to-date source for what's going on, and usually there is a lot going on—lectures, concerts, films, plays. Usually during orientation there will be a number of events of this sort—along with parties. Be sure to go. It will help you get over homesickness, and it will establish a good pattern.

Placement tests in subjects such as mathematics, foreign languages, and English are usually given during the orientation period. Find out what tests you are required to take and which ones might be advantageous to take even if not required. Placement policies vary from school to school, but many colleges will give credit in addition to advanced placement if you score high enough. If you're still in high school and have taken any advanced placement courses, be sure to take the CEEB Advanced Placement Tests. If you do, you may find yourself exempt from some college requirements and ahead on credits.

LEARNING TO COPE
ACADEMIC DEMANDS

Your high school classmates probably represented a fair cross section of American young people, and the student body undoubtedly included many students not headed for college. For this and a lot of other reasons, the pace and standards of work in high school tend to be geared to the average student, not the superior one. You may have discovered that you could do very well without having to work very hard. Or even if you did work hard, the competition probably was not all that stiff, and you didn't have to be too efficient about studying in order to do well.

In most colleges you are going to find yourself in a much faster league. Most college students stood in at least the upper half of their high school classes. In colleges with high admission standards, your fellow students will have been in the upper tenth or above of their high school classes. In short, in college you are likely to be surrounded by students who were at the top of their high school classes. Many of them were also student leaders—class officers, student body presidents, newspaper editors, in short, doers and achievers. Furthermore, college professors are less likely to gear the work to the average student. They may aim their courses at the superior students, and they will expect everyone to meet high standards. The kind of work that got you A's and B's in high school can easily get you C's, D's, and even F's in college.

It is surprising how many students have no idea what demands they will face in college. Because they aren't prepared for a much tougher job of studying, they do badly in their first semester. The result is they are disappointed and discouraged. That's why we think this book is especially useful for the student entering college. If you have a realistic idea of what lies ahead and how to prepare for it, your chances of liking college and of doing well your first semester will be very much better. Many of the students who drop out before graduating are just as able and just as motivated as the people who finish. They might have stayed if they had known a little about how to study properly.

Aside from the competition and standards of work, there's another big difference between high school and college. In high school, even if you have a lot of work, it's pretty well laid out for you. A lot of it is covered in class, and homework can be completed in study halls. Long-range projects, such as term papers, are fewer and less demanding. To a large extent, high school students are graded on what they do in class and in daily homework.

All this is reversed in college. You spend relatively few hours in class, and except for labs, discussion sections, and seminars, you are hardly graded at all for what you do in class. Instead of an hour or two of homework for five classes, you have two or three hours of outside work for every hour in class. Therefore, if you are carrying a course load of fifteen semester hours, you can expect to spend about thirty hours a week in study and preparation. There are no supervised study halls in which you have little choice but to do your work. Instead you will have time between classes that you can use profitably or waste, as you choose.

In most courses you won't be required to do your homework on a daily basis. Rather, you are likely to be given a syllabus outlining an entire semester's work. Nobody checks to see if you are keeping up with the reading or working on the required term paper. You might have an occasional quiz or a midterm exam, but in some courses there will be only one exam, the final. If you let all the reading go to the end of the term, you won't be able to do enough cramming before the exam to perform well, even if the course is only moderately difficult.

You will be thrown on your own, treated like an adult who can be given some general directions and then left to figure out how and when to do what needs to be done. Many college students aren't prepared to take the responsibility that goes with this freedom. To make matters worse, college abounds in distractions and diversions that encourage procrastination. In later chapters we'll deal with the problem of structuring your time so that you can get the most out of studying and still have plenty of time for other things.

SOCIAL PRESSURES

Everyone likes to be liked, and everyone needs friends. Making and keeping new friends will be one of the best aspects of your college years. But if you run into problems in your social life, your academic work will suffer.

Take Suzy, for example. A bright, hard-working student in the small-town high school she attended,

Suzy was respected by her high school classmates. Although she was not the most popular girl in her class, she had a few close friends from school and from her church youth group. She was satisfied with her life. When Suzy entered the state university, she was placed on a dormitory hall whose residents all came from urban areas. They were an unusually sophisticated group of girls. All of them drank. Two were experimenting with drugs, and several of them talked freely about their sexual experiences. Suzy had not faced this sort of thing before, and she felt awkward and uncomfortable. Her roommate, with no intention of being unkind, dubbed her the "country mouse," and one of the other girls changed this to the "church mouse." She could not feel close to anyone, and she became more and more the outsider. As she withdrew from social contacts with them, the other girls became increasingly hostile. Lacking the social skills and the confidence to seek friends elsewhere, Suzy spent most of her time alone. Although she studied diligently, it became harder and harder for her to concentrate. Most of the time she was depressed and anxious. She began to wonder if she were out of step with the rest of the world. By late October she was thoroughly miserable. After a long, tearful weekend at home, she decided to withdraw from the university.

The saddest part of her story is that Suzy made no attempt to seek solutions to her personal problems but rather chose to escape from them. Her problems could have been dealt with. If she had sought the help of her resident advisor, her dean, or someone at the counseling center, she might have been able to rescue her college career. The only way she knew how to do it on her own was to control her environment by withdrawing to the safe, circumscribed world she knew.

There are all kinds of social pressures in college. You will encounter people with different ideas, values, and ways of living. These will challenge things you have always taken for granted. The experience can be a painful and threatening one. But it can be important to you. Perhaps some of your views should be challenged, and those that you stick to can't really be your

own until you have examined them for yourself. The wider social horizons of college can help you do that. Be prepared for some uncomfortable moments. You may be the only person of your race or from your part of the country in your dormitory. You may feel unhappy and isolated. But there are ways of dealing with that problem without giving up or without continuing to be miserable. If you are having trouble coping with social pressures, seek out the help of the support services at your institution.

PARENTAL PRESSURE

Pressure sometimes comes from parents. Most parents are well meaning, but some of them aren't very helpful with the problems their sons and daughters have in adjusting to college, and a few of them seem to go out of their way to add to their children's difficulties.

For one thing, parents are often not aware of the kinds of problems their children face. They don't realize that the competition is keener, that the standards of work are higher, and that their children may not be prepared for the change. Accustomed to seeing A's and B's on high school report cards, they may be upset when their children's first semester college grades are below that level. At their kindest, they may gently inquire why John or Mary isn't doing better, whether he or she is trying as hard as he or she should, and so on. At their worst, they may threaten to take their children out of college, or cut off funds.

Sometimes parents regard their children as extensions of themselves and think it only right and natural that they determine what their sons and daughters do with their lives. In their involvement and identification with their children, they forget that everyone is different and that each person must develop in his or her own way. They forget that their children, who are now young adults, must be the ones responsible for what they do and what they are. When students do things that their parents regard as unacceptable, there is resentment and anger, even when the student feels that whatever he or she is doing is perfectly consistent with his or her own values. If you are in this kind of conflict with your parents, you can help make things better if you acknowledge and respect their feelings without sacrificing your right to live according to your own standards. If you are considerate about small but important things such as letter writing, telephoning, and so forth, and if you demonstrate your adult status by doing your work and handling your finances, you may not eliminate the conflict, but you will keep it to the minimum.

Another big source of conflict between parents and students is the matter of program of studies and course choice. Some parents are convinced that only certain subjects are worth studying and that others are foolish and frivolous. The engineer who can't understand why his son takes courses in art and music, the artist who is horrified by his daughter's enthusiasm for economics and accounting, the physician who insists that his son follow a premedical curriculum, the lawyer who is upset because her daughter has no professional aspiration, the mother who is shocked because her daughter wants to be an electrical engineer are all cases in point. The list could go on and on. In matters of course selection and career planning, students must be guided by their own aspirations, interests, and abilities. Students who merely accept the course that their parents map out for them are usually headed for trouble. They are living out someone else's aspirations, not their own. Sometimes students get entirely through college on someone else's plan. Such people may discover when they are thirty-five or forty that they really don't like what they are doing. A few of the more courageous ones will go back to school to correct the mistake they made earlier.

College is a time for exploring alternatives, for examining life, for moving gradually and smoothly from parental direction to autonomous commitment. At times it is a hard task, hard for students, hard for parents. We hope that some parents will read this book, so that they can have some idea of what college life is for their children and know what they can do to make things as smooth as possible.

FINANCIAL PRESSURES

If you're lucky, you'll have had some experience in managing money before you get to college. Some students, however, have no idea how to budget their funds, and they may discover for the first time in their lives that no one is around to dole out cash when they run out. You'll save yourself a lot of headaches if you learn how to manage your money effectively. College is expensive, and if your parents are supporting you in whole or part, you do them a big favor by not adding to their financial burdens by being careless with money.

Students who go away to college usually open a checking account in the town where their college is located. A common arrangement is for a parent to deposit a certain amount of money in the student's account on a regular basis, usually once a month. The initial expenses are likely to be heavy because you will be buying books and supplies. After a few months, however, you will have a good idea about how much it costs you to live. If you don't get enough money from home, consider looking for a part-time job to help meet your expenses. These are often surprisingly easy to find in a college community. You may have heard—and it's true—that college students who work earn, on the average, better grades than those who don't. Perhaps it is because students who pay part of their own way are more motivated than those who do not. And then, a part-time job forces a student to budget time more effectively. Management of time is the most important aspect of effective studying.

If you've never learned how to balance a checkbook, get some instruction from your parents or your bank. Keeping accurate records is important. It can save you the embarrassment and cost of a bounced check. And get into the habit of drawing enough cash on a weekly basis to meet your ordinary expenses. Most banks charge from ten to twenty cents per check, and if you write a check for every little two-dollar purchase, you are wasting a high proportion of your money.

Many students receive financial aid from their colleges. A typical pattern is to have some funds in direct scholarship, some as a loan, and some in the form of a work-study job. Every institution has a financial aid officer to whom a student can turn if it is necessary to have his or her aid package changed. In addition, many institutions have an emergency loan fund to assist students with temporary difficulties.

Meet your financial obligations promptly. In our credit-oriented society, a good credit rating is a strong asset and a bad one a genuine burden. Delinquency in paying college bills, library and parking fines, etc., may result in some disciplinary action. In any event, your college won't grant you a degree or send out a transcript until you have paid all your bills.

BEING INVOLVED

By now you should be aware that college life has many facets. If you spend fifteen hours a week in the classroom, thirty or so hours in study and review, fifty-six or sixty hours sleeping, you will have more than sixty hours a week left for other activities. You can use that extra time to learn a lot of things that are not part of the formal curriculum, particularly how to work with and relate to other people.

Our advice at the outset is, Take it easy. Don't get involved in too many extracurricular activities during your first few weeks. There is a lot of waste motion in getting started in college, and you may have to work harder at first to learn new study habits and to get into the swing of college life. You will need the time to assess just how hard college work will be for you. Take

most of the first semester getting used to the academic schedule and making new friends. Don't throw yourself into every activity that looks interesting or profitable.

Budget time for recreation. Relaxation is essential to good mental and physical condition. The consensus of a lot of research on work is that productivity declines after fifty-five or sixty hours a week. So, plan on doing something else rather than working beyond sensible limits.

Somewhere in your schedule, allow time for regular exercise. At the minimum, medical experts tell us, it should be the equivalent of a half-hour a day of walking. Jogging is all the rage now, and recent studies show that in addition to its physical benefits, it is a good antidote for depression. If you enjoy some sport, plan to play on a regular schedule. Some colleges even require physical education. If this is the case at your institution, try to get into something that is beneficial or that you enjoy. Or use the opportunity to learn a new sport, such as tennis or golf.

CLUBS AND ORGANIZATIONS

Every campus is crowded with clubs and organizations. There is something for every taste. If drama isn't your thing, how about working on the campus radio station? Some schools even have a TV studio. There is always a student newspaper. There may be a debating society, a chess club, a war games club, a folk dancing club, and even a mountain climbing club on some big campuses. Investigate those things that interest you. Find out what the people are like who are in organizations you might be interested in.

There are two particular reasons for choosing an organization to join. One is to do something you enjoy. The other is to give you experience at something you might want to do later in life or something related to your choice of a profession. If you are headed for medical school, you may join the drama club for fun and the premedical society because it sponsors activities that will help you in your professional goals. And of course, organizations provide opportunities for leadership and for learning how to work comfortably with other people.

A note of caution: Some extracurricular activities place heavy demands on time. Putting out a newspaper or putting on a play is not a small job. You could find yourself giving so much time to these activities that your academic performance suffers. The same applies, of course, to varsity athletics. If you find yourself devoting too much time to some extracurricular activity, curtail it or drop out. Don't run the risk of being put on academic probation.

STUDENT GOVERNMENT

Student government in college is a lot more important than high school student government. On some campuses, the student government assumes the major responsibility for the quality of student life. It may even have sole responsibility for the nonacademic discipline of students. If you have a political streak, or if you would like to have a say in how things are run, this is something to get into.

You will want to start at the "local" level. Go to your dorm council meetings or their equivalent (there are even such organizations for commuting students) and speak up. If you are active, there is a good chance you will be elected to some position sooner or later. That can give you an opportunity to test your skills at management and leadership. Again, however, remember not to spend too much time at it. Some people who are heavily into student government get swamped by it and neglect everything else.

SORORITIES AND FRATERNITIES

Sororities and fraternities offer a way of life that is attractive to many students. They provide opportunities for friendships and for social activities with people who share your tastes. On some campuses they are very important, and on other campuses they are minor.

At some schools the majority of students will belong, and at others only 10 to 15 percent of the students will be in them. Whether they are for you or not depends upon your needs and interests. Don't automatically assume that you should join one or that you should avoid them at all costs, for that matter. For some people they are the most enjoyable part of their college years. For others, they are confining and narrowly conformist. If you participate in rush, the chances are that you will end up either in an organization that suits you or not in one at all. If the latter happens, it is probably for the best. It means that the chances are you would not have been happy in any of the sororities or fraternities on your campus. If you do end up in an organization you don't like, drop out. It's expensive, and if you do drop out, you are more likely to find congenial friends.

Do be involved in some aspect of college life. It will add immeasurably to the quality of your college experience. You will find that you are a part of a living community and not merely an anonymous body in a classroom. And, of course, you know that you will get from an activity what you put into it. If you give some of your time and energy to your college community, you will get back something in return.

Now that we've covered some of the things that help you get off to a good start in college, we're ready to get down to the main topic of this book: how to organize and use your time for effective study.

CHAPTER TWO

THE ART OF STUDYING

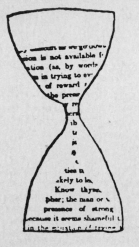

You may not be interested in any of your courses, or you may be interested in your courses but can't seem to do the work for them. People who aren't interested or who don't study usually feel guilty about it. But that doesn't help. In fact, it probably makes it worse by adding anxiety and depression to the problem. Most people who advise students and who know what their problems are believe that lack of motivation is responsible for more failures than inadequate background or lack of ability. Not being motivated is the most serious problem many students face.

Before we can turn to the specific techniques of efficient study, we need to look at the problem of motivation and what you can do about it. We can't make you want to learn, but we can say some things that might help you want to learn. First of all, you might want to assess your motivation for going to college. On page 11 you will find a list of statements about motivation for college. By ranking these yourself, you can determine what things are important to you and what goals and values you have that may make for success in college. Such a self-examination could lead you to change some of those goals and values in such a way as to make your college career a better and easier one.

IMPROVING MOTIVATION

Why do so many college students find it hard to study? Partly it's because of the great difference between high school and college. In high school someone is usually after you every day to do your work, and hardly any internal push is required. In college external pressure scarcely exists, and you are left to move yourself to get the work done.

Another reason has to do with the absence of long-term goals. Most students who go to college express some kind of career interest: They want to be doctors, lawyers, engineers, business executives, teachers, and so on. But these aims are often pretty vague, and they usually shift from time to time. Few students are absolutely sure of what they want to do in life, and even fewer know exactly what they must do in college to prepare themselves for their chosen career. Not being sure sometimes makes them uncomfortable and anxious, but it doesn't provide any real motivation for studying.

There is nothing wrong with not knowing what you want to do, even after you've been in college for a while. In fact, one of the things college can do for you is to help you find your career goals. But occupational choice is often difficult, especially for students in a liberal arts program. In the absence of such a choice, many students can't work up enthusiasm for studying,

MOTIVATION FOR COLLEGE

The following questions are designed to help you think about your motivation and to give you some insight into it. Read completely through each group of items; then rank them in importance by using 1 for the phrase that applies best to you, 2 for the phrase that applies next best, and so on.

I. I came (or will go) to college because—

_____ I know what I want to be, and college preparation is necessary for it

_____ my folks wanted me to, even though I didn't

_____ I thought it would be a lot of fun

_____ I wanted to gain a better knowledge and understanding of the world I live in

_____ many of my friends did, and I wanted to be with them

_____ I wanted to get away from home

_____ I am particularly interested in athletics and student activities

_____ a college degree seems indispensable in this day and age

_____ I like to study and am particularly interested in certain subjects

II. I want to make grades that are good enough to—

_____ let me stay in college

_____ meet degree requirements

_____ let me participate in extracurricular activities

_____ put me on the honor list and give me special recognition

_____ make an outstanding record in college

III. My motivation for making grades is to—

_____ prove to myself that I am learning something

_____ secure a good job recommendation

_____ please my family

_____ do better than my competitors

_____ live up to my reputation of being a good student

_____ be respected by my teachers

IV. I sometimes don't study when I should because—

_____ I worry about my personal problems

_____ I simply can't get interested in certain subjects

_____ I am too involved in extracurricular activities

_____ I am bothered by illness and poor health

_____ I get distracted by things going on around me

_____ I tend to keep putting off my work

_____ I am easily tempted to do more interesting things

or still worse, they feel positively paralyzed without some clear career goal in mind.

We can't do much in this kind of a book to help you make your career decisions. This is something most people work out for themselves. Many campuses have career counseling services, and if you are really concerned about your career goals, you should take advantage of them if they are available to you. They can help you find out what your interests and talents really are, and they can provide you with information about kinds of careers that attract people like you.

But if you don't feel any clear-cut call to a particular occupation, don't make yourself miserable worrying about it. One thing you can be sure of: If you haven't made a career choice by the time you are twenty-one or twenty-two, you won't turn into a pumpkin. And if you're in a liberal arts curriculum, do bear in mind that the subject you major in will probably have little or no direct relationship to what you will ultimately end up doing. A liberal arts curriculum is not designed to train you for a specific occupation, but rather to make you into an educated person and to give you skill in critical reading, writing, and thinking. What you are studying is useful and important in its own right, and it deserves all the effort you can bring to it.

ACADEMIC AND OCCUPATIONAL SUCCESS

If you have a definite purpose, you will find it easier to take on the habits and skills of effective studying. If you lack that purpose now, you might consider some of the things that are true regardless of what you want to do.

Most students seem to be interested in earning a good income when they get out of college. You should note that those who make the best grades in college are generally those who make the best incomes later on. The student who makes Phi Beta Kappa will generally earn more than the average student. People who make *Who's Who* made, on the average, higher grades in college than those who are not listed. Many individual surveys show that college grades are correlated with professional success.

There are a number of reasons why this should be

so. One obvious reason is that those having the highest ability will be more likely to succeed both in college and in their work. You needn't pay much attention to this reason. The other reasons, however, provide you with some strong justification for wanting to learn how to study effectively. Employers and graduate and professional schools are impressed by grades and tend to offer better opportunities to those with high grades.

What is more important, the same habits and skills that make for success in college will also promote success later on. In fact, the habits of work we outline in this book are not at all confined to studying in college. Most college-educated people are employed in positions in which much the same skills are required, though they are appplied to different things. Professional people must be able to read rapidly with comprehension and be able to remember what they have read. They must budget their time much as an efficient student does. They must "take examinations" almost daily, when they answer the questions of their clients, employers, or associates. Most people know how important it is for them to be effective on the job, and many wish they had started earlier to acquire the habits and skills that make for effective work. This is probably the most important reason for acquiring good work habits in college.

IMPORTANCE OF GRADES

Grades are not the measure of a person nor are they the sole measure of academic accomplishment. They are only one rather imperfect measure of how much you have learned in your various courses. People can learn a great deal and acquire a good education without making high grades, and some students who make straight A's may concentrate so much on doing what is necessary just to achieve high grades that they really miss being educated. On the whole, though, grades do reflect what students learn in specific courses, and they foretell what students are likely to accomplish in the future.

If you have any idea at all of going to graduate or professional school, grades are even more important. The competition among applicants for law school, medical school, and certain graduate programs is as keen as ever, and your college grades will probably be the single most important factor in determining whether you are admitted or not. Experienced admissions officers know that grades predict success in advanced training better than do test scores or any other single factor. Of course, a few people with the right connections or with an extraordinary record of achievement in extracurricular affairs will be admitted despite mediocre grades. But it happens less often

than you think. Most graduate and professional schools have two to ten times as many applicants as they have spaces. They can afford to take only the most qualified. In many fields, hardly anyone with less than a B average is even considered, and some schools seldom admit anyone with less than an A− average. So if you plan to go on to advanced studies, you can't afford to dismiss grades as unimportant, even if you have reservations about them, as many of us do.

SATISFACTION IN STUDY

Learning—studying—doesn't have to be a chore. It can even be a source of real satisfaction. In the last chapter we pointed out that if you get no intrinsic pleasure from learning, perhaps you shouldn't be in college. But part of the trick in getting satisfaction from studying is in knowing what to learn and how to learn it. If you can pick up a book, read it with reasonable speed, know how to select the main points and remember them, you're the kind of person who probably does get satisfaction from learning, and you're fortunate because you will be a lot richer person for it. Besides acquiring some useful and interesting information or being challenged to examine some new ideas, you'll have the kind of feeling of pride that a craftsman has in work well done. Having once done a good job at studying, you will be in a better position to do it again. The more you read and learn, the easier it is to read and learn. Instead of being a dull, frustrating chore, studying will be something satisfying in itself. If you develop a high level of skill in studying, we can almost guarantee that you will come to enjoy studying more and that you won't dread it the way so many students do.

Good study habits allow you to get more done in less time. The time you save can be devoted to the things you like best to do. If you earn part of your expenses, you'll have more time for work. We can say with some confidence that if you learn to study in the way this book tells you to, you will benefit in all these ways. A number of investigations show that students who have been instructed in how-to-study methods make better grades with less time spent in studying than do the same kind of students who have not been so instructed.

It is not *how much* you study but *how well*. When students are divided into groups according to how much they study, those who study a great deal—over thirty-five hours a week—actually make poorer grades than those who study a somewhat shorter amount of time. This isn't necessarily because those who study long hours lack academic ability. Many bright and quick students study day and night without getting the grades they ought to. Educational psychologists tell us that the major factor in performance is the quality rather than the quantity of study time. Though every case is different, the odds are very high that you could do more in less time if you learned how.

DEVELOPING PERSONAL EFFICIENCY

Sara is chronically behind in her work. It's not that she doesn't try to study. Every evening after supper she goes to her room and picks up a book. Most of the time, however, something happens to interrupt her. The telephone rings, or someone has an urgent personal problem that he or she wants to talk about, or she can't find the book she needs. By the time she really gets down to work, she's too sleepy to concentrate.

Scott is so worried about his performance in chemistry that he spends four and five hours at a time studying it and neglects his other subjects. He doesn't think about them until exam time, and he realizes how far behind he is. Jack is so anxious about falling behind that he jumps from one subject to another and never stays with any one long enough to master the material.

Sara, Scott, and Jack share the same problem. They have not learned how to organize their time for effective study. Even if you're a student who studies long and hard, the chances are that you're wasting time. In fact, if you study many more hours than other people with the same kind of schedule, you're probably wasting a good deal of your time. This problem can be corrected, but only you can do it. We will suggest some remedies, but you will have to apply them diligently if they are to do you any good.

THE VALUE OF A SCHEDULE

The first remedy—and the most essential one—is a schedule for studying. A well-planned schedule makes time by cutting out the waste motion. It helps keep you from vacillating about what you're going to do next. By assigning time where time is due, it keeps you from neglecting one thing for another. It helps you to study subjects at the best time for those subjects rather than at the wrong time. With your time properly organized, you can avoid the hit-or-miss approach that causes some students to tackle the hardest or dullest subject when they are least able to concentrate. The only way you will really *know* how much time you spend on a given subject is to devise a schedule and then stick to it.

MAKING AND REVISING A SCHEDULE

Someone else can't make a schedule for you. You have to construct your own so that it fits your class hours, activities, part-time work, etc. But we can give you some tips about how to construct a good schedule. Let's start with the example on page 14. There you will find a schedule for a student carrying a fairly heavy load. She is taking the following subjects: economics, psychology, German, organic chemistry, and English literature. She is also enrolled in the ROTC program and holds a part-time job requiring ten hours a week.

We have blocked the schedule off into one-hour periods because many of the gaps in a student's class schedule are only an hour long. These hours add up, and only by using them can you avoid working until late every evening. Research on effective work shows that people do best by working intensively for a reasonable period of time and then resting or switching to another task. There is an optimal cycle of work and rest for every job and for every individual. For the kind of work that studying requires and for the typical student, a period of forty to fifty minutes of work followed by ten minutes or so of rest or change is just about right. Consequently, an hour that is used properly is pretty close to the best unit of time for most college study.

Notice that the hours in the schedule are blocked off for specific subjects. Assigning specific subjects will save you the time you might spend trying to decide what to study next and will ensure that you will have the books and materials you will need for a particular subject. Equally important is scheduling studying for a given subject when it needs to be done. The alternative is to cram when you fall behind in one subject, which, of course, gets you behind in other subjects besides being inefficient.

WHEN TO STUDY

There are other important reasons for blocking out a schedule by specific subjects.

1. You can assign less time to easier subjects and more for those that you find difficult.

2. It spreads out study time. Generally people learn more and remember it better when studying is spread out over several sessions rather than being crammed into one session.

3. Finally, there is a best time for studying anything. As a general rule, study review for a particular subject should come close to the

SAMPLE SCHEDULE

Time \ Day	Monday	Tuesday	Wednesday	Thursday	Friday	Saturday	Sunday
7:00		DRESS	AND	EAT		↑	
8:00	ECON.	Study	ECON.	Study	Study		
8:30	LECT.	Engl.	LECT.	Engl.	German		
9:00	Study	ENGL.	Study	ENGL.	ECON.		
9:30	German	CLASS	German	CLASS	DISC.		
10:00	GERMAN	↓	GERMAN	↓	GERMAN		
10:30	CLASS	PSYCH.	CLASS	PSYCH.	CLASS		
11:00	Study	LECT.	Study	LECT.	Study		
11:30	Econ.	↓	Econ.	↓	Psych.		
12:00		LUNCH					
12:30							
1:00	CHEM.	CHEM.	CHEM.	ROTC	CHEM.		
1:30	LECT.	LAB.	LECT.		LECT.		
2:00	Study		Study		Study		
2:30	Chem.		Chem.	↓	Chem.	Eight hours of	
3:00	Job		Job	Job	Job	study distributed	
3:30						as needed among	
4:00		↓				five subjects	
4:30				↓	↓		
5:00		Recre-		Recre-	Study		
5:30	↓	ation	↓	ation	German		
6:00		DINNER					
6:30							
7:00	Study	Study	Study	Study	Recre-		
7:30	Engl.	Psych.	Engl.	Chem.	ation		
8:00	Study	Study	Library	Study	Recre-		
8:30	Psych.	Econ.	(Papers	Chem.	ation		
9:00	Study	Study	or	Study	or		
9:30	Chem.	German	reports)	Econ.	Library		
10:00		RECREATION					
10:30							
11:00		SLEEP					↓

class period for that subject. This doesn't mean that *all* study time for a subject must be scheduled in this way, but some of it should. This rule really has two parts:

a. If class time is mainly lecture rather than recitation, you should allocate a study period as soon after class as possible.
b. If class time is mainly recitation, you should schedule a review period just *before* the class. Classes in foreign languages may be a mixture, but the emphasis is on recitation, and it is generally a good idea to schedule a study section for a language just ahead of class time.

WHEN TO REVISE A SCHEDULE

The schedule on page 14 is a pretty formidable one. It is for a student taking a tough set of courses who wants to do well. In a sense, it is a kind of ideal schedule. You may not be able to or may not want to settle for so rigorous a routine, but make your own schedule as close to your own ideal as you can. Remember, however, you're supposed to stick to the schedule. Don't make it so impossible that you won't follow it. A schedule that you don't follow is less than useless because it deludes you into thinking you are doing something that you really aren't.

On the other hand, don't get into a fit about occasional deviations from the schedule. As demands vary, you will want to trade around study times, add to them, or take away from them. If you have a schedule, you will be aware of what you are doing, and you can do your trading in a rational way. Finally, you will want to revise your schedule as you get a better feeling for the demands on you, and you will certainly want to set up a separate schedule for final exam time. That is when you must be most efficient about your studying, and a schedule is a necessity.

Put your schedule in a place where you are apt to look at it: in your notebook, over your desk, or even in your mirror or on your "must do" bulletin board.

STUDYING FOR LECTURE COURSES

What do you do in a study period placed right *after* a lecture? First of all, you examine the notes you have taken in class, making sure that you really understand them. It's easy to be misled into thinking that you have assimilated the lecturer's main points just because you could follow them when you heard them in class.

Unless the lecture is unusually well organized and you are a top-notch note taker, you should revise or rewrite the notes, eliminating the trivial points and expanding those that are important or concern difficult matters. You can do this most effectively when the lecture is still fresh in your mind. If you let too much time pass, you'll find it to be a hopeless task. If you rewrite your notes, reorganize them and make them more legible and better arranged for subsequent review.

When a study period comes *before* a lecture class, you can use it to read the assignment that goes with the lecture. Prereading on a topic is an effective study technique because you will become familiar with what the lecture is all about, if nothing more than to get used to the vocabulary. You will be better able to tell the difference between what is important and what is not important. Some lecturers don't follow the same organization as in the reading assignments they give. If that is the case, there are a few things you can do, particularly if you have trouble following the lecture. You can find reading material that does parallel the lectures, or you can ask the instructor for guidance in finding such material. Reading those things may help you understand the lecture. Of course, you must keep up with the assigned reading too.

STUDYING FOR RECITATION COURSES

If a class is mostly recitation, as many language courses are, you can use the study period just before the class to get ready to recite. In most cases this hour won't be enough to be your principal study period. You should prepare the assignment at an earlier time and use the period before class for review and self-recitation. In this way, you distribute your study and bring yourself up to peak performance just before class. You not only will do better in class, but will get more out of it as well.

Although students are warned all through school to be prepared, they don't always heed the advice. Not preparing at the right time often keeps them limping through courses in which they might otherwise do well. Some subjects, such as languages and mathematics, are cumulative. Early in the course you learn things you will need in order to learn something else later on. The consequences of poor preparation snowball for such courses. When students aren't prepared, they don't know what is going on in class. They hesitate to ask questions for fear of revealing their ignorance. As the assignments become more difficult, such students fall increasingly behind. Prepared students, on the other hand, can take each step as it comes. They are less afraid to ask questions in class. And because they know what's going on, they are less bored in class.

MAKING A SCHEDULE

How much time you should allot to study and how to distribute it are highly individual matters. They depend mainly upon your abilities, your work habits, and the kinds of courses you are taking. An old rule says that you should spend two hours in studying for every hour in class, so by that rule, if you take fifteen hours, you should study for about thirty hours a week. But, of course, some people will require more and others can do very well on less. Make sure that you determine realistically just how much you can accomplish in a given period of time. Be sure to take into account honest appraisals of your abilities and work habits as well as the courses you are taking. Don't overdo it. It's just as important to be realistic about the time you need for eating, sleeping, jobs, and leisure. Leisure is essential, not only because you get the most out of college when you are healthy and rested, but because well-spent leisure is an indispensable part of your education. Factory and office workers, as well as students, who try to work very long hours—sixty to eighty hours a week—are less happy and efficient than people who work more moderate hours. If you learn to work efficiently in a shorter schedule of study, you'll be better able to grind for the long stretch if that becomes necessary. If you start out by trying to do too much, you may get discouraged and give up altogether. It is more important to have a moderate and *realistic* schedule than one that is impossibly ambitious.

In the back of this book you will find two pages labeled Provisional Working Schedule. You can use these to plan the allocation of your time. As soon as you know when your classes and laboratories meet, fill these in. Next, fill in the time you spend eating and in other regular activities (job, ROTC, etc.). Now estimate how much time you'll need to do the work in each of the subjects you are carrying. You should modify the rule suggesting two hours of study for each hour of class to suit the demands of the particular courses you are taking.

Adjust the study time to suit your guesses as to how much time you will need to spend on particular subjects. If you're a quick study in languages, you can afford to shave time on French for organic chemistry. On the other hand, if languages are an uphill struggle, be sure to allow plenty of time, particularly at the beginning of the semester.

You may want to compare your provisional schedule with the sample one on page 14. The student who made this schedule has allotted thirty hours a week to study, twenty-two of which are scheduled for particular subjects during the week and eight of which are to be distributed as needed on the weekend. In addition, she has reserved one evening a week for working at the library on papers, reports, etc., and the possibility of another evening being used for this purpose if necessary. In comparing your schedule to this student's, remember that she is carrying a heavy load, that she works outside, and that she is an efficient user of her time.

Of the five courses she's taking, she anticipates that organic chemistry will be the most difficult. It has a laboratory that requires lab reports, and because it is a required course in the premed curriculum, the competition for good and passing grades is tough. Therefore, she assigns six of her scheduled hours to organic and expects to spend additional time during the weekends on it. Three of the scheduled hours come immediately after the weekly lectures. A fourth she puts on Monday evening to prepare for the laboratory on Tuesday. The last two she assigns to Thursday night in order to have a larger stretch to write up lab reports, which she will put in final form on the weekend.

German is the most difficult of the remaining subjects. While she is moderately good at languages, the course has a reputation for being tough. There will be a lot of memorizing and translating. Therefore, she allows five scheduled hours for German, and she suspects she will need an additional two hours during the weekend for it. She manages to put three hours just before the class. Much of the class time in German is taken up with recitation in which students translate portions of the assignment.

In planning her other three subjects, she anticipates little difficulty with economics. It is a course in money and banking, something in which she has an interest. She has a good background in the Federal Reserve system from a course she took in history. She was used to reading the *Wall Street Journal*, which her father, a banker, took at home. Moreover, the campus grapevine has it that the instructor is an excellent lecturer who places the greater emphasis upon lecture material. She schedules four hours a week for economics, scheduling two of them after lecture and one on Thursday evening prior to the meeting of the discussion section for the course on Friday.

She also anticipates little difficulty with her English literature course. She is a fast reader, and she had read some of the assigned reading before she started the course. Rereading these with an eye to putting them in the context created by the instructor will be a pleasure. She need, at this stage, only keep up with the readings to be prepared for class, which is a combination of lecture and discussion. She therefore sets aside four hours a week to do the reading. She anticipates, however, that she will have to find additional time in the second half of the semester when she will have to prepare a major paper.

That leaves psychology. It is a large introductory

course with a heterogeneous group of students. It interests her, and the rumor is that the course, under her instructor, is not too difficult. She learns from the course syllabus that her main task will be to study the textbook. The lectures, according to the instructor, will mainly explain and illustrate the text. So she assigns three hours a week to psychology and reserves a couple of hours on the weekend in case she needs more time for the subject.

Since this schedule was her first guess as to the amount of time she would need for study, she knows that she might have underestimated the amount of work she would have to do. If so, she can still use the time on Friday evening that she had not scheduled, and she will undoubtedly need those hours around exam time.

In totaling up her assigned time, she can expect to be in class or laboratory about twenty hours a week, studying from thirty to thirty-five hours a week, and working ten hours a week on a part-time job. This is a heavy schedule, no doubt about it, but notice how much time she has left over. She can quit studying by ten in the evening, with time left for a snack, a rap session, or TV. She has leisurely meal hours, time for some exercise, and most of the weekend free. A good bit of the time she will be able to take off one or two evenings a week (Wednesday and Friday) in addition to Saturday. Though this schedule calls for more study than many students do, it is still a leisurely one compared with the schedule of a doctor, lawyer, business executive, or someone who moonlights on a second job.

REVISING A SCHEDULE

Your first schedule for the semester should not be your last. The odds are that you have given too much or too little time to some activity. You may have been unrealistic about your total study time. If so, you will want to revise. Use the schedule as a goal to work toward, particularly if you are not doing as well as you should, but alter it when necessary. After you have begun to acquire regular habits of work, you can revise your schedule to better suit the demands on you. The whole purpose of a schedule is to get you into regular

habits of study. After you have established such habits, you won't need to rely so much on your schedule as an incentive, and you can use it mainly as a convenient plan for your week's activities.

We have provided four schedule sheets for you to use in making revisions. If you need more, make them for yourself. Try not to change your schedule more often than every three or four weeks, however, because you'll need to spend at least a week finding out whether it works or not. Besides, it's hard to establish regular habits when you keep changing.

USING YOUR TIME EFFECTIVELY

Many students start out with a schedule and then abandon it because they can't seem to make it work. Although they start off with good intentions, somehow they can't manage to study when they are supposed to.

Take Pete, for example. His schedule called for him to read for English literature from seven until ten o'clock. Determined to do his work on schedule, he sat down at his desk promptly at seven. He opened his book and began to read. But when he reached for his pen to make notes, he discovered that it wasn't in his pocket. He opened the desk drawer thinking to find another pen, but none was there. When he walked across the hall to borrow one from a friend, he became so absorbed in a discussion of the prospects of the Washington Redskins that he forgot he was supposed to be studying English. When he finally got around to leaving, someone said something about a good TV show at eight o'clock. Pete managed to persuade himself that he could study English while watching TV in the lounge. With his attention divided between the TV and the book, he found himself daydreaming about the upcoming weekend and wondering whether he should try to go home to borrow one of the family cars. Ten o'clock came, time to go out for a beer and still no work done.

Dribbling away time is the single biggest block to effective study. If this is a problem for you—and it probably is—it can be solved only with practice and determination. Here are some practical measures you can take.

Establish Definite Study Periods. In your study periods you should do *nothing else but study*. Start by making your study periods short, if you have a problem. Plan for definite periods of rest or relaxation at preplanned intervals. Planning for three hours at one crack and accomplishing nothing is useless. Settle for one hour at a time. If you really have problems concentrating, cut that down. With a modest goal, you'll be more likely to do what you set out to do and have the feeling that you have accomplished something. Start out where you know you can work. If you can't concentrate for an hour, try twenty minutes. Take a ten-minute break and then come back for another twenty minutes. If you can't concentrate for even such short periods of time, you are in serious trouble. You ought to seek some counseling. A counselor, by knowing your unique case, can sometimes help. Or, perhaps, you're not ready for college yet. Most people can study the dullest subject for short periods of time.

Once you've gotten used to an easy schedule, gradually change it. The satisfaction that comes from working well when you work will give you the impetus to work for longer periods. Even students who are very proficient at studying, however, need periodic breaks in order to sustain concentration. A short break every hour or so should keep you alert and relaxed.

Find a Good Place to Study. Some people could concentrate on studying in the middle of the year's biggest party, but most of us need a good place to do our work well. The best place is to sit at a table or desk, not on a bed. If you read or study in a prone position, you're much more likely to daydream or doze off to sleep. Sitting up straight provides the degree of muscle tone necessary to keep you alert.

Keep your table or desk clear of everything not connected with study. That means no pictures, trophies, radio, or any other thing that might distract you from the task at hand. For the same reason, a table or desk that faces the wall or is away from people or objects in the room is a good idea. If you don't see people passing by, or if you're in the library, the other students around you, you'll work with greater concentration.

Good lighting that covers the entire working area is important too. Try to avoid strong shadows on your work. If it is hard to see your work, you'll tire more easily and give up more quickly. Strong light that is comfortable, pleasant, and evenly distributed will make your task easier and more inviting.

Be sure that all the books and equipment you'll need are at hand. Textbooks, notebooks, pens, pencils, erasers, and a good dictionary are essential. Having to hunt for a required book wastes time and invites procrastination. Remember, Pete's wasted evening started with a missing pen.

Any place that provides the best combination of the conditions we have been describing is a good place to work. Your own room, if other people can't disturb you, is a good place. Even if you have a roommate, your room can be a good place, provided your roommate is intent on following the same rules for effective study that you are.

Often, however, other people in your dormitory, fraternity, sorority, or apartment house are on different schedules from yours and are no more disciplined than you are about getting down to work. They interrupt you; they carry on interesting conversations within earshot; they listen to the radio or the stereo. In the war against time dribbled away our worst enemies are our friends, relatives, and roommates.

Find a place to work where other people can't bother you. The best place is usually the library. Find as isolated a spot as you can in the library. Face away from the entrance. Libraries usually enforce rules against talking and other distractions. There are no TVs and no pictures of boyfriends or girlfriends to look at. In addition, the atmosphere generally discourages daydreaming. It's not surprising to find out that students who regularly study in the library make, on the average, better grades than other students.

If you say, as do many students, that you feel uncomfortable studying in the library, it may be that you really are not motivated to study or that you are afraid you might miss out on something interesting in the dormitory or sorority or fraternity house. It is true that some people find it easier to study in familiar surroundings. If this is the case for you, the best thing you can do is to get thoroughly acquainted with the library so that it seems like a good place to be.

In a few large institutions or places in which facilities are tight, the library may be too crowded. Usually, in these places other locations are available. Even unused classrooms sometimes make good places to study. Then, some people who have learned to study effectively can do it in most unusual places—on park benches, on buses and trains, in noisy rooms. But if you're still learning the art of studying, it's safer to pick the library or some other place designed for and restricted to studying.

Many dormitories, fraternity and sorority houses, as well as student centers have special study rooms which are quiet and free from distractions. If you can't be comfortable in the library or you're too far from the library, these make good substitutes.

IMPROVING YOUR ABILITY TO CONCENTRATE

No matter how well organized your time or how ideal your place for study, you will have to use your mind effectively to accomplish something. There are a lot of things that make concentration easier. Physical fitness is one of them. Eat regular meals. Get enough sleep. Don't try to live it up and study at the same time. Save the partying for weekends or for times when you can take off from studying. Getting enough sleep is probably the hardest thing for most students.

Keeping physically fit also means getting a reasonable amount of recreation and exercise. If you enjoy something like tennis or squash, set aside definite times to play. If you're not all that wild about a particular sport, jogging, tossing a frisbee around, or even a regular regime of walking provides exercise that can keep you feeling healthy and fit.

Sleepiness often gets in the way of effective study. If you get sufficient sleep regularly, you shouldn't be sleepy during the day. Study, however, is a quiet activity, and sometimes it is boring. Both of these conditions can make you sleepy, so you may find that you have to fight off sleepiness when you study, even when you have been regularly getting your eight hours. Don't yield to the temptation to put off studying until you are fresh, because doing so will only get you off your schedule to no advantage. The best approach is to fight sleepiness. One way is to take a five-minute break in which you rest or even nap (be sure to have something or someone ready to wake you up). Most people snap back quickly after a short rest. Another is to move around. Pace the floor. Take a brisk but brief walk, or do your work out loud. Still another way to fight sleepiness is to identify those times when you are likely to feel sleepy—for most people, after meals— and schedule those things you find easiest to concentrate on then, or instead of studying, some mildly active form of recreation (don't watch TV).

Different from but related to sleepiness is the feeling of being tired. After a period of reading or study, you may feel mentally fatigued. Research shows that this kind of fatigue is not really very much like fatigue that comes from hard physical work. Rather, it is the result of boredom and a diminished motivation for study. Take it into account in making or revising your schedule. Study for brief periods of time those subjects that appear to make you tired or fatigued. Schedule the longer study periods for those things that absorb your attention. It is also a good idea to study those subjects that interest you the least first and save for later those things that you enjoy more.

Maintaining interest in studying is the goal to be achieved. Anything that will keep you alert is worth a try. For example, you might argue with what you read. As you read something, translate what the author says into the opposite and ask, Why isn't that true? An important feature of effective studying is taking an active rather than a passive attitude. Taking an active attitude promotes attentiveness and helps fight off boredom and fatigue.

STRENGTHENING BASIC SKILLS

How do your basic skills measure up? Are they adequate for the kind of studying you have to do?

Some years ago, Luella Cole Pressey gave questions like those you will find on page 20 to fifty good students and fifty poor ones at Ohio State University. Answer the questions yourself, and compare the pattern of your answers with those given by the good students.

IDENTIFYING YOUR WEAKNESSES

If you have answered the questions honestly, you will be able to pick out those aspects of your basic study skills that need improvement. But the list is almost endless.

Reading, for example, is something that most students take for granted. Don't. Ask yourself, How well do I really read? Some people read so poorly in comparison with others that they are, for all practical purposes, nearly illiterate. Have you thought about how fast you read? Nearly everyone can read faster than he or she does even without special training in speed-reading. How much of what you read do you remember? Most students don't remember more than half of what they read, even right after they have read it. Can you decide what is worth trying to remember? Can you interpret charts and tables? The captions for them? What do you do when you first start to read an assignment? What do you do when you finish reading an assignment? How many times do you read an assignment? When? Do you read a textbook the same way you read a novel? Do you read chemistry and anthropology the same way? If not, what's the difference?

Do you take notes? Not all students do. What kind of notes do you take? Are they adequate? Do you ever have the feeling that the instructor springs things on you in exams that were not in the lectures or in the reading?

Some college students do not know the precise meaning of important words, words that instructors assume all students know. How extensive is your vocabulary? Do you pay attention to new words you encounter? Have you established the habit of consulting the dictionary regularly? Do you know the difference between general and technical words? Can you identify technical words? Are you sure about the meaning of common prefixes and suffixes?

Many students are paralyzed when they have to confront a problem that demands simple arithmetic or elementary algebra. Are you able to do the ordinary operations of addition, subtraction, multiplication, and division rapidly and accurately? Can you translate a word problem into the necessary arithmetic? Do you know how to deal with fractional exponents? Do you know how to read graphs? Can you move a term from one side of an equation to the other?

HOW GOOD A STUDENT ARE YOU?

Read carefully each of the following questions, and answer it honestly by writing a "yes" or "no" in the margin to the left of the question. When you are finished, see the directions for scoring at the end of the test.

1. Can you think of anything that prevents you from doing your best work?
2. Do you usually study every day in the same place?
3. Do you usually know in the morning just how you are going to spend your day?
4. Does your desk have anything on it that might distract you from your work?
5. When studying, do you frequently skip the graphs or tables in your textbook?
6. Do you frequently make simple charts or diagrams to represent points in your reading?
7. When you find a word in your reading that you do not know, do you usually look it up in the dictionary?
8. Do you usually skim over a chapter before reading it in detail?
9. Do you usually glance through a chapter, looking at the paragraph headings, before reading it in detail?
10. Do you usually read the summary at the end of a chapter before reading the chapter?
11. Do you keep your notes for one subject all together?

12. Do you usually take your notes in lecture in outline form?
13. Do you usually take your notes on reading in outline form?
14. Do you usually try to summarize your readings in a sentence or a short paragraph?
15. After you have read a chapter and taken notes on it, do you usually write a summary of the chapter as a whole?
16. Do you sit up studying late the night before an examination?
17. In preparing for an examination, do you try to memorize the text?
18. When you memorize something, do you usually do it all at one time?
19. Do you at times try to analyze your work to see just where you may be weak?
20. Do you often write an answer to a question and then realize that it seems to be the answer to some other question on the examination?
21. Do you consciously try to use facts you learn in one course to help you in your work on some other course?
22. Do you usually take notes in class just as rapidly as you can write?

Some years ago Luella Cole Pressey gave questions like these to fifty good students and fifty poor ones at Ohio State University. Good students more often than poor ones answered them as follows: (1) no, (2) yes, (3) yes, (4) no, (5) no, (6) yes, (7) yes, (8) yes, (9) yes, (10) yes, (11) yes, (12) yes, (13) yes, (14) yes, (15) yes, (16) no, (17) no, (18) no, (19) yes, (20) no, (21) yes, (22) no.

CORRECTING YOUR WEAKNESSES

These are enough questions for the time being. Even the best students can't answer all these questions in the right way. When they do think they know the answers, they are often wrong. In the chapters to follow, we are going to deal with the answers to these questions and others and give you specific suggestions for getting the most from the classroom experience, improving your reading skills, studying textbooks more efficiently, taking examinations, writing papers, and studying foreign languages, mathematics, and the sciences. These suggestions, if you put them to use, will pay off in more efficient study, better grades, and greater satisfaction from your college experience.

We have already made the point that college is very different from high school. Besides facing tougher demands, college students work much more on their own. In particular, the relative importance of classes and homework is reversed. In high school, you probably spent twenty-five to thirty hours a week in class and usually no more than a third of that doing reading and other outside assignments. In college, you can expect to spend fifteen to eighteen hours in classes and laboratories and approximately twice that in preparation outside of class. That is one of the reasons we emphasize the skills needed in study outside of the classroom. But learning both in high school and college starts in the classroom, so that is where we begin.

HOW TO GET THE MOST OUT OF YOUR LECTURE COURSES

College classes vary in size, and size often determines what the course is like. Some small colleges and a few private institutions that have a relatively large faculty-student ratio may maintain class size at no more than thirty. Publicly supported colleges as well as most private ones do not try to keep all classes small. Rather, they will let the nature of the subject set the size of the class. Freshman English courses and foreign languages are taught in small sections because such courses require recitation and discussion. On the other hand, most other freshman courses will be so large that little or no discussion is possible. These courses are planned as a series of lectures. The teacher, often a well-known expert in the subject, will do nearly all the talking. It doesn't matter, therefore, how many students are in the class, for the lecturer can just as easily talk to three hundred as to a hundred students. The chances are that you will find yourself in one or more such large courses, even if you are at a relatively small institution.

ATTENDING DISCUSSION SECTIONS

In many courses, the one-way flow of communication in lecture will be offset by having small groups of students meet once a week in discussion or quiz sections. The purpose of these sections is to allow students to ask questions and to put the lecture and reading material into their own words. Because such teaching is time-consuming, it is usually done by graduate students or by junior members of the faculty who are relatively inexperienced teachers. Moreover, there is likely to be little that is new introduced in such sections. The result is that students who are not particularly interested in the subject have little incen-

CHAPTER THREE

THE CLASSROOM EXPERIENCE

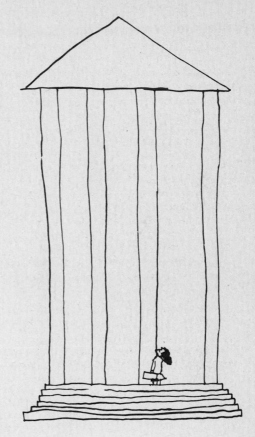

tive to attend. To provide such incentive and to motivate students to keep up with the reading, quizzes are often important features of such sections.

Nevertheless, students are tempted to cut discussion sections, especially if the instructor appears to be inept. Before you do this, make sure that attendance in discussion sections is not required in your particular courses. If it is, your absence will be easily noted, and you may find yourself with a lower grade as the result of poor attendance. And if quizzes are given, it is your responsibility to find out when they are scheduled and what material they will cover. But even when sections are not particularly well taught, it is possible to get a lot out of them if you take steps to do so.

Our advice to all freshman students is attend class faithfully regardless of the way the course is organized. Even if the lecturer goes over the same ground as the textbook, it is worth your while to attend. Students who frequently cut classes usually have academic difficulties. After you have had some experience in college and know your own strengths and limitations, you may be in a position to decide wisely whether or not some classes can be cut.

UNDERSTANDING THE ORGANIZATION

Large lecture courses are usually carefully planned. A teacher of such a course doesn't just assign a textbook, start lecturing, and periodically announce a quiz or an hourly examination. He or she will usually pass out an outline or syllabus that lays out the topics to be covered. The plan of the course will also include a schedule of examinations. The dates of these, because so many students must take them, can almost never be changed once they are set. Hence, you should note when they occur and see if you have hourly exams in other courses scheduled near the same date. If so, you will have to plan your preparation to deal with the problem. It is unlikely that any of your instructors will be sympathetic enough about your plight to allow you an alternate examination date.

If you happen to be sick at the time of an examination, it is your responsibility to notify the instructor or teaching assistant and request a make-up exam at his or her convenience. Instructors differ in their policy on make-ups, but most don't like them and some even assign handicaps or penalties to students who need them. So unless absolutely necessary, avoid missing exams.

Some instructors will tell students how exams will be weighted. For example, half of the exam may be based upon the lectures and half upon the readings. Other instructors are not so clear about the content of

an exam, and they will give you only a rough idea of what is to be covered.

Most examinations in large lecture courses are objective. These are examinations in which you write a little or nothing but rather choose from alternative answers to multiple-choice questions, mark items true or false, or match up items. The teacher will usually tell you early in the course what kinds of exams you will have, and this should determine the way in which you study, as we shall point out later.

Another thing you will want to know about a course is how the lectures are related to the assigned readings. Often the instructor will organize the lectures differently from the readings. Whether or not this is the case, you will want to keep your reading and lecture notes separate. This will be true even when the teacher follows the book closely.

Be sure you understand at the outset how the course is organized. If an outline or syllabus is handed out, be sure you get one. This material is usually handed out the first day of class, and if you have to miss that day for one reason or another, be sure to get your copy of the course outline. It is a good idea to attend the first meeting of any course you think you might take, even if you are undecided or have not yet been able to register for it. But if you don't make the first class, it is absolutely essential that you obtain whatever materials were handed out on that day.

Improving Listening Skills. Listening to lectures in large classes can be a boring and even depressing experience. It makes some people feel that they are part of a faceless herd that is being talked to—often talked down to—by some remote, impersonal figure. Because there is nothing to do but listen, some people adopt the wrong attitude toward lectures. They slump in their seats, take no notes, daydream, and only occasionally catch what is being said. If the lecturer is not particularly inspired or the material dull, it is all the easier to take this attitude.

Good listening, like good studying generally, is an active process. If you sit up, are alert, and are prepared to concentrate, the chances are you won't daydream or fall asleep even if the lecturer is dull or is a poor speaker. Keep your mind on what the lecturer says, not on his or her mannerisms or speaking voice, the pictures on the wall, or the view from the window. You can profit from even the dullest lecturer if you have the right attitude. Taking good notes and keeping your mind on what is being said will repay you at examination time. You won't have that feeling that so many students have of not even recognizing what some of the examination questions are about because you were daydreaming when that topic was discussed.

TAKING GOOD LECTURE NOTES

In addition to being a good listener, you must take good notes for lecture courses. Most students know that they should take notes in class, but many don't know how to go about it. They take either too many or too few notes because they don't know how to pick out what is important. Taking lecture notes is an art developed through practice. It requires a certain amount of effort. That means an alert mind in class and additional time spent after class in editing and rewriting the notes. Time spent developing note-taking skills is time well spent. Good lecture and classroom notes will enrich your college experience.

Surveying, Questioning, Listening. A country politician, explaining how he gave speeches, said, "I tell 'em what I'm gonna tell 'em, then I tell 'em, and then I tell 'em what I told 'em." Most good speeches, chapters, or articles give you some idea ahead of time of what is to come. When you read something, you can generally survey by skimming the headings and reading the summaries. But when it comes to lectures, you can't survey unless the lecture does it for you.

Some lecturers do give you a preview of what they are going to say, and if you get to class on time and are on your toes, you'll pick it up. One very successful lecturer used to make a practice of putting a detailed outline of what he was going to say on the board. Not many lecturers go that far, but if you listen carefully and jot down the points the lecturer says he or she is going to cover, it will help you organize your notes sensibly. You can refer to these topical notes as the lecture proceeds. Surveying helps you to see the orderly development of ideas and to anticipate those places in the lecture where questions you have may be answered.

And questioning is one of the things you should do to get the most out of a lecture. Use the few moments before class to think of questions based upon your reading of the textbook or upon what the lecturer said the last time. If you can't think of anything else, ask yourself, What do I know already about this topic? If you start thinking about the topic of the day as soon as you are settled in class, you will be in the right frame of mind to be an active participant in the course. Continue to raise questions in your own mind as the lecturer talks. This kind of mental activity is one of the principal ways in which you yourself can be a part of the lecture process. Even a dull lecture will be more interesting if you listen to it in this way. If the course is the kind that invites challenging the lecturer's ideas, do so while you are listening and then see how well he or she can give a defense. One of the themes of this book is that effective studying demands active participation. It may seem hard to participate actively in a lecture when all you are supposed to do is listen. But if you listen in this kind of questioning, anticipatory way, you will be as active as you can be under the circumstances.

GETTING THE ORGANIZATION

If you are going to understand a lecture, you must grasp its organization, even if the lecturer does not explicitly tell you what it is. Tone of voice, little phrases such as "And now let us turn to . . ." tell you when a new topic is introduced or what is subordinate to what in the organization of the lecture. Some lecturers talk so fast or are so deficient in telling you about their organization that all you can do is to write down everything that seems to be important irrespective of how it is organized. You must then organize your notes after class. In any event, organizing your notes is an important step in making sense out of them.

To help you provide that organization, here are some of the major clues instructors use to tell you what is important and what is not important: (1) Statements such as "The main point is . . ." or "Remember this . . ." tell you directly; (2) a statement that is repeated often is important to the instructor and ought to be important to you; (3) something may be said in two or three different ways, which is a kind of repetition, though sometimes hard to detect; (4) sometimes a change in pace may serve as a clue: when a lecturer slows down and says something very deliberately, it is probably important.

Lecturers have different styles. Each one will have his or her own way of telling you what is important. Get to know the style of your lecturers so that you know how to identify how each of them tells you what is important. Comparing your reaction to those of others to the instructor will help you in that interpretation. Other students may pick up things you miss, and vice versa.

Identify the major points the lecturer makes. Listening carefully will tell you that the lecturer organizes what he or she says into the equivalent of paragraphs and sections. Your job is to extract the essential information from those paragraphs. When you edit or rewrite your notes, do so in your own words. That way you will be sure you understand what you've taken down. However, watch for technical definitions or statements that are obviously intended to be taken down word for word.

If you have trouble organizing your notes, remember that any kind of notes are better than none at all. If a subject matter is new to you, or the instructor gives you so much information that you are overwhelmed, just try to get it down and to understand it. Perhaps it can only be organized when you put it together with the information you are supposed to pick up from your reading assignments.

How many notes you should take will depend upon a lot of things, but mainly on how fast you can write while listening. If you can't keep up, practice trying to extract the main points. But don't give up altogether. Only a tiny minority of students can get by with no notes whatever. The chances are you're not one of them.

REVIEWING AND REVISING

Your lecture notes, no matter how good you are at taking them, will be, compared with your textbook, incomplete, imperfect, and not too well organized. Revision helps. It also provides you with a chance to review and recite what you have learned. Review and recitation are the only tools you have to fight the inevitable course of forgetting.

Your first review should be right after the lecture or as close to that as you can manage. That way you can fill in information you may not have gotten down in your notes but which is still fresh in your mind. The worst thing you can do is to let your notes go to the point at which you cannot even decipher them before you get around to trying to review them.

Don't just rewrite your notes mindlessly. Having them neatly copied may make them easier to read in the future, but copying will be an empty exercise if you don't engage your mind while you do it. Rewriting will never do any harm, but if you take the time to rewrite, make sure that you do it actively.

KEEPING LECTURE NOTES

In talking to hundreds of students who have done badly on examinations, we have discovered that one of the most common and obvious deficiencies in their study methods has to do with note taking and the use of notes. That is why we spend so much time describing this aspect of studying. Learning to keep a good notebook has been the saving of many a student.

At the very least, you should have dividers for each subject you are taking. Always keep a plentiful supply of blank paper on hand. Many students keep separate spiral notebooks for each course. This is fine, if you remember to take the right notebook with you to class. Nothing is worse than a higgledy-piggledy notebook with a page devoted to psychology and then one to economics or government.

While some good students make do with almost any

arrangement, the best size for most people is letter size—8½ by 11 inches. A notebook of this size allows plenty of room for marginal comments and spare copying, and it cuts down on the amount of page turning you must do.

For lectures, date your notes; for textbook notes, indicate the chapters or pages. Do so for every page of notes so that you can always tell at a glance where you are in reviewing your notes. Keep all your notes in your notebook. If for some reason you are caught without your notebook and have to take your notes on a separate sheet of paper, transcribe them into your notebook at the first possible chance.

THE FIVE R'S OF NOTE TAKING

Professor Walter Pauk of the Study Center at Cornell University describes five essential aspects of note taking. He characterizes these as the five R's of note taking. Here they are:

1. *Recording.* Get down the main ideas and facts.

2. *Reducing.* To reduce is to summarize. Pick out key terms and concepts. You can make from your notes what students sometimes call "cram sheets." These are sheets that list, usually in outline form, the bare bones of a course. You will use them in reviewing by using the key ideas as cues for reciting the details of what you have in your notes. On each page of notes you take, allow room to write down these cues. You will find on example of reducing on page 25.

3. *Reciting.* Review lectures notes as soon after the lecture as possible. But you will also want to review your notes before an exam and from time to time during the semester to keep them fresh in your mind. Do so *in your own words*. That way you will know that you understand.

4. *Reflecting.* Something that many students don't grasp is that ideas from college courses are meant to be thought about. It is easy to fall into the trap of reciting ideas by rote. One of the main purposes of a college education is to help you think. Then, too, if you reflect about what you are learning, you won't be surprised when ideas turn up on examinations in an unexpected form.

5. *Reviewing.* One of the real secrets of successful studying is knowing when, how, and what to review. But however you do it, reviewing is essential. Even the accomplished performer— the pianist or the stage performer—knows that

ILLUSTRATION OF REDUCED NOTES

Original notes	Reduced Notes

Original notes

History 121   February 2, 1979

The Normans (cont'd)
I. Gov't of Henry II 1154–1189
   A. Chancery
      1. Documents became uniform.
      2. All executive orders dependent on written orders from king—per breve regis.
   B. Exchequer
      1. Administrative agents of the king: Sheriff, Viscount.
      2. Revenues were collected at Easter and Michaelmas.
        a. At Easter, Sheriff would pay one-half and be given a notched-stick talley as a receipt for what he had paid. He kept one-half, the exchequer the other.
        b. Revenues computed on principle of abacus.
      3. Every item of income was recorded year by year on pipe rolls (rolled skins of parchment). These are extant from second year of Henry II's reign.
   C. Judicial
      1. Tried to develop a system of courts and judges that would not require his personal intervention.
      2. Itinerant judges on circuit.
        a. Extended over all England.
        b. Broke down local privileges.
        c. Led to Common Law.
      3. Early court was an assembly of the king's barons; after Henry II the court became a body of professional judges.
II. Breakup of Anglo-Norman Empire . . .

Reduced Notes

The Normans (cont'd)
Gov't of Henry II 1154–1189
I. Organization
   A. Chancery
   B. Exchequer
   C. Judicial
II. Administrative reform
   A. Uniform documents
   B. Per breve regis for executive orders
   C. Sheriff, Viscount as administrative agents
   D. Revenues collected at Easter and Michaelmas
   E. Pipe rolls record yearly income
   F. System of courts
      1. Extended all over England
      2. Broke down local privileges
      3. Body of professional judges
      4. Led to Common Law

a review, no matter how well he or she may know the material, is essential to a professional performance.

BY WAY OF CAUTION

Good students often find very eccentric ways to study. If you are such a student, you can ignore nearly everything we've written above. You can take notes on the backs of old envelopes if you want. If you are a virtuoso performer as a student, you can get by with just about anything. But before you try, you had better be sure you are such a virtuoso. And even if you are, there are two things you would be hard put to ignore. The first is to take an active role. Whatever you do, don't just listen passively. Try to anticipate the lecturer. Enter into as aggressive a role as you can without actually challenging the lecturer out loud. The second is to review. Few of us are gifted with the kind of memory and understanding that allows us to reproduce something new and difficult after only one exposure.

HOW TO GET THE MOST OUT OF RECITATION COURSES

Recitation courses, by contrast to lecture courses, require little in the way of note taking. The main thing in these courses is to be prepared to recite. That may mean knowing the assignment, and it may also mean being prepared to contribute ideas of your own to the discussion as well as being attentive to the ideas expressed by your classmates.

CONTRIBUTING TO DISCUSSION

Discussion classes are only as lively as their contributors make them. You can't sit back and expect to be entertained in a discussion section. Don't be afraid of appearing to be ignorant by asking questions. The truly ignorant student rarely asks questions. Usually, it is the intelligent, thoughtful student who does so. Don't be afraid to ask for information. That's what you're there for—to learn. When the instructor asks questions, volunteer, even though you are not sure of the answer. Volunteering for questions is a good, active form of studying, and the chances are you aren't going to be graded on your oral answer.

EXCHANGING IDEAS WITH CLASSMATES

Sometimes small recitation and discussion sections degenerate into a two-way discussion between the instructor and individual students. A lot of discussion sections, however, are run like seminars in which the students are expected to talk to each other rather than to the instructor. If you are fortunate enough to be in one of these, and if it is skillfully managed so that the students do really talk to each other, you will have experienced one of the best and most satisfying forms of education. In a really good discussion, the instructor need only intervene to get people back on the track or supply some missing information. If you are in a genuinely free-wheeling discussion group, you will probably be surprised at the variety of beliefs and attitudes people have as well as by the intensity with which they sometimes hold on to these.

HOW TO GET THE MOST OUT OF INDEPENDENT STUDY

Most colleges and universities offer opportunities for independent study under the guidance or sponsorship of faculty members. Usually, such courses may be taken for variable amounts of credit, a modest project earning one or two credits and a more ambitious one, three or more credits. Independent study may be directed reading or the preparation of a sizable essay on some topic, or it may involve you in original research. In any case, it will give you the chance to plan your own course around a topic that interests you. And you should have the opportunity to discuss your work at regular intervals with a faculty advisor. If the course involves working on a professor's research project, you will gain experience in the laboratory or out in the field gathering data. It may even result in a scholarly publication with your name listed as a coauthor.

PLANNING YOUR WORK

It is tempting, with an entire semester to complete a project, to put off getting started. Don't fall into this trap, or you will end up with an unfinished project and no grade for the course, or what is worse, a hastily done project and a poor grade. Get started immediately. Decide what you need to do and build time into your schedule so that you can work each week toward your goal. If library research is required, set aside the necessary library hours each week. If it is laboratory work that you are doing, schedule it at regular intervals. If your project requires that you conduct interviews or make observations in the field, schedule these so that you will have all your data gathered with plenty of time for analysis.

As with any other course, make provisions to keep your notes or whatever else you will have in an organized way. Nothing makes a worse impression on a professor than to have some student who is working on a research project come into his or her office with a handful of odds and ends of paper with penciled notes and data scrawled every which way on them.

CONFERENCES WITH YOUR FACULTY ADVISOR

Schedule regular conferences with your faculty advisor. Faculty members are busy people, and they are apt to forget about you or be hard to track down unless you have a regularly scheduled time at which you meet with them. Sometimes in independent study, you will be part of a research team, and you will meet regularly with a group. But if you are on your own, be sure you have a regular time for conferring with your advisor, even if it is only for a few minutes. When a faculty member agrees to sponsor you in independent study, he or she makes an implied commitment to spend time with you. You have a claim to your advisor's time, no matter how busy he or she is.

PREPARING YOUR PAPER OR FINAL REPORT

Decide at the outset what form your final report will take. Allow plenty of time to prepare it. If it is a paper, follow the procedures described in Chapter 7. If something not quite like a typical paper is expected, be sure you know what it is and begin to gather the materials you will need as soon as possible. Any independent project that you have worked on for an entire semester is worth the effort of a presentation that will do it justice. Don't let a hasty or sloppy presentation of your efforts disguise all the work you have done.

Some Tips about Independent Study. Independent study is one of the best features of a college education, but don't overdo it. A student who spent half his or her junior and senior years doing independent study may be looked upon with suspicion when applying to graduate school. If you have really done a lot of independent study, be sure you have copies of whatever product resulted. You may want to submit these with your graduate application or to a prospective employer. But if you have put a lot of time in on independent study with little to show for it, those who examine your record will entertain the impression that you were looking for easy A's or a way to boost your grade point average without too much work.

If you do a really good job on an independent project in, say, your sophomore or junior year, keep in touch with your advisor. He or she will know you well and be able to write a good letter of recommendation for you.

A FINAL WORD

This chapter is the shortest in this book. And for a good reason. We've already pointed out to you that in your college years you will spend about twice as much time in study outside of class as you will in class. In high school you were taught. In college, to a surprising extent, you teach yourself. It's not that going to class is not important for most students it is an absolute must—but it has a different flavor in college. Chances are your high school teacher monitored your work carefully. That was part of his or her job. In most colleges the role of the teacher is different. Your professor knows more than you do, and it is his or her job to tell you what he or she knows, or lead you to discover it yourself, or better yet, show you how to discover knowledge completely on your own. Learning how to teach yourself is vastly easier if you go to class. If you take advantage of your new freedom to cut class, to sleep, or to ignore what is going on, you're just making trouble for yourself. Once again, let us remind you that if you find going to class such an awful chore that you can't bring yourself to do it, you ought to think about whether or not you are ready for college.

CHAPTER FOUR

THE ART OF READING

*But thanks to my friends for their care in my
breeding,*
*Who taught me betimes to love working and
reading.*

ISAAC WATTS (1674–1748)

Isaac Watts is a bit stuffy for modern tastes (he also wrote "For Satan finds some mischief still for idle hands to do" and "How doth the little busy bee improve each shining hour"). But he has a point. You are fortunate if you have learned to read well and like reading. Generally, these things go together. People who read well like to read, while those who do not, find it to be a chore. In college you must do more reading than you have ever done before, and if you don't read well, you will need to work hard on doing better at it. When you are better at it, you will like it more. Even if you are a good reader, the chances are you can improve some aspect of your reading skills. This chapter is designed to help you do that. If you really have trouble reading, you may need some special instruction in improving your skills. Some of the information in this chapter may help you decide whether you need special help or not.

The following questions are meant to help you find out if you are deficient in any of the most basic aspects of reading. Answer them carefully and honestly. If you cannot answer a question, keep the question in mind, and when you are next reading something—this book will do—try to determine whether you have one or more faulty habits of reading. Any question to which you answer "yes" marks a fault.

1. *Do you move your lips or vocalize when you read?* Silent reading isn't as old as reading itself. Through much of recorded history, readers read aloud (even in a library!). But that was when books were few and much of learning was oral. Reading aloud is too inefficient for the modern world. When you move your lips, you are going through exactly the movements made in reading aloud. It is inefficient because it slows you down.

   We could go on to tell you that moving lips is a bad habit that you ought to break. It is a bad habit all right, but it is a symptom rather than a cause of poor reading. Simply holding your lips still will not improve your reading, but if you learn to read better and faster, lip movements should all but disappear. Then, too, there are going to be some times when you will want to read in a way that encourages lip movements—when you are reading something very carefully or when you are reading something that is difficult to follow.

2. *Do you read each word one by one?* Good readers know that some words are more important than others, and they do not give equal emphasis to each word. Reading words one

by one is more a symptom than a cause of poor reading, and it is usually a symptom of very poor reading indeed. People who read word by word generally have a hard time putting together the words to make sense. They can understand each word as it comes, but they have no idea what the words are saying when they are put together in phrases and sentences. Such people are probably deficient in all aspects of literacy. The chances are they write poorly and do not understand English grammar.

3. *Do you often find words you do not understand or are unfamiliar to you in your assigned readings?* If you do, you need to work on your vocabulary. There are some ways to improve your vocabulary, and we will discuss them later in this chapter.

4. *Do you backtrack and find it necessary to reread what you have just read?* This is a symptom of inattention. And sometimes, even when you attend you don't always remember what you read as well as you need to. The result is that you have to read and reread. If, however, you do a good job of *studying* what you are assigned, you won't have to reread when you review. We will give you some suggestions for studying in Chapter 5 so that you won't have to reread the same material many times.

5. *Do you read everything at the same rate and in the same way?* Francis Bacon told us that "Some books are to be tasted, others to be swallowed, and some few to be chewed and digested." Some things should only be skimmed. Other things, such as entertaining stories, can be read as rapidly as possible by a mixture of reading and skimming. Still others must be read very carefully. You must go through each sentence as if every word were a mine ready to be exploded. If you don't adjust your rate to the nature and difficulty of the material you are reading, you are not a good reader and you probably don't enjoy reading as much as you should.

6. *Do you often complain that you don't understand what you read?* Some things you won't understand. All of us are going to have trouble understanding some of what we read, simply because we are ignorant of the technical details of the subject. But you should be able to understand *most* of the textbooks assigned at your college. If you feel that you do not understand a significant part of what you read, you are a poor reader. The chances are that it isn't just because you don't have the technical background (though that may be part of the problem), but because you are deficient in basic language skills and because you have developed poor reading habits.

There are other faults, but these are diagnostic. If your reading is characterized by any of these things, then you have room for a lot of improvement. And as we will point out, with a little application, nearly everyone can improve his or her reading skills in some respect. There are a very few people whose difficulties with reading are so fundamental and deep-seated that their problem must be described by a special word, *dyslexia*. Most people *can* improve.

READING WITH A PURPOSE

Most students, when they sit down to study, select a book and begin to read. They don't give any thought to the special purpose they may have in reading, with the result that they read everything—literature, history, chemistry, political science—the same way. But there are as many different ways to read as there are purposes in reading. How you read should depend upon your purpose at the moment.

SKIMMING

One aim in reading is to find out what something is about. You want to know what kinds of things are in a particular book, or you may want to know if something you are interested in is mentioned. One way is to look for signposts. In textbooks and some technical books, that is relatively easy to do, for the headings do most of the work for you. You can page through a book or chapter simply examining the headings and subheadings. Another way, particularly in books that do not have headings, is to examine the first sentence of each paragraph. While it isn't necessarily true that the first sentence contains the main idea of that paragraph, most of the time it does. On the same principle, you may want to read the opening paragraph of each chapter or section. Finally, a third way to skim is to run your eyes over the page looking for certain critical words. This may be necessary in books that do not have indexes. And even for books that do have indexes, you may learn as much by leafing through the book, looking for words here and there, and reading sentences here and there as you would by going through the index.

Skimming is an important and first step in studying,

and we will have more to say about it later in this chapter and in the next.

GETTING THE MAIN IDEA

Sometimes we read just to get the main idea. That is important in business and professional reading, and in many courses in which you have extensive supplementary reading, you may have to read with the sole idea of understanding the main idea. It is also the thing you do in the first stage of study, as part of your survey. Even when you read carefully, you will want to be able to pick out the main idea in each section of the book you are reading.

How do you find the main ideas? This depends upon the level you are looking at. There are main ideas for entire chapters, sections, subsections, and paragraphs. Paragraphs are the smallest unit, and we will start with them. The usual definition of a paragraph, as a matter of fact, is that it is a section of prose that contains a single topic. Everything in a paragraph centers around that single topic. Most writers know that, and they usually put one topic and only one topic in each paragraph. Students sometimes don't, and we will have more to say about that in Chapter 7. Suffice it to say here, learning to identify the main or topical idea in reading will help you structure your own writing better.

In writing, you are told to begin a paragraph with a topical sentence, then explain it, illustrate it, support it with additional sentences, and finally wind up with a summary statement or a transitional sentence. To have the topical sentence come first in a paragraph is not, however, always practicable or desirable. Sometimes a transition sentence comes first. Such a sentence shows the connection between one paragraph and the one that comes before or after. Sometimes the author can't give you the main idea first. A good way to present something new, for example, is to illustrate the principle you are going to state first. Thus, it will remind the reader of something which he or she already knows before you state the principle. It is the principle, not the illustration, that is the main idea. It is what is new to you, not what you are familiar with that is the main idea. On page 31 you will find an exercise to help you locate main ideas.

In looking for the main idea, don't look for whole sentences. Sentences usually have more than one idea in them. The main idea is likely to be the principal clause or phrase in a sentence. You can usually boil it down to a couple of words in your own mind.

To see what we mean, pick up one of your textbooks and find some sentences with main ideas. Now try throwing away the modifiers. Keep only the subject and the essential words in the predicate. The chances are you will have the main idea.

Remember, however, that sometimes qualifiers are important to the main idea of a topical sentence. If you throw away the adjective in the sentence, "Even tame lions bite," you will miss the essential point of the sentence. On the other hand, if you read, "The person who reads rapidly, scanning each line in the fewest number of glances and not stopping to daydream, is typically the person who learns a great deal in a short period of time," you can eliminate most of the words, translate them, and come up with "The fast reader is usually the fast learner" as the main idea.

You will occasionally encounter paragraphs in which the main idea is not expressed at all. That doesn't happen very often in textbooks, but it does happen in literature generally and in fiction in particular. A writer may spend a paragraph describing a house. The purpose, however, is not to tell you about the house, but by describing it to tell you about the people who live there. From the description you may know that they are old, fussy, and aloof. You need to be alert to these kinds of things in reading imaginative literature. Incidentally, almost nothing you read is complete in itself. The writer doesn't bother to tell you everything essential about the subject. A writer who did so would bore his or her readers beyond endurance. He or she takes for granted that you know certain things already—that you have had certain experiences. Writers expect you to be able to draw implications from what you read. If you don't understand something you read, perhaps it is because you don't know something that is essential to make sense out of the material or because you do not draw the correct implications about what is not said.

Practice finding the main idea of paragraphs. If you do, you may become so skillful that you will do it unconsciously, without thinking about it. To do that is to have at your command one of the most important aspects of efficient reading.

EXTRACTING IMPORTANT DETAILS

Because students aren't always able to spot the *important details* in what they read, they think that instructors maliciously look for unimportant or trivial details for examination questions. More often than not, this is just a rationalization for poor reading. While an occasional student may get the main idea and not be able to remember the details, they usually go hand in hand. The main idea is something that cognitive psychologists often call a *macrostructure*. A macrostructure is an idea that encompasses or summarizes the details. For example, you may read in your European history textbook that "the Congress of Vienna was a triumph of reaction." If you know the text you will be able to relate this main idea to all sorts of important details—that the reaction results included the restoration of the balance of power, the elimination of republican governments everywhere, and the attempt to reestablish old values and systems.

What is an important detail? It is often an example of the principle stated in the main idea. This happens regularly in science textbooks. For example, a biology textbook may tell you that sparrows in urban England during the nineteenth century were darker and grayer than sparrows in the country. The text may then go on to tell you that this is an example of protective coloration in natural selection. Because the city birds lived in an environment of sooty, coal-dust-stained stone rather than woods, the ones not seen by predators (alley cats, for example) survived to breed. The result was that the urban sparrows became darker than the rural sparrows. The important idea is that protective coloration results from natural selection. The sparrows of England provide an example.

Of course, what is important is a matter of judgement, and people will not always agree. But most of the time, particularly in textbooks, which are organized to present information in an orderly way, it is easy to pick out the main idea and at least the *most* important details. If you get in the habit of reading in such a way

as to identify them without thinking about it, you will be more efficient at absorbing information than you would be if you just read along without any thought to what is important and what is unimportant.

READING FOR PLEASURE

The more you read for pleasure, the better reader you will become. Some people read little beyond *TV Guide* and the sports section, the comics, or the gossip columns in the newspaper. We all have things we like to read for pleasure, but one of the things a college education should do for you is to broaden the limits of the kinds of things you read. Also accept the fact that you can read for pleasure in all the same ways you read in order to learn. Some things you will want to read very slowly, even out loud or saying the words to yourself as you read. Other things you will want to skim. Some things you won't want to remember after you have finished reading; others you will. Here you will want to be an active reader, searching for important ideas and making them a part of your pool of knowledge. Some things you will want to read for the way in which they are written. Be alert to the style of what you read. If you are, you will increase your pleasure in reading, and when you increase your pleasure in reading, you will become a better reader.

ANALYZING PARAGRAPHS

Here are two paragraphs from C. R. McConnell, Economics: Principles, Problems, and Policies, *7th ed., McGraw-Hill, New York, 1978. In the first of these paragraphs, we have analyzed the words and phrases to illustrate how to analyze paragraphs. The second paragraph is for your own practice. Underline the important words and phrases and then write your diagnosis of them in the margin.*

Main Idea →

Explanation by Example →

Economists put forth the idea that specific consumer wants can be fulfilled with succeeding units of a commodity in the law of diminishing marginal utility. Let us dissect this law to see exactly what it means. A product has utility if it has the power to satisfy a want. Utility is want-satisfying power. Two characteristics of this concept must be emphasized: First, "utility" and "usefulness" are by no means synonymous. Paintings by Picasso may be useless in the functional sense of the term yet be of tremendous utility to art connoisseurs. Second—and implied in the first point—utility is a subjective notion. The utility of a specific product will vary widely from person to person. A nip of Old Tennishoes will yield tremendous utility, to the Skid Row alcoholic, but zero or negative utility to the local WCTU president.

← *Important Detail*

← *Important Detail*

← *Explanation by Example*

By marginal utility we simply mean the extra utility or satisfaction which a consumer gets from one additional unit of a specific product. In any relatively short time wherein the consumer's tastes can be assumed not to change, the marginal utility derived from successive units of a given product will decline. Why? Because a consumer will eventually become saturated, or "filled up," with that particular product. The fact that marginal utility will decline as the consumer acquires additional units of a specific product is known as the law of diminishing marginal utility.

EVALUATING WHAT YOU READ

Another purpose that will guide your reading from time to time is *evaluation*. You will often read controversial materials, interviews, news stories, and other things that cannot always be taken at face value. You may even read things that offend your beliefs and values. Determine why. Even textbooks often do not agree with your beliefs and preconceptions. When they disagree, examine your beliefs and determine whether or not you want to keep them. If you do that, you will discover that you are in a much better position to defend those beliefs.

If you take an evaluative stance when you read, it will keep you alert and you will absorb knowledge more selectively. You will become more skillful at dissecting arguments. You will become less satisfied with accepting everything you read at face value.

EXPANDING WHAT YOU READ

Another purpose in reading is to expand or amplify what you read so that it can be applied to situations not mentioned by the author. You may want to apply what you read to your own problems. When you read this book, for example, certain things will apply to the way you do things and others won't. Are you alert to these, and can you expand upon what we say so as to make this book more relevant to your own problems? Once again, this is part of the process of making your reading an active experience.

USING YOUR EYES

It may help you to improve your reading if you know something about what goes on when you read. You use your eyes, of course, when you read, but you use them in a special and in some respects a rather strange way. In this section we're going to tell you how your eyes work in reading and how knowing that may help you improve the use of your eyes in reading. You need to know, however, that your eyes are only tools. It is your purpose, your attentiveness, and your attitude that really control how you read. When these are improved, proper use of the eyes nearly always follows.

EYE MOVEMENTS

You probably know that your eyes don't move smoothly across the page as you read, but you may not know the details of how they actually do move. When your eyes move across a line of print, they move in a series of quick movements broken by very brief pauses. The movements are called *saccades*. They are so fast that you are not aware of them. Your brain manages to blank out whatever signals come from your eyes during these saccadic movements so that you are only aware of what you see during the pauses.

Most of us aren't aware of the pauses themselves, so we have the impression that our eyes move smoothly across the page. If you watch another person read you can clearly see the quick, jerky movements. The easiest way to do that is to get some likely guinea pig, such as your roommate, to sit next to you and read. You then train a hand mirror on his or her eyes so that you can see them as they move.

What you probably can't do, because they are so quick, is to count the eye movements. The pauses, which are called *fixations*, last only one-quarter to one-fifth of a second. The number of pauses per line varies, of course, with the length of the line of print, the nature of the material read, and other things. But what is more important, the number varies with the skill of the reader. Good readers fix, on the average, once every three words of print. The typical college reader, however, is going to average about one and one-half words per fixation. Surprisingly, however, there is very little difference in the speed of the saccade between good and poor readers. About 90 percent of the total reading time is spent in fixations anyway, so the speed of the saccadic movements makes little difference.

There is another difference between good and poor readers that may be even more important than the length of the fixation or how many words can be taken in per fixation. It is the frequency of *regressive movements*. Regressive movements, or regressions, are saccades in the reverse direction. All of us make regressive movements at one time or another; that is to say, we backtrack along the line of print. We aren't aware of doing it, but once again, if you have a handy guinea pig to observe, you can probably detect those regressive movements.

These regressive movements are far more common in poor or unskilled readers than they are in good readers. Beginning readers make them on just about every other word, while the average college student may go along for nearly an entire line of print without making one.

Another difference between skilled and unskilled readers is in the return movement. Good readers make a single return movement from the end of one line of print to the beginning of another. Poor readers overshoot or undershoot, and they have to make corrections to find the beginning of the line.

IMPROVING EYE MOVEMENTS

The eye movements in reading are automatic and reflexive in character. That means that there isn't much you can do directly and consciously to improve them. In fact, knowing about them may make you a little uncomfortable and self-conscious about reading for a while. Some reading clinics do have devices that may be of some help in correcting poor eye movements, but nowadays the emphasis is upon improving eye movements indirectly by improving the *mental* habits of reading. As you improve the way in which you approach reading, your eye movements will almost automatically improve. As we will point out later, keeping a record of your reading speed helps to increase your speed.

There is an upper limit to reading speed. You can't push your fixation time down to much less than one-fifth of a second. You can't increase the speed of your saccadic movements, and even the best readers must make a fixation, on the average, about once every three words. Thus, even if you make no regressive movements and if your return movements are absolutely on target, you can't read faster than 900 words a minute. No matter what anybody tells you, reading faster than that is skimming. Some things, of course, can be skimmed, and it is useful to know how to skim well. But remember, any claim that someone can read faster than 900 words a minute is based upon skimming, not reading.

Most people have a lot of room for improvement in their reading speed. A typical student reads easy textbook material at a rate of between 200 and 300 words a minute. That rate can be pushed quite a bit higher, and as it increases, your eye movements will improve.

HOW TO IMPROVE YOUR READING

There are a few things nearly everyone can do to improve reading ability. Some of these will come naturally as you learn better habits of study, for often poor reading is the result of wandering attention, or an inability to organize what you are reading into coherent knowledge. But there are some specific steps—aside from general improvement in study skills—that you can take which will improve your reading.

BUILDING A VOCABULARY

If you're going to make sense out of what you read, you're going to have to enlarge your vocabulary as the material you read becomes more difficult. In college,

you are going to learn about a lot of things that are new to you. It stands to reason that you will acquire many new words. Many of these will be technical terms, peculiar to a discipline. If you take economics, you will learn about *demand curves* and *marginal utility*. In psychology you will encounter *libido* and *ganglion*, in philosophy, *epistemology* and *positivism*. You must learn what these mean, either by reading about them and hearing about them or by consulting a glossary or dictionary. In addition to these technical terms, you will find that the books you will be asked to read will contain words that are unfamiliar to you, words such as *heuristic, peroration,* and *reticular.* Finally, you will find familiar words and phrases used in new and quite specific senses.

One of the most obvious marks of a good student (and good reader) is vocabulary. Good students not only recognize and define more words than do poor ones, but they also discriminate more carefully among the meanings of words. This helps them read faster. They perceive the meanings of words at a glance. They don't need to stop and think. They are not baffled by an inability to comprehend what they read. Hence, part of learning how to study and to read faster is to become a master of the words you read. There are several ways to do this.

Paying Attention to New Words. Be on the lookout for new words. When you see a new word or encounter one that you have seen before but which you can't pin down, don't pass it by. Not only is that being lazy, it's a sure way to poor academic performance. The meaning of a whole sentence may hang on the new, unfamiliar word. And this may be the sentence with the main idea. Being alert to new words is one more way for you to make the reading process active.

Using the Dictionary. Once you have spotted a new word, an old word in a new context, or a word you think you know but are not sure of, the first thing to do is to look it up in a dictionary. *Your dictionary is the single most important study aid you own.* Use it. And make sure it is a good dictionary. There are a lot of cheap dictionaries available in drug stores and supermarkets, but a cheap dictionary is like a cheap automobile tire. If that's all you can afford, okay, but you are better off sacrificing something else to get a good one. If you don't already have one, get a dictionary intended for use at the college level. Though some of these are available in paperback, you are better off getting one in a sturdy binding. If you really are going to make the most of it, it will get a lot of hard wear.

When you look up a word in the dictionary, find out its particular meaning in the context in which you

HOW FAST CAN YOU READ?

Here are two short passages that you can use to get a rough idea about how fast you can read. Before you read them, get a watch or a clock with a second hand. When you are ready to begin, write down the exact time to the second at the head of the passage (for example: 7:23 and 15 seconds). Then read the passage as rapidly as you can. Do not, however, read so fast that you do not understand and remember what you read because you will want to check yourself on the comprehension test we have provided for each passage. When you are through reading, mark down the exact time at the bottom of the passage. Then go directly to the comprehension test. Do not look back at the passage while taking the test. You should get nearly all the items right (at least nine). If you miss too many items, you have not read carefully enough. You can find a rough index of your speed of reading by checking the facing table against the time it took you to read the passages

---

Passage 1

Workers for the bureaucracy are recruited through competitive examinations administered by the Civil Service Commission throughout the nation on a regular basis. Anyone may take the tests, and the tests and the scores determine who is eligible for federal employment, with war veterans spotted extra points. An agency with a job opening notifies the Civil Service Commission and is given three names from which to choose.

Although fairer than the spoils system, this method of recruitment leaves some groups still discriminated against. Those with fewer educational opportunities are less likely to score well on the exams, which may be imperfect predictors of job success. And the force of tradition has discouraged members of some groups, such as women and blacks, from seeking work beyond a limited range of categories. Jobs in the higher-paying categories are held primarily by white males.

To help insulate the system from political pressures and the evils of the spoils system, public employees in the civil service have their political activities limited by law. They may vote, make financial contributions, and express their opinions. They may attend political rallies or hold some local offices. But the Hatch Act, first enacted in 1939, bars them from taking an active part in party politics and campaigns. Nor may they hold any state or federal elective office. Another limitation to the activity of government workers is the agreement which a job seeker makes upon applying to the civil service not to strike against the government. In recent years, this pledge has not been a total barrier to collective bargaining. In 1962, President Kennedy recognized the right of government employees to organize when he signed an executive order to that effect. Today, a majority of civil service workers belong to unions. The no-strike pledge has not always been strictly observed. Postal workers walked off the job in 1970, and this action was followed by a "sick out"—workers calling in sick instead of reporting to work as a way of protesting their job conditions—among a substantial number of the Federal Aviation Agency's air traffic controllers.

The substitution of a merit system for a spoils system has produced a stable and capable bureaucracy but one which absorbs a good deal of time and energy in internal administration. It also creates a conservative bias by insulating agency decision makers from electoral constraints and by discouraging innovation. Government policy has been removed yet another step from popular control. If law is what the judges say it is, policy is what the administrators say it is. And when administrators do not change with elective officials, political interests can continue to operate inside the government long after they have been repudiated by the voters.

(From D. J. Olson, and M. Meyer, *Governing the United States: To Keep the Republic in Its Third Century*, 2d ed., McGraw-Hill, New York, 1978, p. 401.)

Comprehension Test for Passage 1 *Mark each statement true or false.*

_____ 1. The Civil Service Commission supplies each agency with one name for each job.

_____ 2. Public employees in the civil service have their political activities limited by law.

_____ 3. The Hatch Act was enacted in 1962.

_____ 4. Though civil service workers are not supposed to strike, they are allowed to engage in collective bargaining.

_____ 5. Almost no civil service workers belong to unions.

_____ 6. The merit system has resulted in instability in the bureaucracy.

_____ 7. Agency decision makers are insulated from electoral constraints.

_____ 8. The merit system requires much time and energy in internal administration.

_____ 9. The merit system has removed government policy another step from popular control.

_____ 10. Once political interests have been repudiated by the voters, they cease to operate inside of the government.

The key for scoring the questions is as follows: (1) F, (2) T, (3) F, (4) T, (5) F, (6) F, (7) T, (8) T, (9) T, (10) F.

Passage 2

Geological changes affecting the geography of North America have profoundly influenced the course of American history. Paramount in importance among the continent's geographical characteristics is its isolation, shared of course by South America, from the great, interconnected land mass of Europe, Asia, and Africa. Homo sapiens or modern man apparently evolved from hominids or manlike creatures somewhere in the "old" world roughly 200,000 years ago. He lived in fact on each of the old world's three continents. No human beings set foot on American soil until, at the earliest, some twenty thousand years ago. Thus for roughly 90 percent of the period of man's existence on earth the New World had no human habitation.

New World plants and animals differed also from those of the Old World because of the water barrier between the two great land areas. Until the coming of the Europeans America had no cattle, hogs, sheep, or goats. Horses and camels had once inhabited the Western Hemisphere, but had become extinct before the coming of Columbus. Of man's major domestic animals only the dog, fellow immigrant with man from Asia, preceded Columbus to these shores. Cultivation of crops such as wheat, rice, rye, oats, and barley had helped the inhabitants of the Old World to progress from nomadic hunters and food-gatherers to settled tillers of the soil. With the exception of wild rice, none of those crops grew in pre-Columbian America, but corn, a hybrid plant developed by the Indians, had enabled some of them to make the same transition from hunting and food gathering to settled agricultural life.

Those geological conditions which isolated the New World from the Old were not constant. Alternate warming and cooling of the earth have raised and lowered sea level dramatically. In the warm periods glacial ice has melted in such quantities as to raise sea level, perhaps in association with other factors, high enough to inundate about half of North America, including large portions of the South and the Middle West. In such periods forms of tropical life existed on the fringes of the Arctic. On four occasions, the last one some nine thousand years before Christ, cooling of the earth permitted glaciers a mile or two in thickness to blanket the northern half of North America.

The effects of the glaciers stagger the imagination. They swept New England's topsoil out to sea, leaving a rocky and infertile land behind. As if to compensate the region for its loss, however, the glaciers apparently were responsible for endowing it with a vast coastal shelf of relatively shallow water which still provides one of the world's major commercial fishing areas. Farther west the glaciers scooped out the Great Lakes and converted two northward flowing rivers into the Missouri and Ohio River systems as tributaries to the Mississippi.

By holding so much of the world's water supply on land, the glaciers also lowered sea level sharply. In the narrow Bering Strait between Alaska and Siberia there appeared a land bridge linking the Old World and the New. Archaeological and anthropological evidence has established beyond any question that by this bridge man and his friend the dog first emigrated from the Old World to the New.

(From N. A. Graebner, G. C. Fite, and P. L. White, *A History of the American People*, 2d ed., McGraw-Hill, New York, 1975, p. 3.)

Comprehension Test for Passage 2 *Mark each statement true or false.*

_____ 1. No human beings set foot on American soil until twenty thousand years ago.
_____ 2. Horses had not existed in North America until the coming of Columbus.
_____ 3. Indians cultivated wheat, rice, rye, oats, and barley before the coming of Columbus.
_____ 4. No pre-Columbian Indians had made the transition from hunting and food gathering to settled agricultural life.
_____ 5. Geological conditions which isolated the New World from the Old remained constant.
_____ 6. Glaciers swept New England's topsoil out to sea.
_____ 7. The glaciers produced a vast coastal shelf of relatively shallow water.
_____ 8. Glaciers scooped out the Great Lakes.
_____ 9. During the glacial period there was a land bridge across the Bering Strait.
_____ 10. There is no evidence as to how man came from the Old World to the New.

The key for scoring the questions is as follows: (1) T, (2) F, (3) F, (4) F, (5) F, (6) T, (7) T, (8) T, (9) T, (10) F.

Minutes	Seconds	Reading speed (words per minute)
5	34	80
4	28	100
3	43	120
3	11	140
2	37	170
2	14	200
1	52	240
1	35	280
1	23	320
1	14	360
1	7	400

found it. Many words have general meanings, to be found in the dictionary, but also particular meanings in particular contexts. This is particularly true of words that are used as metaphors (if you don't know what "metaphor" means, or even if you think you know but aren't sure, look it up). Once you understand the meaning and the *uses* of a new word, it's a part of your personal property.

Every educated person needs the dictionary habit. Accomplished writers, who have a better command of English than most people, often have a half-dozen different dictionaries for different purposes. They are forever looking up new words and even words they have used all their lives, simply to sharpen their use of these words for particular purposes.

Vocabulary Cards. If you have a poor vocabulary, you will have to work extra hard to improve it. One way to do that is to use vocabulary cards. Three-by-five index cards are best for this purpose. Carry some around with you, and when you come to a new word or a word about which you have some question, write it on the card. Also write the phrase or sentence in which you found it, so that you know something about its context. Then when a dictionary is handy, look up the word and write its definition on the other side of the card.

When you have accumulated a batch, take the cards out and look at the side with the new word. Rehearse the meaning of the word, then turn to the other side to see whether you are correct. Some people keep tabs on themselves by putting a dot on the corner of a card each time they miss the definition. The use of vocabulary cards is particularly helpful when you are in a course that makes heavy use of unfamiliar technical terms. Some people use the technique for general self-improvement. They set goals for how many new words they are to learn each week.

General vs. Technical Terms. Be sure, in building your vocabulary, to keep in mind the distinction between general and technical terms. The definitions you find in an ordinary dictionary are for general use, not for technical use, unless the word has *only* a technical meaning. For many technical words and technical uses of ordinary words, you will need to consult a glossary or a special dictionary. Many introductory textbooks carry glossaries of the special terms in the field. And there are special dictionaries for nearly every natural science and social science as well as for such professional fields as medicine and law. While you will probably not want to buy one of these (they tend to be expensive) unless you are seriously committed to a

WHAT YOU CAN LEARN FROM A DICTIONARY

Here is a reproduction of the entry for "memory" in Webster's New Collegiate Dictionary. The entry tells you how to pronounce the word and how to spell the plural; it also tells you what part of speech the entry is (n = noun). It gives the etymology of the word (ME = Middle English; MF = Middle French; L = Latin). It then gives a series of definitions, and finally under synonyms (syn) it gives a number of words with similar meanings. A careful reading and study of this one entry can teach you about the correct use of a half-dozen words. (By permission. From Webster's New Collegiate Dictionary, copyright 1977 by G. & C. Merriam Company.)

mem-o-ry /'mem-(ə-)rē/ *n. pl.* -ries [ME *memorie,* fr. MF *memoire,* fr. L *memoria,* fr. *memor* mindful; akin to OE *mimorian* to remember, L *mora* delay, Gk *mermēra* care, Skt *smarati* he remembers] **1 a:** the power or process of reproducing or recalling what has been learned and retained esp. through associative mechanisms **b:** the store of things learned and retained from an organism's activity or experience as evidenced by modification of structure or behavior or by recall and recognition **2 a:** commemorative remembrance <erected a statue in ~ of the hero> **b:** the fact or condition of being remembered <days of recent ~> **3 a:** a particular act of recall or recollection **b:** an image or impression of one that is remembered **c:** the time within which past events can be or are remembered <within the ~ of living men> **4 a:** a device in which information esp. for a computer can be inserted and stored and from which it may be extracted when wanted **b:** capacity for storing information <a computer with 16K words of ~> **5:** a capacity for showing effects as the result of past treatment or for returning to a former condition—used esp. of a material (as metal or plastic)

syn MEMORY, REMEMBRANCE, RECOLLECTION, REMINISCENCE *shared meaning element:* the capacity for or act or action of remembering or something remembered *ant* oblivion

field, you will find them in the library. If you have any doubt as to whether or not you are using a technical term correctly, particularly in a term paper, consult the appropriate specialized dictionary.

Technical terms are often more important than students realize. In some courses, half or more of the subject matter is knowing what the technical terms mean. Good students list these terms separately and study them. Sometimes they have separate places in their notebooks just for technical terms. Sometimes they underline such words in their notes. They review these terms systematically before an examination.

Dissecting Words. You can improve your vocabulary by learning something about how words are put together. The English language, particularly the part of it derived from Latin, is built of elements, many of which are used over and over again in combination to produce new words. There are three kinds of elements: prefixes, suffixes, and roots. If you know the meaning of a particular prefix and root or a particular suffix and a root, you can guess the meaning of an unfamiliar word that combines these.

The root is the main part of a word, while the prefix and the suffix are special syllables added at the beginning and the end. In the word "premeditation," *pre-*

is the prefix, *meditat(e)* is the root, and *-ion* is the suffix. The prefix *pre-* means before, and the suffix *-ion* tells you that the word is a noun. "Meditate" means to contemplate. So premeditation refers to an act that is contemplated beforehand, as in murdering someone with premeditation.

In a separate table (page 38), we have listed some of the more common prefixes and suffixes. As an exercise, guess at the meaning of these (we have provided a space for that), then check by looking up the meaning in a dictionary. If your guess is off the mark, rehearse the correct meaning.

We have also provided a short list of some common Latin roots and their meanings. Since most of you will not have taken Latin, it would be unfair to expect you to know the meaning of these, though you will probably be able to guess some of them from English words that contain them. These Latin roots appear over and over again in an enormous number of English words.

If you have a good dictionary, the chances are that it will give you (before the definition and after the key to pronounciation) something of the origin of the word in question. For example, one of the dictionaries college students commonly use tells us that *domestic* is an adjective and that it derives from the Latin word *domesticus*, a word itself based upon another Latin word, *domus*, meaning house. The word does not come directly from Latin into English, however. Instead, the dictionary tells us, it is directly derived from the French word, *domestique*. Indeed, there are two major routes for Latin words into English. The older of these is through French, for if you have studied English history, you will know that the language of the ruling classes in England, following the Norman conquest in 1066, was French. When the nobility began speaking English, they imported many French words into English. More recently, words have been taken directly from Latin into English, partly as the result of the shift from using Latin for all learned and technical writing to using English.

A few Greek words have found their way into English, mostly by way of Latin. While these are much less frequent than words of pure Latin origin, some of them are very important. *Logos,* which in Greek had a broad meaning including word, speech, thought, and knowledge, is the basis for the English word "logic" and for the suffix *-ology* (as in psychology, sociology, etc.), as well as for the root of words such as "prologue." Learning about words can be an absorbing matter, and if you find reading the derivation of words in the dictionary to be interesting, you might want to consult historical or etymological dictionaries. At least one of these (Skeat, *A Concise Etymological Dictionary of the English Language*) is available in paperback.

COMMON PREFIXES, SUFFIXES, AND LATIN ROOTS

The prefixes and suffixes we have listed below occur often in English words. Any good dictionary will list and define almost all of them. You can help improve your vocabulary by looking up their meanings and writing them in the space provided. We have also listed a few of the many Latin roots upon which English words are based. The English meaning is given for each. Try listing beside each as many English words derived from these roots as you can.

Prefixes	Meaning
ab-, abs- a-	
ad-, a-, at-, ap-	
be-	
bi-	
co-, com-, con-	
de-	
dis-	
en-	
in-, il-, im-, ir-	
non-	
per-	
pre-	
pro-	
re-	
sub-	
un-	

Suffixes	Meaning
-able, -ible, -ble	
-al	
-ance	
-ent	
-est	
-ful	
-ing	
-ion	
-ity	
-ive	
-ize	
-less	
-ment	
-ous	

Some common Latin roots	English equivalent	English words containing them
capio	take, seize	
duco	lead	
facio	do, make	
fero	bear, carry	
mitto	send	
muto	change, alter	
probo	test	
recipio	take back	
specto	look at	
tendo	stretch	
terreo	frighten	

LEARNING TO READ FASTER

We pointed out earlier in this chapter that there is an upper limit to how fast we can *read*. Most of us, however, seldom even approach that upper limit, so there is room for improvement. Also, we sometimes read when all that is necessary is that we skim. There are different ways to skim. Those of you who have taken one of the so-called speed-reading courses may know that you can skim a whole page in a few seconds. However, you can also skim in a more detailed way, so that you pick up almost as much information as you would reading. In fact, many expert readers mix skimming and reading, and all good readers, when reading, adjust their rate to the difficulty or unfamiliarity of the material.

Practice at Reading. "I get plenty of practice at reading," you might say. "I read several hundred pages a week." True enough, you do get a lot of practice, if you are a college student. But practice doesn't necessarily lead to improvement. Many years ago, a famous educational psychologist, Edward L. Thorndike, demonstrated a fundamental truth: You can't improve your performance the next time unless you know how well or badly you did the last time. Thorndike asked blindfolded people to draw a line exactly three inches long. People could go on drawing hundreds of lines without coming close to making their lines exactly three inches long. But if they were told after each attempt how long the line was that they had just drawn, they could draw a line almost exactly three inches in length after only a few repetitions. Obvious, you say. Perhaps, but we still often ignore the principle. People do try to improve their reading speed without knowing how fast they are reading. The first step toward improving your reading speed is to keep a record of how fast you read.

Devote a special period each day to training yourself in fast reading. It can be at any time, as long as you can count on it and don't allow other activities to interfere with it. Figure on spending a half-hour—certainly no less than ten or fifteen minutes—at your practice in fast reading.

Choose some material that you like to read and that is not too difficult: a novel, a book of short stories, a magazine such as *Time* or *Newsweek*. However, try to choose something that will not distract you with illustrations and that does not ask you to look at tables and graphs or read formulas. Whatever you choose, keep the same kind of material for the duration of the first phase of your self-training course. If you choose something like *Time*, which has multiple columns and an irregular format, keep on reading that kind of material.

If you choose a book with only a single column per page, keep on reading other books like it.

Get a watch or clock that has a second hand and note the time to the second when you start reading. Read as rapidly as you can and still get the meaning of what you read. When you have finished reading three or four pages, note the time again. Subtract the first time from the second and divide by the number of words you have read. You don't need to count all the words. Count the words in ten or so lines through what you have read, average the result, and multiply by the number of lines.

You'll find a chart on page 40 in which you can record your results. List on the chart the source and page numbers that you have read, the number of words, the time, and your rate. You will also find it useful to make a graph of the results. Put on the horizontal axis of the graph the practice session—first, second, third, etc.—and on the vertical axis the words per minute. Make a mark on the graph for the reading rate at each practice session. That way you will not only be able to tell if you are improving or not but whether you are improving at an increasing rate, and furthermore, you will find it easier to see the irregular fluctuations in your rate this way.

Be sure that you do not sacrifice comprehension. You will want to check from time to time to see how much you remember of what you have read.

If you are an average person, you ought to reach a near maximum rate of reading after a couple of weeks of daily practice sessions. You should be able to tell that from your chart or from the graph. It will not be the best you can do, but it is good enough for a start. Then it is time to begin practicing material that is more difficult, such as the textbooks you use. You will need to work on material in which the words are bigger and the sentences longer. If you have been practicing the right way, you should be reading more slowly during the first few sessions with the more difficult material.

At the same time you should be conscious of reading your regular assignments more rapidly and efficiently. Reading efficiently means gearing reading speed to the difficulty of the material. When you move on to more difficult material, you must make doubly sure that you are not missing something. Also, you will need to practice adjusting back and forth between reading and skimming.

One psychologist who spent a lifetime studying how people learn complex skills gathered evidence to show that we never stop improving. He studied workers who had been operating the same machine for more than twenty years. Even after all that practice they still got better year by year, though naturally the improve-

CHART FOR INCREASING READING SPEED

Use this chart to keep track of your progress in your daily practice in reading faster. For instructions see text (to find reading rate, multiply the number of pages by the number of words per page and then divide by time).

Magazine or book	Pages	Time	Rate

ment was small. The chances are you can improve your reading skills all your life. The biggest improvements are going to come early, however, and just a few weeks of practice will help you greatly, particularly if you are not a good reader to begin with.

If, when you start out to measure your reading speed, you find that you are a very slow reader, you will want to get help. If you cannot read easy material at more than 150 words per minute, you may want to go to some special place for remedial work. Most campuses have study skills centers, reading clinics, or other places where students who are deficient in particular skills can be helped. Or if after a good bit of practice on your own, you find that you cannot read easy material faster than 250 words per minute, the chances are that you are doing something wrong. Once again, it might be worth your while to look into places (or courses) that might give you special help.

Practice at Skimming. You will need practice at skimming too. Here the emphasis need not be so much on speed—if you skim in the right way speed will take care of itself. Skimming is mainly a matter of knowing what you are doing.

There are two kinds of skimming. One is to look for key words and phrases. Often that may mean a search through headings. But sometimes it means more than that. While writing the material a few pages back, one of the authors wanted to check his memory on how Latin came into English. He took an appropriate book, looked up Latin in the index, and then skimmed through the indicated pages looking for entries such as "Latin," "Norman French," "growth of the vernacular," and similar words and phrases. In less than a minute he had skimmed through some ten pages and found out what he wanted to know. Although it was in a book he had not previously read, he was familiar with the material and knew what to look for. For this kind of skimming you must have some idea of what you are looking for. It is the kind of thing you do when you review, or when you are looking for some specific statement which you may want to read in detail.

Another kind of skimming is the kind you do on initial reading. This is more like the sort of thing advocated in so-called speed-reading courses. You simply let your eye wander down the page, getting a feel for what the book or article is about, how it is written, and what kind of a vocabulary you are going to have to have to read it. In short, it is a kind of scouting expedition that, among other things, can tell you how fast you are going to gear your reading rate.

Probably even more useful to many people is a mixture of reading and skimming that we might call *browsing*. When you browse through a book, you let your eye run down the page, catching a word or phrase here or there. When you find something interesting or important, you read in detail. We ordinarily think of browsing as a kind of passive activity—the sort of thing we do when we are waiting in the dentist's office—but it does have its uses in studying as well as in leisure reading.

One use of browsing is as a technique to examine secondary reading—the kind of thing your instructor may put on the reserve shelf in the library. Make it a practice early in the semester to browse through some or all of the books on reserve. You'll have an idea of what they are about, how interesting and how difficult they are. When you find a topic that interests you later in the course, or if you find something that you don't understand, you will have a better idea of where to go.

CHAPTER FIVE

STUDYING FROM TEXTBOOKS

Let's assume that you have read the first four chapters and have tried to carry out the advice in them. You have made a workable schedule, found a good place to study, and assured yourself that your reading skills are up to college level. You understand the plan of the course you are taking, have set up a notebook in the right way, and have begun to take notes.

You have a copy of the textbook for the course, and it is on your desk along with all the other materials you need, including a notebook and writing implements. You are now ready to read the assignment in the text. How do you make the best use of the time you've allotted for this study period?

Every student has his or her own approach to studying textbooks. Two students, both outstanding, can go about studying the same material in very different ways. There are, nevertheless, some general principles for the effective study of textbooks. People who are good at studying use these rules in one way or another, even those who don't realize they are doing so, just as the man in Molière's play was surprised to discover that he had been talking prose all his life. Where they will differ is mainly in their individual styles and the degree to which they emphasize different aspects of the principles of good studying.

What are these principles? One way of phrasing them originated with the late Francis P. Robinson, of Ohio State University, who spent a long career guiding students in their study habits. Robinson put it in a formula: Survey Q 3R, or merely SQ3R. It is a good slogan and one that is easy to remember.

It is a way of summarizing five specific steps in effective study. These steps are:

Survey
Question
Read
Recite
Review

Robinson's plan has been widely adopted, and while there have been suggestions to change it in minor ways, it is still, after all these years, a very good approach to studying from textbooks. It is something that all students, good and poor, can do, and if they do, their study habits will improve.

SURVEY

The first of the five steps is survey. It tells you to get the best possible overview of what you are going to study before you study it in detail. Surveying an assignment ahead of time is important for the same reason that reading a road map beforehand is important when you are about to take a trip on unfamiliar roads.

Know what you are going to run into before you start. If you have a general idea about what you are going to do, you can make more intelligent decisions about the details.

SURVEYING A BOOK

Surveying a book goes in steps, from big ones to little ones. When you first pick up a book, survey the whole book. Start by reading the preface to get an idea of why the author wrote the book and what he or she says in it. By reading what the author has to say you can find out what kind of book it is and for whom it was written. It may even tell you what background you need for reading the book.

Next, look at the table of contents. Go through it to find out what's in the book. You will want to do this repeatedly as you get into the course. The more you read in the book, the more meaning the table of contents has.

Finally, leaf through the book. In a short period of time you can turn every page of a good-sized textbook, glancing at the headings, reading sentences here and there, and looking at the illustrations. The effort is worth the trouble. It will give you a feel for what is in the book, how difficult it is, and how it is organized. Most textbooks have summaries. Read them too when you survey.

SURVEYING A CHAPTER

When you settle down to read a chapter, survey it first. When most authors write textbooks they go to some pains to organize what they have to say under various headings. They do this mainly to help the student to know what to expect. In most textbooks you will find scarcely a page without headings.

Yet many students ignore the headings and try to read textbooks the way they would read novels. When they do that, they ignore a lot of the author's work, and they throw away the most significant and useful clues to the content of the book. Use the headings. They tell you what a section is about. When you actually read that section, you should have located certain points that bear on the headings. Anything else in the section will be secondary.

Pay attention to the *order of headings*. Most textbooks use two or three orders. This one, for example, has three: a main heading in the center, two or more side headings under each main heading, and sometimes, two or more indented headings, called run-in headings, under these. In many textbooks there may be even more complicated schemes, with different levels of heading distinguished by type size or style.

We have gone into some detail about headings because you use them at nearly every stage of the study process. You first use them in making your initial survey of the book. Then when you begin to study a particular chapter, first go over the headings in that chapter. Also, as part of your survey of the chapter, read the summary.

We have taken a bit of space to write about the survey step in the Survey Q 3R method because we know that most students do not do enough surveying. They have acquired the habit of plunging right into the text without first making a map of what they are going to find. We also know that the survey methods pay dividends.

QUESTION

The Q in Survey Q 3R means question, and it emphasizes the importance of asking questions while learning. Most things worth remembering are answers to some sort of question. Moreover, people seem to remember what they learn in answer to a question better than things they have merely read or memorized.

Questions help because they make us think about what we want to know about the material we are reading. They give a purpose to our learning. A person with a question is a person with a purpose. He or she is looking for an answer, and usually a specific answer. Such a person is not just satisfied with listening or reading in a kind of vaguely attentive way. He or she is looking for something specific, and the chances are that person will remember the answer when it is found.

Your Questions. If you make use of the question technique in reading this book, you should already have a number of them about this section. Why did the authors make a separate heading, "Question"? What good are questions in studying? What kinds of questions? Who makes them up? These are a few things you might have asked by now. Some questions will have been partly answered for you, and if you keep them in mind, you will find that the rest will be also.

Who asks the questions? You are the best source, for you are the one who is trying to learn. Every time you come to a new section, you should have your head full of questions. At the very least, you must ask what the word or phrase that provides the heading means. You can also ask, What do I know about this topic already? or What does this have to do with the general topic of the chapter or book?

How do you learn to ask the right sorts of questions? The answer, you should know by now, is, It takes practice. Often you will want to ask the simple question: "What is _____?" This will happen when the heading is in the form of a new technical term. In an astronomy text, for example, you might find a heading that says, "Retrograde Motion." You will ask yourself, Do I know what "retrograde motion" means? If not, what is it? Some people advocate writing down questions, but this is probably too time-consuming. Even-

tually, the art of asking questions will become so habitual that you won't even have to stop to formulate them. Remember, the purpose of asking questions is to direct you to the main idea in a section and to help you to assimilate that idea into your general body of knowledge.

The Author's Questions. You can learn something about how to ask questions from looking at the questions in workbooks and textbooks. Authors sometimes provide questions. Usually these are to be found at the end of chapters or sections, but occasionally at the beginning. Use them. They are often the most neglected parts of textbooks, particularly when they are stuck at the end of chapters. They have many uses. You can use them in your survey. You can use them while you read, and again when you have finished reading. You can use them as a way of testing yourself. If you test yourself before the instructor does, you will do much better when you are faced with an examination.

Stop for a second. In starting to read this section, did you pause to ask questions? What are author's questions? Where are they? How do you use them?

THE USE OF QUESTIONS

Here is a sample paragraph from a textbook (P. William Davis and Eldra Pearl Solomon, The World of Biology: Life, Society, Ecosphere, McGraw-Hill, New York, 1974, p. 46). The kinds of questions you would want to ask about this paragraph are written in the margin.

What is the function of the cell membrane?

What does selectively permeable mean?

How does the cell control its own composition?

Every cell is surrounded by a delicate limiting membrane, the cell membrane (also called plasma membrane). Its most obvious function is to prevent the contents of the cell from spilling out. It also regulates the passage of materials between the cell and its environment. Because it permits the passage of certain types of molecules while restricting the passage of others, the cell membrane is described as selectively permeable. Responding to varying conditions or needs, the cell membrane may present a barrier to the particular substance at one time and then actively promote passage of the same substance at another time. By regulating chemical traffic in this way the cell controls its own composition.

Here is another paragraph from the same source (pp. 46–47). Try writing your own questions.

In animal cells the cell membrane is coated externally by a thin layer of protein and carbohydrate which is thought to be an adhesive that holds the cells of a tissue together. This cell coat helps cells recognize one another and so determines which cells will associate with one another to form tissues. Plant cells are surrounded by a much thicker coating called the cell wall. Secreted by the cell itself, the cell wall is composed of a carbohydrate, most often cellulose. It forms a tough, protective covering that makes plant cells quite rigid. The cell wall does not present a barrier to materials passing in and out of the cell because it is studded with tiny pores.

Nowadays some textbooks, particularly in the social and natural sciences, are accompanied by workbooks for students. These workbooks contain a lot of different things, but they nearly always have several kinds of questions, some to be used in studying. Others are for review and still others are samples of the kinds of examinations you might expect.

READ

The next step is reading. This is the part many students put first because they think that studying is mainly a matter of running their eyes over the text. The book is, of course, meant to be read. But this is neither the first, last, nor even necessarily the most important part of studying a textbook. It provides the details. It fills out the framework you should already have if you have surveyed.

Reading Actively. A lot of things you can read passively. In reading a good adventure story or something interesting in the newspaper, you can usually go along without thinking much about what you are doing. Such stories are mainly for your entertainment, and you can read without much concern about whether you will remember the details of what you read. It is true that some stories must be read in such a way that there is a kind of dialogue between you and the author, but much of the casual reading that people do can and should be done in a relaxed and passive way.

Most textbooks have to be explored. You can't just walk through them. You must be alert to your surroundings every step of the way. Questioning while you read is one way to avoid reading passively. You must keep asking yourself, Am I following what I am reading? Can I remember what I have just read? What is the main point of what I have just read? If you do this, you will no longer voice the familiar complaint: "My head is just like a sieve; I forget what I read the minute I am through."

Although reading important novels, plays, stories, and poetry requires more than passive reading, the specific recommendations we give here do not apply to them by and large. Such works require a different set of skills. Toward the end of this chapter we'll have a few words to say about reading history and literature. The suggestions we give here apply mainly to reading in the social and natural sciences, to applied subjects such as business management or medical technology, and, perhaps, to a lesser extent to such subjects as art history and philosophy.

Reading for Main Ideas and Important Details. In the last chapter we wrote about the purposes of reading. Of those purposes, two are especially important in studying from textbooks. One is to read for main ideas, and the other is to read for details. Rather than repeat ourselves here, we suggest that you try to remember what was said in Chapter 4. If you draw a blank, you might look at page 30.

Noting Important Terms. Italicized words and phrases usually are important. Authors use italics for emphasis. They are signs to stop and take heed. The author is now saying something that *he or she* thinks is *important*. (If you don't know what italics are, "he or she" and "important" in the last sentence are printed in italics.)

If a technical term is italicized, repeat it to yourself and make sure you know what it means. Also, though it seems like a small point, make sure you know how to spell important terms. Instructors sometimes get impatient with students who can't seem to learn to spell important words.

Of course, authors do not always emphasize important words or phrases by italics, in which case you will have to look out for them yourself. That is another aspect of reading actively. Some authors place special and technical terms in boldface type. Be doubly sure that you know these, know what they mean, and can spell them.

Reading Graphs, Tables, Illustrations. When you read, read everything. One of the worst things you can do is to skip tables, graphs, and diagrams. Give them more than just a casual glance. Some things are easier to understand when they are in diagrams and graphs rather than in words and formulas, and some things can only be presented in diagrams. Even a simple photograph or drawing can tell you what a whole section is about. They sometimes help make the material vivid to you, and in that way make it easier for you to remember. The old saying "A picture is worth a thousand words" isn't always true, but there are a lot of times when it is. If there are tables, be sure to read them carefully. We'll have more to say on the topic of tables and graphs in Chapter 9 (pages 101–103).

RECITE

Reciting is the oldest way of learning. Long before books were invented, recitation was the heart of learning. In parts of the world where books are scarce, it still is. Have you ever seen a TV documentary about some school in a remote part of the world with all the children reciting in unison? Such rote recitation is less valuable than the kind of recitation we want you to use because it downgrades understanding and questioning in favor of sheer memorization. Rote recitation does have its uses, however. Getting the multiplication tables into your head so that you can do fast calculations requires a lot of plain rote recitation. To a lesser extent rote recitation can also be applied to the study of foreign language vocabularies and similar things. Our main emphasis, however, is going to be on reciting for comprehension rather than for rote memory.

Reciting as a Means of Recall. Reciting is probably the best single way to keep your reading active. As long as you merely read a book, you can, without challenge, comfort yourself with the belief that you understand and will remember. But if you recite to yourself as you read, you may make the unpleasant discovery that you don't really understand, that you can't really remember, even for a few seconds.

The only way to find out if you really understand and can remember what you have read is to recite it to yourself just after you have read it. Recitation is an effective study method because it immediately reveals to you your own ignorance. If you recite, you can correct yourself right on the spot. In this way, it is very much like programmed learning.

Reciting is recalling. Stop as often as you need to and try to recall what you have just read. At this point, for example, you might stop and ask yourself, What have I learned thus far in this chapter? Try to remember the main headings and the important ideas. Can you summarize what you have read? Check your recall against what is actually written down. In practice, you will want to recite at every important step. Recite the main idea in each section.

The general rule is as follows: As you read, stop at intervals to recite the substance, in your own words, of each major section in a chapter. When you do your first reading of the material, the amount of time you spend in reciting will probably be less than that spent in actual reading. But when you review for an examination, the bulk of your time will be spent in reciting rather than reading.

Recitation *both* at the original reading and at the review is necessary. Older research on the value of recitation for remembering what you have read showed that the earlier you recited, the less the forgetting later on. So you need that first recitation to keep the forgetting process from getting started. Because some forgetting is almost inevitable no matter what you do, you need that review just before the examination to correct for the fact that you will have forgotten some things, despite your earlier review.

More recent research tells us why early review is so important. Remembering the kind of material you will find in a textbook is not merely remembering how

to string a bunch of words together, as you might do if you had to remember a poem in a language you don't know. What you do when you read something is form a structure in your own words, in your own way of thinking. Just reading is a lazy process, and the structure you form from just reading is so simple and bare of detail that it will never do for an examination. In one investigation in which college students were asked to write down what they had just read, some students read so superficially that all they could say was, "This passage was about how evolution makes different species of animals." All the details that were in the passage about the classification of animals, about the relations between genetics and evolution, about natural section, just weren't absorbed by these students.

How Much Recitation? How much time should you spend in recitation? That depends upon what you are studying. If what you are learning is rich in detail and contains a lot of confusing relations, or consists of disconnected facts, you need to spend a lot of time reciting. That is because it is harder to form a rich structure for such material in your own head. In some cases, you may want to spend as much as 90 percent of your time in recitation. If, for example, you have to learn a number of rules, items, names, laws, or formulas, then recitation should be the principal mode of study.

If, on the other hand, the material is organized, or in the form of a story or history, less recitation is needed. Here you may need to stop only now and then to recite what you have read, pausing perhaps more often to recite dates and names when they occur. It is hard to recommend a figure, but perhaps as little as 20 percent of your total study time would be spent in recitation for this kind of material. For courses such as economics, political science, and the like, 50 percent of the time is as good a figure as any. But remember, these are ball park figures. How much time you actually need to spend in recitation will depend upon how active your normal reading is (if you really read attentively all the time, you needn't spend so much time reciting), your particular course, and a whole host of other specific circumstances.

This you can be sure of: The time spent in recitation pays off. In one study, for example, students who spent up to 80 percent of their time reciting did better than people who spent the same amount of time reading without reciting. Also, the time you spend reciting actually saves time. The amount you remember when you recite is so great that you don't need to spend nearly so much time later in rereading and review.

When do you stop to recite? To wait until you have finished a chapter is too long. Forgetting has already taken its toll, and you have too much material to form into a sensible structure. On the other hand, stopping to recite every paragraph—except where the material consists of a lot of more or less unrelated facts—breaks up the material too much. You can't form a sensible structure because you haven't got a complete scheme to do it with. Probably your best guides are headings. Stop each time you get to a new heading and recite what you have read in the section you have just finished.

Besides giving you a chance to organize things in your own words, recitation serves to keep your attention on your task. When you just read, it is easy to do so with only a half a mind, to read the words without really taking them in. When you know you have to recite something, you can't daydream.

Recitation also helps you correct mistakes. It shows you where you have missed something or where you have misunderstood it. And if you make notes of these mistakes when you recite, you'll know exactly what points you're going to have the most trouble with in a review.

REVIEW

The fifth and final part of Survey Q 3R is review. We don't need to make a big thing out of this because most students review anyway, especially before examinations. Many students even review things they haven't read before! We can, however, make a few suggestions about how to review and when it should be done.

SURVEYING THE MATERIAL

Reread enough to make sure that you haven't omitted anything and to refresh your memory. Recite both before and after you read. The recitation before reading a section will tell you how carefully you need to read. Reciting after your reading will tell you what you have learned. If you have taken notes on what you have read, use these to guide your reviews and as a prompt for the recitation before your review.

WHEN TO REVIEW

If you have done a good job of surveying, questioning, reading, and reciting, you won't have trouble knowing what to do when you review. You may not know, however, when you should review and how often. Most students wait until just before an exam to do their reviewing. This is a good time for a final review, but not for the first review.

The first time to review is immediately after you have studied something. For example, after you have read a chapter, reciting between each of its sections, you should immediately go back and review it. This means trying to recite the important points of the whole chapter and rereading as necessary to check yourself. It also means reading over and then reciting the notes you have made. This first review may be fairly brief, for there hasn't been much time for forgetting, and it should be mainly one of recitation.

If you are really well organized, you will plan for one or two reviews between the first review and the final review before an examination. These intervening reviews are often skipped by students, but they will make the final review easier.

The final review should consist of as much unprompted recitation as possible. Use the book to check the accuracy of your recitation, but try to recite without first reading. This review, of course, is intensive. Go over all the material you think you will be responsible for on the examination. Plan your time so that you review all the material. Don't run out of time when you are about halfway through. It goes without saying that reviewing should not be crammed into the last few hours before an examination.

In this section we have stressed studying for examinations. But we really have been writing about studying for mastery. Mastering something doesn't mean that you will not "forget" it, though in a sense we probably never forget anything that we really learn. When faced with a problem in statistics years after you have studied the subject, you may feel that you remember nothing. But a few minutes of working with the problem will revive the whole thing for you, if you really mastered the material in the first place. Things that you really master—that you have studied well— become a part of you. They never leave you, and they allow you to understand and appreciate your world in a deeper and more knowing way.

UNDERLINING AND OUTLINING TEXTBOOKS

Most students, in studying textbooks, underline or make notes or do both. These are good ways to prepare for review, and note taking in particular, if you do it the right way, provides for recitation. Because underlining and outlining are so important to studying from textbooks, we have included a special section on them.

UNDERLINING

A typical practice of poor students is to sit down with a chapter in front of them, read away in a listless manner, and then when they think they see something important, underline it or mark it with a magic marker.

They do this without surveying the chapter or asking questions. The result is a hit-or-miss selection of passages, one that represents a chance judgment rather than any sense of the overall organization of the material. Unfortunately, such students are then stuck with what they have done. They think they have underscored the important points. But they will have missed many important things and selected others that are not important. In reviewing, they don't think to check their underscoring to see whether it is right, and if they do, they find it impossible to erase lines and put in others, especially if they have underlined in pen or underscored by using a magic marker.

Incidentally, if you are buying a secondhand textbook, insist on getting one that has not been underlined. Otherwise, buy a new one, because the handicap of seeing someone else's underlining is far too serious to be worth the amount of money you save by buying a used book.

Underlining has its place. Some people find it useful and others do not. One of us consistently underlines, the other does not. But if it is to be useful to you, it must be done wisely at the right time and according to a plan. The plan is this: First you should survey a chapter. Then ask yourself questions about it and try to answer these questions as you read. In this first reading *it is best not to underline*, because you really don't know what is important until you have grasped the whole. As your questions are answered, or as you think that you spot main ideas and important details, put a check mark in the margin. The next time you read, read for the main ideas, important details, and technical terms. It is these you want to underline.

Even on the second, careful reading, don't underline the sentences as you read them. After you have read one or two paragraphs, go back and decide what it is you are going to underline. As a guide, use your check marks in the margin. If they do not designate the really important points, you can change them or ignore them.

Don't underline sentences wholesale. Many of the words in one sentence that contains an important idea are unimportant. Decide which these are and leave them out when you underline. Underline only the words and phrases which are essential. If you do this, when you go back at reviewing time you can read only the underlined words and phrases. This way you will grasp at a glance what is important. On page 49 you will find an example of good underlining. Examine this example carefully and try to figure out why we have underlined the things we did.

If you follow these rules, you probably will not underline as much as most students do. On the average, a half-dozen or so words per paragraph will do the trick, though, of course, the amount depends upon the nature of the material you are studying. Underline lightly. A book with heavy underlining is hard to read and sometimes confusing.

TAKING READING NOTES

For most subjects you will also want to take notes, preferably in an outline form, as you study the material in your textbook. There are several good reasons for taking such notes:

First, to do so forces you to participate actively in the learning process. If you try to write down in short form what the author says, you make it a part of your own mental processes. You can't fool yourself into believing that you have really been reading, when your mind has been elsewhere. You have got to find out how the author organizes things if you're going to take sensible notes in outline form.

You already know that we remember what we read actively. Taking notes helps us to read actively. Also, taking good notes on reading assignments makes reviewing easier and more effective. If you outline a chapter carefully, you reduce to a couple of pages what may be contained in twenty pages of print. You eliminate those things that the author puts in to make it easier for you to understand but which, once you understand, you don't need to remind you of the basic ideas. If your outline is good enough, your reviews can be simply a matter of making sure you know what is in it. And since you wrote it, it should be easy to recite or relearn, if necessary. If you understand, you can fill in the details and give examples.

METHODS OF OUTLINING

How do you go about outlining? The first step is to use whatever clues the author gives you for her or his own outline. If there are a number of headings in the text you can get the skeleton of your outline from these headings. Most headings, however, are not sentences; they are just a few key words. You will want to write full sentences, so if you use the headings, make sentences out of them (doing this will give you the main idea). To make a sentence out of the heading you will have to read the section marked by the heading.

Your outline should be orderly. You can make it so by using two simple devices. One way is to indent one order of statement under another. The highest order starts at your left margin. All the statements subsumed under this will be indented to the right. Indicate statements subsumed under each of these by indenting further to the right.

The other way of indicating the structure of your

UNDERLINING A TEXTBOOK

Here is an example of underlining to pick out the main points (from C. R. McConnell, Economics: Principles, Problems, and Policies, *7th ed., McGraw-Hill, New York, 1978, pp. 48–49).*

Extensive Use of Capital Goods

All modern economies—whether they approximate the capitalist, socialist, or communist ideology—are based upon an advanced technology and the extensive use of capital goods. Under pure capitalism it is competition, coupled with freedom of choice and the desire to further one's self-interest, which provides the means for achieving a rapid rate of technological advance. The capitalistic framework is felt to be highly effective in harnessing incentives to develop new products and improved techniques of production. Why? Because the monetary rewards derived therefrom accrue directly to the innovator. Pure capitalism therefore presupposes the extensive use and rapid development of complex capital goods: tools, machinery, large-scale factories, and facilities for storage, transportation, and marketing.

Why are the existence of an advanced technology and the extensive use of capital goods important? Because the most direct method of producing a product is usually the least efficient.[2] Even Robinson Crusoe avoided the inefficiencies of direct production in favor of "roundabout production." It would be ridiculous for a farmer—even a backyard farmer—to go at production with bare hands. Obviously, it pays huge dividends in terms of more efficient production and, therefore, a more abundant output, to fashion tools of production, that is, capital equipment, to aid in the productive process. There is a better way of getting water out of a well than to dive in after it!

But there is a catch involved. As we recall our discussion of the production possibilities curve and the basic nature of the economizing problem, it is evident that, with full employment and full production, resources must be diverted from the production of consumer goods in order to be used in the production of capital goods. We must currently tighten our belts as consumers to free resources for the production of capital goods which will increase productive efficiency and permit us to have a greater output of consumer goods at some future date.

Specialization

The extent to which society relies upon specialization is astounding. The vast majority of consumers produce virtually none of the goods and services they consume and, conversely, consume little or nothing of what they produce. The hammer-shop laborer who spends his life stamping out parts for jet engines may never "consume" an airplane trip. The assembly-line worker who devotes eight hours a day to the installation of windows in Chevrolets may own a Ford. Few households seriously consider any extensive production of their own food, shelter, and clothing. Many farmers sell their milk to the local creamery and then buy oleomargarine at the Podunk general store. Society learned long ago that self-sufficiency breeds inefficiency. The jack-of-all-trades may be a very colorful individual, but he is certainly lacking in efficiency.

In what specific ways might human specialization—*the division of labor*—enhance productive efficiency? First, specialization permits individuals to take advantage of existing differences in their abilities and skills. If caveman A is strong, swift afoot, and accurate with a spear, and caveman B is weak and slow, but patient, this distribution of talents can be most efficiently utilized by making A a hunter and B a fisherman. Second, even if the abilities of A and B are identical, specialization may prove to be advantageous. Why? Because by

[2] Remember that consumer goods satisfy wants directly, while capital goods do so indirectly through the more efficient production of consumer goods.

---

outline is to use a consistent system of lettering and numbering the different orders. There are several ways of doing this, and if you already have one, there is no need to change it. If you don't, try using Roman numerals (I, II, III, . . .) for the highest-order headings, capital letters (A, B, C, . . .) for the second order, Arabic numerals (1, 2, 3, . . .) for the third order, and lowercase letters (a, b, c, . . .) for the fourth order. If you need additional orders, you can use lowercase Roman numerals (i, ii, iii, . . .) or use parentheses around letters or numerals, for example, (I), (II). Look at the sample outline on pages 50 and 51.

CONTENT AND FORM OF NOTES

Your notes should contain the main ideas and important details at each level of the outline. Be sure to put enough into your notes so that you can understand them later. If, for example, you are outlining a section in a physics text on the idea of the *wave front,* don't simply write down "Huygens's Principle." Tell what Huygens's Principle is. You might write: "Huygens's Principle: Every point on a wave front is a point source for waves generated in the direction of the wave's propagation."

We add only one other warning: Write legibly. Even people who have a good hand get in such a hurry when they take notes that they can't read their own scrawl later on. If your writing is hard to read anyway, make a special effort to improve it when you take textbook notes. If you practice writing clearly, you may learn to write well enough for instructors to read your writing. While almost no one admits it, clear writing is probably worth some points on an examination.

OUTLINING FROM BOOKS

Here is an outline of Chapter 4, "The Art of Reading." It illustrates how you might outline material found in a textbook.

I. Reading well and liking to read go together.
II. If you are deficient in reading you will:
   A. Move your lips or vocalize when you read.
   B. Read each word one by one.
   C. Find many unfamiliar words while reading.
   D. Backtrack and reread what you have just read.
   E. Read everything at the same rate and in the same way.
   F. Not understand what you have read.
III. Reading with a purpose.
   A. Skimming.
      1. Look for signposts
         a. Look for headings.
         b. If there are no headings read the first sentences of paragraphs.
      2. Skimming is the first step in studying.
   B. Read to get the main idea.
      1. Finding the main idea.
         a. At different levels: chapters, sections, paragraphs.
         b. Paragraph contains a single topic.
         i. Topical sentence usually at beginning of paragraph.
         ii. But sometimes it occurs elsewhere in paragraph.
      2. Main idea not necessarily whole sentence.
         a. May be the principal clause of a sentence.
         b. May need to be boiled down in your own words.
         c. Often can throw away qualifiers.
      3. Sometimes main idea not expressed, only implied.
   C. Extracting important details.
      1. Details often examples—particularly in science.
      2. Often a matter of judgment.
      3. Make identifying them habitual—without thinking about it.
   D. Reading for pleasure
      1. The more you read for pleasure, the better reader you will be.
      2. Read for pleasure in all the different ways you read to learn.
   E. Evaluate what you read—examine your own beliefs.
   F. Expand what you read to apply to situations not mentioned by author.
IV. Using your eyes.
   A. Eye movements.
      1. Saccades are quick movements broken by brief pauses.
      2. Pauses are fixations.
         a. Fixations last one-quarter to one-fifth of a second.
         b. Read during fixations.
      3. Very little difference between good and poor readers in speed of saccades.
      4. Good readers fix on the average only once every three words.
      5. Poor readers make more regressive saccades.
      6. Good readers make a single return movement at the end of a line; poor readers overshoot or undershoot.
   B. Improving eye movements.
      1. Eye movements in reading are automatic or reflexive.
         a. Can't improve them much consciously.
         b. Major emphasis now upon improving mental

Making outline notes of textbook material helps you understand what you read and remember it when exam time comes. There are some kinds of things, however, for which outline notes are inappropriate. You would not want to outline a foreign language text. Some textbooks, especially in the physical sciences, are often almost in outline form to begin with, and it is hardly worth your while to copy outlines from a book. In this case, you'll do better to emphasize silent recitation, or written recitation of things that are important.

If your instructor follows the textbook closely when he or she lectures, you would do well to keep your textbook notes and lecture notes together in parallel format. You might plan to read and outline the textbook material before you go to class. Then your lecture notes will highlight what you have already extracted from the textbook plus any new material introduced in the lecture.

READING WHICH YOU DON'T OUTLINE

Some kinds of reading do not lend themselves to notes in outline form. When you read a work of literature, you do not read in order to understand some particular facts or theories. Rather, you will be expected to interpret what you read. Here, a commentary on reading rather than an outline is appropriate. You will be expected to appreciate why the story or the essay is written the way it is. You will be expected to be alert to the author's imagery and to any symbolic interpretation the work may have. Some people prefer

habits of reading.

  c. Keeping a record of reading speed helps to increase speed.

2. Upper limit to reading speed about 900 words a minute.

3. Most students read at a rate of 200 to 300 words a minute.

  a. That rate can be pushed quite a bit higher.

  b. As you do so, your eye movements will automatically improve.

V. How to improve your reading.

  A. Building a vocabulary.

    1. Lots of new words encountered in college.

    2. Vocabulary mark of a good student and good reader.

    3. Be on the lookout for new words.

    4. Use the dictionary often.

      a. A good dictionary is essential.

      b. In looking up a word, find out its meaning in the context in which you found it.

    5. Use vocabulary cards to improve a poor vocabulary.

    6. Distinguish between general and technical terms.

      a. May need glossary or special dictionary for technical terms.

      b. Sometimes half or more of the subject matter may be in knowing what technical terms mean.

    7. How to dissect words.

      a. Many words consist of roots, prefixes, and suffixes.

      b. Knowing the meaning of commonly used prefixes and suffixes may help you guess the meaning of new words correctly.

      c. Many English words built on Latin and Greek roots.

  B. Learning to read faster.

    1. Very few people read at their maximum rate.

    2. Reading faster requires practice.

      a. For practice to be effective, you must know whether you are improving or not.

      b. Therefore, you must keep a record of how fast you are reading.

        i. Devote a special period each day to practice at fast reading.

        ii. Use the same kind of material every day.

        iii. Use the same format.

        iv. Use material of moderate difficulty.

        v. Time yourself.

        vi. Count the words and calculate your reading rate.

        vii. Make a chart or graph of your reading rate.

        viii. Be sure you are not sacrificing comprehension for speed.

    3. If your reading is exceptionally slow or you don't improve, you will need help.

    4. Practice skimming.

      a. There are two kinds of skimming.

        i. Searching for key words.

        ii. Searching for key words and phrases on your initial survey.

      b. Use browsing for secondary or less-important reading.

---

to make notes in the margin of the book; others keep a separate notebook for the purpose of writing commentaries.

You will probably want to read through a story the first time without making notes. Then on rereading, you may want to take notes. A useful form for making such notes is to cast them in the form of questions, which you can then answer. Some of your questions might be very general and about the whole story. Is a particular story mainly an account of certain incidents, or are the incidents mainly there to reveal something about the character of the people in the story? Is there any significance to the names the author gives the characters?

In some high school texts and in a few college anthologies, you will find questions of this sort, written by an editor and intended to help you understand and appreciate the stories contained in the anthologies. These can provide a guide for the kinds of questions you should be thinking about on your own. However, most literature courses in college now use paperback editions without these special guides. Here, your best guide is your instructor. Try to imagine the kinds of questions he or she would like you to ask about what you are reading.

Some aspects of what you will read for courses in literature cannot be approached in this way. You need to be alert to features of the story that may appear to be quite incidental but which are central to the idea or the mood the author wishes to convey. There may be allusions, for example, to stories from classical mythology or to biblical texts. Jot these down in your notes and, if you can, look them up and see why they might be relevant to the story.

Not all works of literature are fiction, of course. You will read some essays, and you may be asked to read some great classical treatises, such as Darwin's *Origin of Species* or Marx's *Capital*. Or you may be asked to read excerpts from works like these. Essays and treatises are not like textbooks. They are apt to be more discursive. And the chances are that you are asked to read them in much the way you might read stories. That is to say, you ask yourself, Why did the author say things in exactly that way? Is there anything in the work that reflects the author's personal life? In brief, you will read such works in a literary and historical context.

You are, however, expected to know what the literary works you read are about. It is a good idea to write summaries, and we will deal with the problem of writing summaries next.

WRITING SUMMARIES

Summaries can be helpful for almost any kind of reading assignment. They are useful for textbooks, particularly when the textbooks do not have summaries at the ends of the chapters. A few authors deliberately do not provide summaries because they believe that students profit most when they write on their own. For textbooks, don't try to write the summary until you have studied the material thoroughly and after you have outlined. Summaries should be as brief as possible, but they should contain all the essential information.

If you write a summary of a story, be sure that it is more than a bare recital of the narrative. Characterize the people in the story, and make sure you refer to the author's symbols and any symbolic interpretation the story may have. Be sure you can, in your own words, comment on the atmosphere of the story, the feeling the story evokes, whether or not there is irony in the story, and all the other features you may have jotted down when you made notes about the content of the story.

TAKING NOTES FOR HISTORY TEXTS

History texts often have a unique organization; things are usually arranged chronologically. It is true that modern texts and history instructors place less emphasis upon particular dates—your instructor may not care if you don't have the exact dates for the treaty of Ghent or for the founding of the Federal Reserve system, but you had better have these in their right eras and in the right context.

A typical organization for a history text is to deal with a span of time that has some natural historical significance. The history of France (or the whole of Western Europe, for that matter) has a kind of continuity from 1815 and the Congress of Vienna to the revolutions of 1848 and, in France, the establishment of the Second Republic. So after you have surveyed and read your text, you might make notes by blocking off in your notebook a couple of pages devoted to the period from 1815 to 1848. Then you can indicate the significant events, ideas, and people in something like a chronological order. Also, since modern history courses stress social, intellectual, and technological history as well as the traditional political history, you might rule your note pages into parallel columns with these things as headings. This way you can see, for example, how the development of railroads and industry paralleled changes in where people lived and in the kinds of clothes that they wore as well as in the kinds of ideas they espoused.

While it is not strictly a matter of making notes, there is one feature of studying from history texts (and lecture notes) that is of particular importance. Make sure you know how to use maps. Examine the maps in your textbook very carefully, and make sketches of them if that is the way you can impress them upon your mind. On an examination, you may be given a blank map with the instructions to indicate certain features on it. You could be given a blank map of, say, North America and be asked to indicate the limits of French and British settlements on the eve of the French and Indian War. Even if maps are not given on tests, maps are a good way to hold information that you may be required to produce. For example, it is much easier to remember that the provinces of Alsace and Lorraine were ceded by France to Germany after the war of 1870 if you know roughly where Alsace and Lorraine are on a map of Europe. Otherwise you have merely memorized a statement that has no real meaning to you.

SUMMARIZING A CHAPTER

The time to recite what you have read in this chapter is now. If you haven't already made an outline, do it now. Then run back through the chapter to make sure you haven't missed something. Write a summary, using your outline.

EXAMPLE OF A SUMMARY

Here is a summary of Chapter 4, "The Art of Reading." Compare the statements in this summary with the headings and main ideas in the chapter. Also, compare it with the outline on pages 50 and 51 to see how an outline and a summary differ.

In college you will have to do more reading than you have ever done, and you will need to work at doing better at it. When you read better, you will like it more. If you move your lips when you read or read word by word, or find a lot of unfamiliar words, or backtrack, or read everything the same way, or fail to understand what you read, you are a poor reader and will need to improve.

There are different purposes in reading and different ways to read. Skimming is one way to read. In one kind of skimming you look for headings and subheadings. Another way to skim is to search for ciritical words. We also read to get the main idea. The main idea of a paragraph is the topical sentence, often found at the beginning of the paragraph. In looking for the main idea, don't look for whole sentences. Pick out the key words and phrases. Sometimes the author will not state the main idea but only imply it. This happens often in literary texts. Sometimes you will want to read to extract important details. Important ideas are often examples, particularly in scientific texts. Often you have to use your judgment to find important details. When you read for pleasure, you will want to suit your reading to your purpose, just as you do when you read to learn. Keep an active attitude toward reading; evaluate what you read.

When you read your eyes move in a series of quick movements broken by brief pauses. The movements are called saccades, and the pauses, fixations. The pauses last about one-quarter to one-fifth of a second and they occupy about 90 percent of the total time in reading. There are also regressive movements. These occur more often in poor readers. Another difference between good and poor readers is in the return movement at the end of a line. Poor readers overshoot or undershoot.

The best way to improve your eye movements in reading is to improve your mental habits. You can't read faster than 900 words a minute, but since the typical student reads only 200 to 300 words a minute, there is a lot of room for improvement. To improve your reading you need to build your vocabulary. You will learn many new technical terms in college, and you must pay attention to these. Use your dictionary frequently. If you have serious trouble with vocabulary, use vocabulary cards. For technical terms you will need to consult glossaries and technical dictionaries. Learn to dissect words into prefixes, roots, and suffixes. Know the meaning of as many prefixes and suffixes as you can.

Practice timing yourself at reading. Do this every day with the same kind of material. Make a chart or graph of the results to see if you are actually improving. If your reading rate is very poor or if you don't improve, you will need to find special help. Practice at skimming as well as at reading.

CHAPTER SIX

TAKING EXAMINATIONS

If you're used to miracles, then perhaps you may believe that you can pass examinations without studying for them. For most of us, however, that's not possible. After all, the main purpose of examinations is to determine how effectively you have studied. If you have followed the rules for effective study, you have done most of what is necessary to be ready for examinations, and you will have no need of miracles. In this chapter, we offer you a few additional ideas particular to taking examinations.

PREPARING FOR EXAMINATIONS

The best rule is, Be prepared. Be prepared for the kind of exams you are to take and for *all* the questions you might be asked, not just for some of them. Master the subject matter thoroughly and organize it well in your mind. Be in good physical condition, rested, and in a good frame of mind.

THE FINAL REVIEW

If you have kept up with your studying, preparing for an exam is mainly a matter of review. This review should be an intensive one. You will go over your lecture notes and textbook notes, look at the main ideas, and review lists of technical terms.

A review is just that—a review. It is not an attempt to learn things you should have learned earlier. If you're still reading material for the first time just before an exam, you had better hope for a miracle. You are seriously handicapped. If the exam is easy and the material not too strange to you, you might be able to scrape by. But you would have done much better if you had studied the way you were supposed to.

In some subjects, you may want to make a set of review notes. These can be of two kinds. They can be condensations of your detailed notes, or they can be compilations of all the things you found difficult, are apt to forget, or need to commit to memory.

SCHEDULE OF REVIEWS

Most students overestimate the time they will need for review. If you have kept up with your work, reviewing for an exam need not take a lot of time. For weekly quizzes, a few minutes will do. For a midterm or hourly exam, two or three hours will be enough, and for a final exam, five to eight hours. Moreover, keep your review periods short, no more than an hour or an hour and a half. Intersperse them with periods of doing something else, particularly rest and recreation. If you work too hard at reviewing a lot of material at once, you will have trouble organizing it.

Make a definite plan for review, just as you schedule your regular hours of study. For the week prior to the exam, revise your regular study schedule. If it is midterm time, set aside particular hours for review of particular subjects. Take some of the time from the hours regularly scheduled for the subject in which you are to be examined, and also use some of your extra hours for review. You may need to cut down on some of your free time, but don't cut into it too deeply; you won't need to if you have been following a good study regime.

This brings up the subject of cramming. All of us like to boast about how much cramming we have to do. We have all heard tales of studying all night and living on black coffee. Most students do more talking than cramming, but the fact is that this kind of frantic, disorganized studying is inefficient and perhaps even harmful. Going without food, sleep, and rest is physically draining; if you have been doing that, it may take a superhuman effort of will to do your best at an exam. And if you are really in poor shape, your judgment will be affected, and you may not even know whether or not what you are doing in the exam is right. It doesn't take pep pills to disorient you. Students who have spent all night studying and drinking endless cups of coffee have been known to write gibberish on an exam under the impression that they were making sense. Even if you are not in that bad shape, if you don't have your wits about you, you can't organize your answers or recall easily, and you are apt to lose your ability to discriminate the right from wrong answers in an objective exam.

Then, after the exam, you will need to make up for lost sleep, and that will result in cutting classes and falling behind in your other work. Once you start cramming and shortchanging your sleep and other studies, you set up a vicious circle. You're always behind in something and always having to resort to further cramming.

It ought to be obvious to you that it is much better to organize your life so that you can live as normally as possible during times of preparing for exams. Get your meals, sleep, and recreation. Keep up with your other subjects. You may not have much to offer in a bull session on cramming, but you will be way ahead in taking examinations.

HOW TO REVIEW

Emphasize recitation. Keep rereading to a minimum. Go after the job chapter by chapter, topic by topic. First try to recall the main ideas without referring to notes. Then check your recollections against your notes. For each main heading of a chapter, do the same

thing. First recall the main points, then check. If you can't recall something or can't explain or understand a point, go back to the book and reread the passage covering it. If you attempt to do more rereading than this in a chunk, you will lose sight of the important points or skip around so aimlessly that you will accomplish little.

It is easy to fall into the trap of trying to outguess the instructor. Some students try to anticipate what will be on the exam by guessing what the instructor's favorite topics are. They then study only those topics. But instructors seldom make up exams by their favorite topics, or even by cribbing from exams given last semester or last year. They more often try to keep a balance in all the material they presented or asked students to read. If you try this route, you will end up saying those famous sad words, "I studied the wrong things."

If you try to predict all that *could be* asked instead of concentrating on a few topics or questions, you will be in good shape to deal with anything that turns up. As you review, ask yourself the following questions: Is this something that could be a question? Is this an important point? How might a question be asked on this topic? Take advantage of the hints that most instructors give, either directly or indirectly, about the kinds of questions they tend to ask. One way or another, you should be able to spot many questions that are likely to appear. If you are thorough and comprehensive about this, you will be prepared to deal with any question that comes your way.

TYPES OF EXAMS

Most exams are either objective or essay. Objective exams do not require you to write. All you do is decide whether certain statements are true or false, which of several statements is true, or how statements should be matched. Objective exams stress your ability to *recognize* the right answers when you see them, not your ability to recall or organize the information you have learned.

The essay examination, on the other hand, requires you to *recall*. You must organize what you know in a coherent way. In science and mathematics courses, you will be given problems to solve. Like essays, problems stress your ability to recall rather than recognize information. That is true even when they are presented in a multiple choice or some objective format. If you aren't just going to guess at the most plausible answer, you must recall how to solve the problem and then work it out.

There are some kinds of exams that are in between traditional essay and objective exams. Completion

SCHEDULE OF REVIEW FOR FINAL EXAMINATION

Here are two schedules of review for final examinations. The first is a sample schedule for the week of finals; the second is a blank schedule which you can complete before your own final exams. Note that specific times are allotted to each subject and that time has been set aside for meals, study breaks, and recreation. Note all that the last study time scheduled is 10:00 P.M.

Sample Schedule of Review for Final Examinations

Time \ Day	Saturday	Sunday	Monday	Tuesday	Wednesday	Thursday	Friday
8:00	— — — — — — — Breakfast — — — — — — — — —						
9:00	Study Chem.	Study Engl.	INTRO.	ELEM.	Study Psych.	Study Psych.	Study Hist.
10:00	Study Engl.	Study French	CHEM.	FRENCH	↓	↓	↓
11:00	Study Chem.	Break	EXAM	EXAM	Break	Break	Break
12:00	↓	Study Chem.	Break	Break	↓	↓	↓
1:00	— — — — — — — Lunch — — — — — — — — —						
2:00	Study Engl.	Study Chem.	Study Engl.	ENGLISH	Study Hist.	INTRO.	U.S.
3:00	↓	↓	↓	LIT.	↓	PSYCH.	HIST.
4:00	Study Chem.	Break	Break	EXAM	Break	EXAM	EXAM
5:00	↓	Study Engl.	Study French	Break	Study Psych.	Break	Break
6:00	— — — — — — — Dinner — — — — — — — — —						
7:00	Study French	Study Chem.	Study Engl.	Study Psych.	Study Hist.	Study Hist.	
8:00	Free	↓	↓	Study Hist.	↓	↓	
9:00	Time	Break	Study French	Free	Break	Free	
10:00	↓			Time	Study Psych.	Time	

questions, for example, require you to fill in a word or phrase. Or sometimes, the instructor will ask you to identify or describe something in a short sentence. These kinds of questions do not require you to organize a lot of information, but they do test recall.

Students often ask whether they should study differently for these different kinds of examinations. You should prepare *somewhat* differently for each type, but not so differently as many students think. Because objective exams require only that you select (or guess at) the right answer, many students don't study as thoroughly for them as they do for essay exams. This is a mistake. It is just as difficult to do well on an objective exam as on an essay exam for the simple reason that all students have the same advantage or disadvantage. Most objective examinations are graded relatively (on a curve of some sort), so that on the average you will finally end up just where you belong.

Students also feel that objective exams overemphasize details. This feeling, however, is in many instances an illusion. When students take objective exams, they are confronted with many detailed statements. When they take essay exams, they may not realize that they are required to supply details, to invent examples, to produce formulas, etc.

Schedule for Review for Final Examinations

Time \ Day	Saturday	Sunday	Monday	Tuesday	Wednesday	Thursday	Friday
8:00							
9:00							
10:00							
11:00							
12:00							
1:00							
2:00							
3:00							
4:00							
5:00							
6:00							
7:00							
8:00							
9:00							
10:00							

You may feel that objective exams are sometimes picky and based upon trivial detail. Occasionally that is the case (as it may well be for essay exams too), but more often than not, it is not. Compare the questions on the next objective examination you take with the headings and important points in your notes. You will find that they are likely to correspond. Exams usually cover precisely the points you should know if you were to organize answers into essays.

The principal difference between the two types of exam is one of organization, not of details. Essay exams are harder in the sense that they require you to organize the information, but they do not require you to *know*

any more than will a good objective exam. Because essay examinations do require organization, if you are to take one, you should practice organizing answers ahead of time. Since objective tests place a premium upon recognition, you should be ready to recognize general points when they are given in specific examples. In general, you will probably want to spend more time in reading and less in reciting if you know you are to take an objective exam.

Don't go to extremes in your preparation. All reviews should include some rereading and some recitation. All reviews should stress knowledge of the main ideas and the important details.

EXAMINATION ANXIETY

Many students approach exams with dread. They are upset both before and during an examination. A few students become physically ill before or during an examination, and many students break out in a sweat and show all the other symptoms of acute anxiety. This negative approach is reinforced by the fact that grades depend so heavily upon examinations. Students who are not doing well may easily approach a particular exam with the feeling that it is going to cut them out of academic life.

Try not to develop these feelings. They will only make you miserable. If you develop good study habits, you will approach examinations with more confidence, and you will have less cause to get yourself into a state of anxiety. Exams that come early in a course provide an opportunity for you to assess your preparation. Use this opportunity to correct any deficiencies you find.

Another symptom of anxiety many students show is to get rattled during an examination. They forget things they knew just a little while before, and they make careless mistakes. The best way to prevent going to pieces during an exam is to be thoroughly prepared. If you have a tendency to fall apart, you need to be better prepared than other students. Then as you gain confidence in your ability to cope with the stress of an exam, you will gradually lose that tendency. Sometimes students who fall apart during an exam are unconsciously providing themselves with an alibi for doing poorly. Test anxiety can be a defense against taking the blame for poor preparation.

Besides being well prepared, there are a few other things you can do to reduce your anxiety. Some of them are little things such as getting to the exam well before it begins. Avoid rushing. It merely aggravates your nervousness. Another thing you can do is to relax before the exam. Don't try to do a last-minute frantic review while waiting for the exam to be handed out. Don't talk about the exam with other students. That merely invites being upset. The only thing hectic, last-minute reviewing or exchanging ideas about what is going to be on the exam does is to confuse you with details and increase your tension. Rather, spend the few minutes before an exam engaging in small talk, reading the newspaper, or doing anything that will put you in a relaxed mood.

The last and most important thing you can do to bolster your confidence is to have a strategy for taking the exam. People who know what to do in emergencies don't panic or get upset, and this holds for taking examinations. You probably know what kind of exam to expect. There is a sensible way to go about taking each kind. Know what it is and be prepared to carry out your plan as soon as you get the signal to go ahead.

If, in spite of being well prepared and rested before an examination, you are still crippled by anxiety, you will need to do something about it. Many counseling services offer special sessions on how to reduce examination anxiety. And even if such a particular service is not offered at your institution, being counseled about your problems with examinations may help you. Panic before examinations even when you are well prepared is a symptom of something being wrong. Doing something about it may not only help you with examinations but in other problems of personal adjustment as well.

TAKING OBJECTIVE EXAMINATIONS

Here is what you do when you are faced with an objective examination:

1. *Survey.* When you pick up an objective exam, flip through the pages to see how long it is and how many kinds of questions are on it. Note how many questions there are of each type—true-false, multiple choice, matching—so that you can determine how to divide your time among them.

2. *Read directions carefully.* Make sure you know what you are supposed to do. Indicate your answers in exactly the way the directions tell you to. If you don't, you will lose points.

3. *Be sure you understand the scoring rules.* If there is no penalty for guessing, you can try to answer every question. If you leave some questions unanswered, you may lose some points. If, on the other hand, there is a definite penalty for guessing by taking off points for a wrong answer, follow a conservative strategy. How conservative your strategy should be will depend upon the penalty. If the instructor takes *two* points off for a wrong answer and gives only one point for a correct one, you will want to be very careful indeed. True-false tests are more likely to have such a severe correction for chance because you have a fifty-fifty chance of getting any answer right just by flipping a coin.

If on a true-false test, the instructor arrives at a score by taking the number right minus the number wrong, you should guess and try to answer every question because, on the average, your guesses will be right more often than wrong. But as we pointed out earlier, if the instructor corrects for this by taking the number right minus *two* times the number wrong, be very careful about your guesses.

Guess only when you have a strong feeling that you may be right.

Whatever you do, read the instructor's directions. If the instructor says, "There is no penalty for guessing" or "Don't guess, because wrong answers will be penalized," adjust your performance accordingly. If you don't know or don't understand, ask.

4. *Answer easy questions first.* Sometimes speed is a factor in objective tests, and you will want to work as rapidly as is consistent with care. After you have surveyed the test and gotten the instructions straight, begin to answer the questions. Some will be easy and some will be hard. Some are so easy that you can answer as soon as you have read the question. If you have to stop and think, put a check mark in the margin and go on to the next question. Come back to those hard ones after you have done all the easy ones. Whatever you do, don't get bogged down on some particular question. Unless the test is unusual, every question of a given type will have equal wieght, and you're just wasting good time fussing over a particular question. Knowing how much time you have left and how many tough questions remain to be answered, you can apportion your time sensibly.

This is particularly good advice for an objective test in which the questions are problems that must be worked. Work those that you are sure you know how to work first and then, if you have time, go back to those that you must figure out in order to know how to work.

5. *Place the question in context.* As you read the questions, remember their context. Ask yourself how this question ought to be answered in the light of your textbook or what has been said in class. Identify the source, if possible. Don't fall into the trap of answering a question with your own personal opinion or what has been said in some other course you are taking. Most answers are relevant to a given context. Don't handicap yourself by ignoring that context. Even if you think the instructor or the textbook is wrong, it is still your job to show that you know what the correct answer is from the point of view of the course you are taking.

ANSWERING TRUE-FALSE QUESTIONS

True-false questions usually state the relation between two states or qualities. "Attitudes are learned," "Roses are red," "The stock market crashed" could be examples. Such statements may be true some of the time and not others, or true in some contexts and not others. You can't be expected to answer anything so ambiguous as these examples, and instructors don't intend that you should. They are usually interested in knowing whether you know when and under what circumstances something is true or not. So statements in true-false exams are usually provided with qualifiers.

1. *Analyze qualifiers.* There are a great many possible qualifiers, but the most often used ones come from the following series:

All, most, some, few, none, no
Always, usually, sometimes, rarely, never
Great, much, little, no, none
More, equal, less
Good, bad
Is, is not

Scrutinize the qualifiers carefully. You can test the qualifiers by substituting for the one in the question one of the others in the same series. If your substitution makes a statement that is better than the one in the question, the statement is false. If your substitute does not make a better statement, the question is true. For example, take the statement, "Some roses are red." The alternatives are "All roses are red," "Most roses are red," "Few roses are red," and "No roses are red." The two extreme statements are clearly not true. You may have some question about "Most roses are red" and "Few roses are red." But even if one of them is true, "Some roses are red" would also have to be true. None of the substitutes makes a better statement than the original.

Don't labor over qualifiers, however. Take the time to test them only if you suspect you might be misled by the one that is in the question.

2. *Pick out key words.* Much more important than analyzing the qualifiers is finding the key word or words. There is always a key word. It will be a word or group of words upon which the truth or falsity of the statement depends. All the other words in the statement form something that could be either true or false, depending upon the key word or words.

Some students have picked up the idea that certain words automatically make a statement true or false. And, to be sure, it is difficult to construct true statements with such qualifiers as "no," "never," or "every." But don't automatically mark statements containing them as false. Instructors discard statements that can be answered correctly by taking a cue from extreme

EXERCISE IN KEY WORDS

The following quiz (from Clifford T. Morgan, Introduction to Psychology, McGraw-Hill, New York, 1961, p. 2), specifically designed both for students who have had a course in psychology and for those who have not, illustrates the importance of key words in objective questions. Take the quiz, picking out the key words and writing them in the space provided. In most cases, there is only one key word, but in a few instances, there are two or three. Also indicate in the right-hand column whether you think the statement is true or false. When you are finished, look below for the correct answers.

1. Geniuses are usually queerer than people of average intelligence.
2. Only human beings, not animals, have the capacity to think.
3. Much of human behavior is instinctive.
4. Slow learners remember what they learn better than fast learners.
5. Intelligent people form most of their opinions by logical reasoning.
6. A psychologist is a person who is trained to psychoanalyze people.
7. You can size up a person very well in an interview.
8. When one is working for several hours, it is better to take a few long rests than several short ones.
9. The study of mathematics exercises the mind so that a person can think more logically in other subjects.
10. Grades in college have little to do with sucess in business careers.
11. Alcohol, taken in small amounts, is a stimulant.
12. There is a clear distinction between the normal person and one who is mentally ill.
13. Prejudices are mainly due to lack of information.
14. Competition among people is characteristic of most human societies.
15. The feature of a job that is most important to employees is the pay they get for their work.
16. It is possible to classify people very well into introverts and extroverts.
17. Punishment is usually the best way of eliminating undesirable behavior in children.
18. By watching closely a person's expression, you can tell quite well the emotion he is experiencing.
19. The higher one sets his goals in life, the more he is sure to accomplish and the happier he will be.
20. If a person is honest with you, he usually can tell you what his motives are.

The keys words for each question were as follows: (1) usually, (2) only, not, (3) much, (4) better, (5) most, (6) psychoanalyze, (7) very well, (8) better, (9) in other subjects, (10) little, (11) stimulant, (12) clear, (13) mainly, (14) most, (15) most important, (16) very well, (17) usually, best, (18) quite well, (19) sure, happier, (20) usually. All the statements are false. The reasons for their being false can be found in the book from which they were taken or, very likely, in any general course in psychology.

modifiers, and they do manage to construct some statements containing such modifiers that are, in fact, true. So judge each statement in the light of what you know. The exercise above will give you practice in identifying key words.

ANSWERING MULTIPLE-CHOICE QUESTIONS

Multiple-choice questions are basically true-false questions arranged in groups. A lead phrase at the beginning of each question combines with three or more endings to make different statements. Sometimes the questions are made so that more than one answer is possible. For example: Roses most often grow (1) on bushes, (2) on trees, (3) in winter, (4) in summer. Identifying the key words as "most often," we see that "on bushes" and "in summer" are true. In such cases, the directions will probably tell you to mark all words or phrases that complete the statement correctly. Be sure, however, to read directions carefully, for sometimes the instructions are different.

More often, however, just one of the alternatives will be correct. Here, your job is to pick out the alternative that is best—that is *most nearly true.* It is usually a relative matter, not one of absolute truth or falsity. For this reason, you will want to adopt a strategy of elimination in dealing with the question. Take for example the following question: The American philosopher most influential in the philosophy of education is (1) William James, (2) Bertrand Russell, (3) John Dewey, (4) Nathaniel Hawthorne. If you remember that Hawthorne is the author of *The Scarlet Letter,* you will realize that he is not, technically speaking, a philosopher and can be easily eliminated. The other three are all philosophers, and unless you know something about philosophy and the philosophy of education, you will have a hard time reaching the right answer. The key words that will help you are "American," "philosopher," and "most." Bertrand Russell is English, so you can eliminate him. We have already established that Hawthorne is not a philosopher, and thus, you must choose whether William James or John Dewey is the more influential. Here, it is essential that you know something about the philosophy of education. Both were influential in education, but John Dewey is incomparably more so. In fact, he is probably the single most important influence on the course of American education.

Once you have made your decision, mark the answer and go on to the next question. If you can't make up your mind, place a check mark at the side and leave the question until you have worked all the easier problems.

ANSWERING OTHER TYPES OF OBJECTIVE QUESTIONS

You can apply similar methods to matching questions. Read all the items to be matched so that you know all the possibilities. Then take the first item on the left and read down the items on the right until you find the one that you're sure is the best match. If you're not certain, leave the item and go on to the next one. The best strategy is to fill in only those you're sure about. That way you will reduce the number of possibilities for the difficult matches.

Some matching questions consist only of words and brief phrases to be matched. Others contain whole clauses, similar to those in true-false or multiple-choice statements. If that is so, try to spot the key words.

One kind of question used fairly often in large courses is the completion question. This provides a statement with some key element left out. You're supposed to supply it. In answering this kind of question, choose your words carefully. The chances are that the instructor has something pretty specific in mind—a technical term or a pet phrase. Try to recall the very best wording so that you will get full credit,

not half. But if you can't think of the exact answer, write down something. Instructors seldom deduct for guessing, and while you may look a bit silly to the grading assistant by giving some far-out answer, you just might have the right idea.

FINISHING THE EXAMINATION

We have said that you should answer the easy questions first on an objective exam and then come back to the hard ones. Before you begin to work on these harder questions, note how much time you have left and allocate it among the remaining questions. Leave some time for a final glance over the exam. Before you turn your paper in, read through it to check for such careless mistakes as putting down an unintended answer or skipping a question that you know how to answer.

When you reread your examination, you will be tempted to change some of your answers. If you feel strongly that an answer should be changed, do it. If, however, you have a hard time making up your mind between two answers, don't change the answer you wrote the first time. Almost everyone agrees that if you are guessing, first guesses are more likely to be right than second guesses. Change your answer only if you are reasonably sure that your first answer is wrong.

TAKING ESSAY EXAMINATIONS

An essay examination is one in which the questions are relatively short, and most of your work consists of writing the answer rather than reading the questions and trying to figure out the right answers. At one extreme, essay exams consist of short-answer questions. These require you to write down something very specific. At the other extreme, they will consist of questions that ask you to "discuss" some general issue. Sometimes exams will be mixtures of these. Short-answer questions, or identification questions as they are sometimes called, require somewhat different strategies than discussion questions, but there are some principles that apply to both.

PLANNING YOUR TIME

Planning and allocating time are essential in taking essay exams. Most students know enough to write more than they have time for, and it is easy to get carried away on a question you really know something about. If you're not careful, you will spend too much time on some questions and end up by giving others too little. You will, consequently, get a low grade because the instructor or grading assistant will expect you to have budgeted your time.

Read through the whole exam first and make a tentative decision about how much time you can afford to spend on each question. If you have a choice of which questions to answer, choose all your questions at the beginning.

FOLLOWING DIRECTIONS

The key words in essay exams are instructions you are supposed to follow. They are words such as "list," "illustrate," "compare," "outline," "state," "discuss," etc. Usually an instructor chooses such words carefully, and he or she expects you to do what you're told. Students who aren't prepared as well as they should be are tempted to "write around" a subject—to tell everything they know about a subject whether relevant to the question or not. This is a waste of time. Graders and instructors ignore what wasn't asked for and may even penalize a student for evading the question. Stick as close to the directions as you can. If you're told to list, do that; don't illustrate or discuss. If you're told to compare, be sure you do that.

IMPORTANT WORDS IN ESSAY QUESTIONS

Here are some of the words that provide the critical instructions for answering essay questions. We've provided a brief summary of what each tells you to do.

Compare
Look for similarities and differences between the things mentioned (*e.g.,* Compare the U.S. and Confederate Constitutions).

Contrast
Stress the dissimilarities.

Criticize
Make your judgment about the item in question. Stress the deficiencies. (*E.g.,* Criticize Paul Valéry's views on the poet's language.)

Define
Give a concise and accurate definition of what is called for.

Describe
Mention the chief characteristics of a situation or retell the essential features of a story (*e.g.,* Describe France on the eve of the revolution, or Describe Conrad's *Heart of Darkness*).

Diagram
Provide a drawing, chart, or plan.

Discuss
Be analytical. Give reasons pro and con.

Evaluate
Provide both positive and negative sides of the topic (*e.g.,* Evaluate the role of Disraeli in forming the modern Conservative Party).

Explain
Give reasons for what is asked for. Provide the causes. (*E.g.,* Explain the reasons for the notion of penetrance in population genetics.)

Illustrate
Use examples. Or, where appropriate, provide a diagram or figure.

Interpret
Translate, solve, or comment on a subject, usually giving your judgment about it.

Justify
Provide the reasons for your conclusions or for the statement made in the question (*e.g.,* Justify Henry Clay's interpretation of the Constitution).

List
Provide an itemized list. The items should be numbered.

Outline
Organize your answer into main points and subordinate points. While it is not necessary that your answer be in outline form, it helps to prepare it that way.

Prove
Provide factual evidence or, where appropriate, a logical or mathematical proof.

Relate
Show the connection between the things mentioned in the question. Note this does not mean to compare, so if you are asked to relate the American and French revolutions, you are not to compare them but to show how one influences the other.

Review
Provide a summary, usually a critical one. A review usually also implies commenting on important aspects of the question.

Summarize
Provide a summary, usually without comment or criticism.

Trace
Describe the progress of some historical event or, where appropriate, describe the causes of some event.

ORGANIZING ESSAY ANSWERS

Here are two examples of brief answers to an essay question. Read them to see what you think of them, and then compare your judgment with our comment at the end. The question is: What were the important results of the (English) revolution of 1688?

The first answer

I will summarize the most important results of the revolution under three headings:

1. *Parliament's victory.* The most direct result of the revolution of 1688 was the final victory of Parliament in the conflict between it and the crown that had gone on all during the 17th century. Parliament, by declaring the throne vacant because of James II's desertion to France, finally established that the king ruled by choice of the people and Parliament and not by divine right. Parliament established a Bill of Rights, which said that the king was not above the law but was himself subject to the law. In the early years of the reign of William and Mary, many additional acts were passed which curtailed the powers of the crown.

2. *The end of religious conflict.* The revolution itself did not entirely end the religious troubles of the 17th century, but Parliament passed a Toleration Act which brought an end to many of the difficulties of the Dissenters. The Catholics, however, were still subjected to many infringements of civil liberties.

3. *A new political class.* The important general result of the revolution and the victory of Parliament was the beginning of a long era during which political power in England was divided between the landed gentry and the merchant class.

The second answer

The revolution of 1688 was very important. It was so important that it is sometimes called the "glorious revolution." Parliament won, and it passed a lot of acts which were against the king, and it invited William and Mary to rule jointly in England. William and Mary still had to fight though, especially in Ireland where James II was finally defeated. William and Mary cooperated with Parliament so there wasn't so much trouble between the King and Parliament. James II was very unpopular because he was a Catholic, and Parliament made it so no Catholic could ever become king again, although parliament made things easier for the Dissenters. This was the end of the Divine Right of kings in England, though at first the country was ruled mostly by the aristocracy and the rich merchants. Real democracy didn't come until much later, so the revolution of 1688 wasn't a completely democratic revolution.

Notice that these two answers differ more in organization than they do in content. The first answer is not perfect, but it is balanced, clear, and factual. The second is much poorer because it is vague, disorganized, and full of irrelevancies and loose statements.

ORGANIZING YOUR ANSWERS

The difference between a good essay answer and a poor one is often a matter of organization. The best way to make sure that your answer will be coherent and organized is to outline. When you're sure you understand what is asked for in a question, decide what points you will make and sketch these out in outline form. Use this outline as a guide to writing the answer. After you are through with it, you can cross it out so that it won't be taken as part of the answer. The grader won't mind if you do this; instructors expect good students to outline. If you don't outline, you will get off the subject more easily, and in the rush of writing, you may forget one of the important points.

You can even write most answers in some kind of outline. Don't make it skimpy or use incomplete sentences. If you do, the grader may not know what you mean. Number the main points and possibly even indicate the subordinate points by letters and by indenting. One of the reasons for giving essay exams is to help you organize the material in your own mind, and you're much more likely to get credit for what you know if you express it in a well-organized, outline form. Study the two examples we give to see the difference organization makes in the quality of an answer.

CHOOSING YOUR WORDS

Most students don't take the trouble to choose their words carefully in answering a question. Instructors are not mind readers. They can't guess what you intended; they can only judge what you actually said. So say what you mean. Say it precisely. Give illustrations (if appropriate) and important relevant details, but make it clear that you know what you're talking about. The two examples on organizing essay answers illustrate the difference between precise, accurate statements and statements that, while they may be intended to say the same thing, don't say it in quite the right way.

Know the difference between padding your answer and elaborating your points. Bringing in extraneous points, repeating what you have already said, and being unnecessarily wordy are all padding. Look at the two essays. If you can't tell the difference between them in this respect, you may need some remedial help in writing. Even though the poorly organized answer is shorter, it is full of padding. The other is not.

WRITING LEGIBLY AND CORRECTLY

Poor handwriting handicaps many students in essay exams. Instructors can't give you credit for something they can't read. Some instructors try hard to decipher illegible writing, but others have no patience with it and will mark down the illegible or barely legible paper. One investigation of the matter showed that an answer written in a poor hand was judged a whole grade point lower than the same answer written in a clear hand. And the graders in this study were told to ignore handwriting.

Take the trouble to put your answers in good English. Punctuate properly and spell correctly. Poor writing implies disorganized and confused thinking as well as inadequate command of the subject matter. Poor spelling, especially of important or technical words, suggests careless reading and study. It is only natural that mistakes of this sort will pull your grades down.

TAKE-HOME AND OPEN-BOOK EXAMS

Take-home and open-book exams are fairly common in college. They are most often to be found in courses in which there is an emphasis upon problem solving—courses in mathematics, statistics, philosophy, or organizational management. The purposes of take-home and open-book exams are slightly different, and each requires a slightly different approach.

TAKE-HOME EXAMS

First of all, know the rules. Are you allowed to read the exam before you study for it? How much time are you allowed in taking the exam? Usually, you are told that you may consult any references you wish but that you may not talk to another student about the exam. It doesn't take much sense to realize that take-home exams do not emphasize factual information. They are not the sort of thing on which you can make a high grade by just copying out of a book. More often than not they require you to solve a particular problem. In a take-home statistics exam, for example, you may be

given the data from a study and asked to treat those data statistically. That will require you to understand the purpose of the study, to select the right statistical measures, and to apply those measures to the data correctly. In philosophy, you may be asked to apply different sets of ethical principles to some problem of life.

If you are allowed to read the questions beforehand, and in most instances that will be the case, read them and decide what technical information you will need. Then read or review the books or your notes that cover the problem you are faced with. In some instances you will have to decide whether the problem on the exam is to be solved with one method or another. In short, you will have to make a decision about what to read. That is a critical decision, for you could elect the wrong method or the wrong set of principles.

When you have decided what background you will need to solve the problem in a particular question and have done the necessary reading, plan your answer. Plan it carefully. You might even outline the steps that will be required to find the answer. Then go about solving the problem or synthesizing the information needed to answer the question. Work deliberately and carefully. Minor mistakes that might get by on a regular exam will not get by on a take-home exam. If you have to do some calculations, double-check them, for once again, while you might at least get partial credit if you make arithmetical mistakes on a regular exam, you will not get credit for a wrong answer on a take-home exam.

After you complete the exam, put it away for a while. If you have the exam only overnight, you can only afford to put it away for a couple of hours at the most. But if you have several days, put it aside for a day or so. Then take it out and go through all the steps you went through originally. Decide what it is you need to answer the question or solve the problem. Be sure you consider alternatives. Make certain you have made the right choice. Then review the reading or your notes, and finally recheck your calculations or reread your answer and make whatever changes you think necessary.

OPEN-BOOK EXAMS

Open-book exams are usually based on the same principle as take-home exams. They emphasize problem solving, thinking, and discovery. However, they require a slightly different approach because you will likely have only a limited time to complete them. You can't afford to review all the relevant material. Rather, at best, you can afford to check certain important points in the textbook or your notes. Therefore, like an ordinary essay exam, you will have to do all your studying ahead of time. It is a fatal mistake to assume, because an exam is open-book, that you don't need to study as hard as you would for a regular exam. Be thoroughly prepared. Then you won't need to waste time flipping through your notes or the book looking for something that you studied only hastily.

Check in your sources when necessary, but spend as much time as possible with the exam itself. As with take-home exams, however, plan your answers. Make sure you have picked the right technique or the right material with which to answer the question, plan or outline the answer, and then write it or do your calculations. Keep your work legible and easy to read. Show how you got intermediate answers if the problem is mathematical or in the physical sciences.

Otherwise, all the strictures for essay exams apply. Allocate your time among all the questions carefully, write legibly, and use sensible English. Remember, however, you may have *less* time per question than you would in an ordinary essay exam because at certain points you might be expected to look something up in a table or read some result off a graph in a textbook.

LEARNING FROM EXAMINATIONS

Most students think of examinations only in terms of grades. In fact, the major excuse for examinations in education is to give you a chance to learn from them. Sometimes students don't realize that, and they fail to use their exams for their educational value. When they get their papers back, they may count up the numbers assigned to the various questions to see if the instructor made a mistake, or they may look for something in their answers to quibble over, and then put the exam aside and forget about it. Errors in grading do occur, and if you believe that you have been unfairly graded, you should certainly discuss the matter with your instructor or the grading assistant. It is more important, however, to read your exam over so that you can correct your past methods of preparing for exams and so that you make sure that you really understand what you should have written.

See where you made your mistakes and lost credit. Was it because you misinterpreted something? Did you fail to get something in your notes? Did you fail to notice the important qualifiers? These and other questions can be answered by studying your exam and looking up the answers to questions you missed or did not do well on.

When you do that, you will achieve a deeper and better knowledge of the subject, and you can uncover characteristic faults in your study habits or gaps in your understanding. Mistakes, when promptly corrected, provide an important tool for learning.

CHAPTER SEVEN

WRITING PAPERS

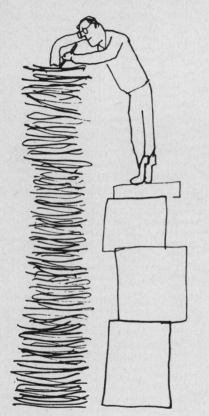

How well can you put your ideas into words? The most important thing most students get out of the whole of formal education is the ability to read and to write in a sensible and organized way. This chapter is concerned with writing. It concentrates on writing papers in such different courses as history, psychology, and marketing, but what we have to say here is a way of telling you, through some specific examples, how to express ideas and how to put those ideas so that you reveal yourself to be an educated person.

Nearly everyone who goes to college is required to take a course in English writing. Given half a chance, this course can help you learn how to write accurately and in such a way that you can express complicated ideas without getting hopelessly mixed up. In most writing courses you write some themes or compositions, and the instructor goes over these carefully so that you know what it is that you are doing wrong.

Lots of students hate writing. The composition course is a chore, and they will often do as little in it as they possibly can. They try to find easy topics to write about and then write in such a way as to risk the least challenge by the instructor. Too bad. However, even if you don't cotton to the English writing course, you will have to face the challenge of writing in other courses. College instructors—good college instructors, that is—are sticklers on the subject of teaching you how to write (and well they might be). So if you are in a college that is aiming really to educate you, you are going to have to write. We can't instruct you in writing—only someone who goes to the trouble of correcting what you write can do that—but we can provide you with some rules to make it easier for you to write well and to concentrate on learning how to write well rather than on getting the mechanics of term papers just right.

You may never become a professional writer, but you can learn to write clear, direct, sensible prose. No matter what you do after college, there will be times when you will have to write well enough to communicate something to other people. Writing is *the* basic skill for educated people.

This chapter is mainly about writing term papers. We can't cover everything. Most students find it useful to buy one of the many good handbooks of composition and manuals on writing that can be found in any college bookstore. These books will go into greater depth than we do on many of the things we cover in this chapter.

STEPS IN WRITING A PAPER

In this section, we will go over the steps in writing a paper. After that, there is a section on using the library and taking research notes. In the final section we will give you a little advice about the mechanics of writing.

CHOOSING A SUBJECT

Sometimes topics for a paper will be assigned to you, but usually you will have some freedom in picking your own topic, and in the case of themes for English compositon, you may have the freedom to write about anything that interests you.

If you pick a topic that is too broad or too narrow, too personal, or too controversial, you make trouble for yourself. Most instructors will warn you against picking a topic that is too broad or too difficult, but you will also have problems if you pick a topic that is too narrow or one in which you have a lot of personal involvement. Then, too, a lot of students flounder around because they just "can't think of anything."

One way to find topics is to thumb through the indexes of textbooks and scholarly books on the subject you want to write about. Suppose, for example, that you are taking a course on American political parties. You may find an entry in your textbook: "Conventions, beginnings of." You turn to the pages indicated and you find three or four paragraphs on the matter. You read that at first, presidential candidates were nominated in secret by caucuses of congressional representatives, but that by the 1830s this system was replaced by open nominating conventions. How this came about might interest you, and so you tentatively pick the topic "the rise of nominating conventions." By way of practice, pick up a textbook and see how many topics you can identify that might be suitable for a term paper.

Lecture notes will provide another source of possible topics. If you know that you are going to write a term paper for a course you are taking, make special note of things that come up in lecture that might be interesting or useful. Be alert to topics that might relate to your major or potential major. If you are a major in speech pathology taking a course in the psychology of language, you might find the instructor alluding to problems of language development in the deaf. That could provide a topic for you.

For some kinds of papers, this approach won't work. In one institution, for example, all engineering students are required to write papers on the design of common household articles. The student must pick out something such as a stove, a vacuum cleaner, or even a broom and decide what is wrong with its design and how to improve it.

In fact, you will find that many of your courses will ask for papers based upon your daily experience. Most of us write best when we write about things we know about and are interested in. If you are taking a course

in social organization, you might want to write a paper about the role of your hometown high school basketball team in the social structure of the town.

Other good topics come from relations between subjects. You may be taking simultaneously a course in United States history and one in twentieth-century American literature. For the literature course you may have read and liked one of the novels of Sinclair Lewis. For the history course you could write a paper on the social changes of the 1920s as depicted in three Sinclair Lewis novels—*Main Street, Babbitt,* and *Elmer Gantry.*

Choosing a topic that is likely to interest the instructor is, by the way, a good rule. This isn't as crass as it sounds. Good writers take into account their potential audience, and your main audience for a term paper is the instructor and the grader. If you don't know what the instructor would be interested in, choose an important topic, one that would likely interest a number of people.

Even more important is to choose a topic that interests you. You will spend a fair amount of time working on that topic, so it should be something that you care about learning more about or about some idea or experience that you want to understand better.

GATHERING THE MATERIAL

Where and how you gather the material for your paper depends upon the subject you are writing about, the type of paper required, and its length and complexity. Sometimes you may have to do little reading and instead write an informal essay on something of personal interest. More often, however, you will have to learn something new. In this case you will probably make heavy use of the library and you will have to take research notes.

To get started, you should do some background reading. Your textbook or other books you have read in the course usually can supply some background. If you get stuck, your instructor can help you clarify or limit a topic and provide some background reading sources. In many cases, these background sources will furnish a bibliography that will lead you to other materials. In other cases, you will have to go to abstracts, cumulative indexes, or special bibliographic sources to compile a list of things you should read. And, of course, once you begin reading in earnest, you will find additional references.

As you consult your references, you will prepare a working bibliography. The working bibliography should be kept on 3 × 5 or 4 × 6 file cards. For each book or article you consult, prepare a card which contains the following information: (1) author(s) of book or article (also editor or translator of books where applicable); (2) title and edition (if not the first) of book (as copied from the title page, not the spine) or title of article and the name of the magazine or journal. Then, for books you will need (3) place of publication; (4) name of publisher; (5) copyright date. For articles you will need (6) volume number of journal or magazine, if given; (7) the year; (8) the page numbers of the article if the journal or magazine cumulates page numbers through the year; if page numbers are not cumulative, you will need to note the month of issue as well as the page numbers.

In the upper-right-hand corner of the card, write in the code number (1, 2, 3, . . .) that you assign to each card. Later, when you take notes, you can simply refer to this code number instead of duplicating all the bibliographic information on the note cards. Study the sample bibliography cards given on page 69. If you are careful and accurate in preparing your cards, you will save time and grief when you are ready to compile your final bibliography.

As you read, take notes. Notes for a paper based upon library research are not like the notes you take from textbooks. Research notes are not outlined. Instead, they are in the form of summaries. How lengthy or detailed your summary is depends upon the length of the reading, on what the instructor has suggested that you do, and your purpose in reading. You can make rough reading notes as you go, perhaps in the form of a rudimentary outline, but when you have made your summary, you can throw the rough notes away. Be sure your summaries are in your own words. If you use the author's words for anything, you must not forget to put quotation marks around them or otherwise indicate that you are quoting directly from your source. Be sure to note the page of the quote.

Another thing about note taking for a research paper is that you don't know exactly how many notes you will use for your paper until you have finished reading almost all your materials. Your original topic may turn out to be too big, or some of the sources you consulted may prove to be irrelevant or unimportant for your purposes. Neither do you know as you read just how you will organize your paper. And it's a sure thing that no matter how you organize your paper, you are not likely to use the notes in the order in which you took them. Moreover, when you begin to write the paper, you will refer to the notes from some sources many times and to others hardly at all.

All of this means that you have to use a system for taking and keeping research notes different from the system you use for lecture and textbook notes. If you take your notes on sheets of notebook paper and then keep them in a notebook, you will find it hard to organize and reorganize them when you begin to write

your paper. *You should keep research notes on 3 × 5 or 4 × 6 cards.* If you have one card for each main idea you come across in your reading, you can later arrange the cards in any order that fits the organization of your paper. For a large paper requiring a lot of cards, you will need a card box in which to file them. If you buy a thousand cards at a time (that isn't as expensive as it sounds), you will get a reasonably sturdy cardboard box. Otherwise you can buy a metal or plastic box (or improvise one on your own). People who write factual books or articles almost invariably use this method of note keeping because it is so efficient.

Because you have all the bibliographic information on your bibliography cards, you won't need to repeat the material on your note cards. But you will have to keep track of where your notes came from. If you have assigned code numbers to your bibliography cards, just enter in the upper-right-hand corner of your note cards the right number. If you haven't used code numbers, you should place in the upper-right-hand corner the last name of the author, an abbreviated title, and the date.

On the top line of the note card indicate the topic covered by the notes on that card. For example, if you are summarizing an article about smoking and heart disease, the topic heading on your card might be, "Smoking—effects of nicotine on heart rate." Most summaries will fit on one card, but if you do need more than one card for a given topic, label the cards a, b, c, etc., and be sure that you have some way of telling, on each card, which bibliography card is the right source.

When you copy an author directly, copy accurately and put quotation marks on your card. If you use only part of a direct quotation, use an ellipsis (three spaced periods) to indicate that you have left something out. Once again, don't forget to write down the pages for the quote.

All this may seem to be complicated and cumbersome at first, but once you are used to the card system for taking research notes, you will use no other.

CONSTRUCTING AN OUTLINE

Just about when you are finished taking notes, you will want to begin an outline of your paper. First read through your note cards and rearrange them according to the topic headings. This will give you some idea about how your paper should be organized. When you construct your outline, arrange your main and subordinate topics in good logical order. If you haven't read it yet, see what we have to say about the format of outlines (pages 48–49).

One thing to remember is that you can't have fewer than two subheadings of a topic. If you have only a

BIBLIOGRAPHY CARDS

#1

Lewis, C. S.

Surprised by Joy.

New York: Harcourt, Brace + World, Inc. (Harvest Books), 1955.

1. Reference to a book

Code number

Author

Title

Publication facts

#2

Schakel, Peter J., ed.

The Longing for a Form: Essays on the Fiction of C.S. Lewis.

Kent, Ohio: The Kent State University Press, 1977.

2. Reference to an edited work

Code number

Editor

Title

Publication facts

#3

Walsh, Chad.

"Back to Faith,"

Saturday Review, 39 (March 3, 1956), pp. 32-33.

3. Reference to a magazine or journal article

Code number

Author

Title of article

Magazine, volume, date, and pages

NOTE CARD, CORRESPONDING BIBLIOGRAPHY CARD, AND QUOTE CARD

Study the sample note card and its corresponding bibliography card.

Influence of Charles Williams on C.S. Lewis ⟨#1⟩

   Williams was a great friend of Lewis's and given a warm welcome when he arrived in Oxford. He became a regular member of the Inklings. Though Lewis denied being consciously influenced by Williams in his work, Green believes that the unconscious influence of Williams made the war years productive for Lewis.

                    p. 184

- Code number
- Topic heading
- Note
- Page reference

⟨#1⟩

Green, Roger L. and Hooper, Walter.

C.S. Lewis – A Biography.

New York & London : Harcourt, Brace Jovanovich (Harvest Books), 1974.

The code number on both the note card and the bibliography card tells you the source of the note.

Suppose you had decided not to code your reference. Your note card would then be in the following form:

         Green & Hooper
        C.S. Lewis – A Biography

Lewis – Early childhood

   "I am a product of long corridors, empty sunlit rooms, upstair indoor silences, attics explored in solitude..."

Written by Lewis in his autobiography

             p. 20

- Abbreviated version of author and title
- Topic heading
- Note (a direct quotation)
- Use of ellipsis, indicating part of a sentence is missing
- Page

single subheading, you don't need it. It can be incorporated into the main heading. Don't use too many main headings. Four or five should be enough, even for a longish paper. Use a sentence rather than a topical outline (don't include minute details). This will give you a start on writing your paper.

Spending time on an outline is worth it. It will make your paper better organized and make your writing job an easier one. After you begin writing you will probably want to revise your outline. You may also discover that you may have to do some more reading to fill out your notes or to make a thin section into a substantial one.

WRITING THE FIRST DRAFT

Very few people can get by with just one draft. This book went through an outline and at least three drafts. Two drafts should do for a term paper. But for a difficult, an important, or a particularly long paper, you may need as many as three.

First rearrange your note cards in the order of your outline. Then write. For writing, allow yourself a large block of time during which you can work without interruption. Writing a long paper all in one session is a big undertaking, but for a short one that ought to be possible, and it's a good idea. For a first draft, don't worry about getting everything just right. Once you get your ideas down, you can correct them easily enough.

Leave plenty of room for corrections and alterations. Of course, your final draft will be double spaced, but do your first draft that way, too. If you write by hand, write only on every other line.

When you have completed the first draft, go over it once for obvious changes. Then put it aside for a while. When you plan your time for writing, allow as much time as possible between the first draft and your revision. You will have a fresh perspective, and it will be easier for you to detect mistakes and lapses in grammar and writing if you do.

REVISING THE PAPER

After you have put your work aside for a day or so (preferably longer), begin your revision. *Check first for coverage.* Did you get everything in that you should? Is there anything that slipped by the first draft? Did you not explain certain topics sufficiently? You may need to go back to your notes for something that you left out or something you think you might not have gotten quite right. You may even have to go back to the library to check on something or dig up additional

material. If you want to write a really good paper, it is worth the effort.

Then, check the organization of your paper. Does it hang together logically? Are the headings and subheadings (assuming you incorporate these into your paper) in the right places? Are the transitions between sections smooth? Should you have a summary and a conclusion? If you're not satisfied with your organization, change it. That may mean simply a cut and paste job (if you don't have glue or paste, stapling cut-out portions on new blank pages will do), or it may mean rewriting sentences and even paragraphs. Be critical.

Finally, check the mechanics. Are your sentences grammatical and understandable? Do you have some wordy and awkward constructions? Look at your verbs. Do you overuse such all-purpose and sometimes meaningless verbs as "involve"? Do you monotonously use the passive voice? (If you don't know what that is, look it up.) Are your spelling and punctuation correct? Of course, you will always have a good dictionary handy, but in addition refresh yourself by glancing at a concise handbook of style such as *The Elements of Style* by William Strunk, Jr. and E. B. White.

DOCUMENTING THE PAPER

When you write a paper using other people's ideas, you must give credit to your sources. Using someone else's ideas, or discoveries reported by other people, without acknowledging your debt is described by a single word. The word is "plagiarism." That is a serious offense. In many colleges and universities detected plagiarism is grounds for dismissal.

In a research paper, documentation may be given in the text by footnotes keyed to a bibliography. If the reference is well known and short, you can acknowledge it in the text. A Biblical reference is an example. "When I was a child, I spoke like a child. . . ." (I Corinthians 13:11). Note: If you use a new or not well known translation of the Bible, you should refer to it by footnote. An other example: "Good night, sweet prince; and flights of angels sing thee to thy rest." (*Hamlet*, V, ii, 59).

Footnotes belong either at the bottom of the page and numbered consecutively or in a list at the end of the paper. Sources that you use merely for background material and that you do not directly draw upon can simply be cited in your bibliography.

There are several ways to do footnotes. You should consult a style manual, such as the *MLA Style Sheet*, the *Harbrace Guide to the Library and Research Paper*, or the College Outline Series *Preparing the*

PAGE WITH FOOTNOTES

The following is a page from a term paper on Margaret Fuller, a nineteenth-century feminist. This excerpt illustrates the use and form of footnotes in term papers.

In Mount Auburn cemetery in Cambridge, Massachusetts, is a memorial stone raised following the death by shipwreck in 1850 of Margaret Fuller, Marchesa Ossoli. The inscription on this stone reads in part: "By birth a child of New England, By adoption a citizen of Rome . . . In youth . . . seeking the highest culture . . . In maturer years, earnest reformer in America and Europe."[1]

If a few words carved on a gravestone can sum up the span of a life, these words do so for Sarah Margaret Fuller. This paper explores briefly her passage from the rarefied culture of New England Transcendentalism to the European revolutionary movement of 1848. For, although Margaret Fuller was formed by the New England of the early nineteenth century and molded in its image, she left the peace of Concord, the familiar intellectual world of Cambridge, for the bustle of New York, and then, beckoned by her long cherished dream of Italy, she arrived finally at Rome where she found her spiritual home.[2] From a youth devoted to culture of self she moved to reform and finally to participation in the Roman revolution of 1848.

The young Margaret's worship of genius and power and her disdain for the "vulger herd"[3] became the faith of the mature woman in the unspoiled nature of the people.[4] Her early desire to remain aloof from such experiments in

---

1. Mason Wade, <u>Margaret Fuller: Whetstone of Genius</u>, Viking, New York, 1940, pp. 271–272.
2. R. W. Emerson <u>et al.</u>, <u>Memoirs of Margaret Fuller Ossoli</u>, v. 2, Phillips, Samuels & Co., Boston, 1852, p. 216.
3. Ibid., v. 1, p. 134.
4. Ibid., v. 2, p. 225.

Research Paper. These sources will give you the correct forms of citation and keys to standard abbreviations (op. cit., ibid., etc.). Whatever you choose, be consistent in your use of it.

In psychology, sociology, and a few other subjects in which you might have to write a term paper, your instructor may prefer that you use the journal form of citation. In that form you do not use footnotes. Instead you key the citation to the publication date given in the list of references. For example, you might write: "It is well known that autonomic responses may be influenced by cognitive activity (Jones, 1976)"; or alternatively, "Jones (1976) argues that autonomic responses are influenced by cognitive activity." If there are two or more references in the same year by the same author, add letters to the year (Jones, 1976a; Jones, 1976b). Be sure to find out whether or not your instructor wants you to use this form. But be sure *not* to use it where it would be inappropriate.

There is an art to knowing what information needs to be acknowledged by a footnote or citation and what information is general knowledge. It is better for a student to err on the side of too much documentation than too little. When in doubt, acknowledge your source.

The final bibliography will consist of all the works you consulted in your paper, even if you do not refer to them directly in a footnote. Since you already have your working bibliography on cards, all you need do is to go through the cards, eliminate the references which you did not use and prepare a list alphabetized according to the author's last name of those works you did consult. If you cite more than one work by the same author, list these in alphabetical order by title. Your bibliography will be the final page(s) of your paper.

Once again, the rules for the journal format used in psychology, sociology, and other courses are slightly different. You will include in the bibliography only those works that you actually cite in text. General references that you may have consulted will not be included. And while you alphabetize by author's last name, for several works by the same author you list these in order of publication date rather than alphabetically by title.

PREPARING THE FINAL DRAFT

At this point, you will no doubt feel that your job is finished and that you will want to get the final version typed as soon as possible. But if you can, set the paper aside for a day or more. You will probably be able to make a few more corrections before you prepare the final version.

A research paper has three parts: the title page and (if the paper is a long one) table of contents, the body of the paper, and the bibliography. The title page contains the title of your paper, your name, the class and section, and any other information the instructor requires. If your paper is long enough to require a table of contents, prepare one from the outline you made while writing the paper.

If at all possible, type the paper or have it typed. Use a good grade of paper, standard size (8½ × 11 inches), and double-space. If you place your footnotes at the bottom of the page, they should be single spaced and set off from the text by a line extending across the paper. You will find a sample page with this form of citation on page 72. Number every page except the title page in the upper-right-hand corner. If you must write the paper by hand, use lined paper and skip lines between each line of text. This will provide room for your instructor to write comments and corrections. When you prepare the bibliography, double-space between each entry, but single-space lines within each entry (see example below).

When the paper has been typed or copied in its final form, proofread it carefully. Mistakes are made by everyone. Make sure that you have a duplicate copy before you turn the paper in.

Your instructor will likely make notes and comments on the paper before handing it back to you. Go over these carefully. You will learn something, and besides, you don't want to make the same mistake twice. If you can't tell from the instructor's comments what you might have done the wrong way, ask for a conference to go over the paper.

SAMPLE BIBLIOGRAPHY

Here is a sample bibliography for a term paper in education, entitled "Teaching the United Nations in Social Studies."

Bibliography

Books
1. Arndt, Christian O., and Samuel Everett, eds. Education for a World Society: Promising Practices Today. New York: Harper, [c. 1951].

2. Carr, William G. One World in the Making. Boston: Ginn, [c. 1946].

3. Jones, Goronwy J., and Evan T. Davis. United Nations for the Classroom, 2d ed. London: Routledge & Kegan Paul, 1957.

Periodicals
1. Brickman, W. W., "Ignorance of UNESCO," School and Society, 87 (May 1959), p. 272.

2. Bruce, W. J., "Education and the United Nations," National Elementary Principal, 37 (May 1958), pp. 12–14.

3. Educational Policies Commission Official Statement, "UN, UNESCO, and American Schools," NEA Journal, 42 (February 7, 1953), pp. 77–78.

4. "From Citizens to School Board," Life, 33 (September 15, 1952), pp. 125–127.

5. Haines, A. B., "Hubbub over UNESCO," Nation, 175 (September 20, 1952), p. 221.

6. Miller, R. I., "New UN Teaching Materials," NEA Journal, 49 (April 1960), p. 48.

7. "Pressures in Los Angeles," New Republic, 127 (September 22, 1952), p. 7.

8. Smith, P. E., "How to Teach about the UN," NEA Journal, 49 (April 1960), pp. 47–48.

9. Staines, R. G., "UN and the Future of American Education," Teacher's College Record, 54 (February 1953), pp. 256–268.

10. Terrian, F. W., "The Sociology of the Attacks on the Schools," California Journal of Secondary Education, 28 (March 1953), pp. 134–141.

USING THE LIBRARY

The library is the heart of any college or university. You will go there to gather material for the papers you write, to find the required or supplementary reading lists for your courses, and to study when your dormitory or home is too noisy.

You may not know all the things the library, even a small library, can do for you. If so, you can never make proper use of its resources. If you are in a big school, don't let the size of the library overwhelm you. All libraries are organized on logical principles, and you can easily learn to locate anything you want.

LAYOUT OF THE LIBRARY

The first thing you have to do is to learn the layout of your library or libraries (in larger universities some collections are decentralized and separately housed; in the biggest places decentralization may extend all the way down to the departmental level, so that each department will have its own library). Generally, where there is more than one library, there is a certain amount of duplication so that many things will be found in both the main library and in the branches.

During orientation, or as soon as possible after you start classes, go to the main library and look around. At many places, the library staff will provide orientation meetings for students. If so, go to one of them. Most larger libraries have directories posted at various points to guide you to locations for the various collections. Some libraries publish manuals that list their services, or they provide guided tours for new students. Take advantage of whatever opportunities your library provides for you to familiarize yourself with what it offers.

You must know the location of the following:

1. **Card Catalogs.** The card catalog is the backbone of the library. It is where you start when you are looking for a particular book, and it is often the place you start when you begin your term paper. We have included a special section on pages 75–76 about using card catalogs.

2. **Reading Rooms.** Large libraries usually have several reading rooms, one for each of several functions or subjects. Smaller libraries may have one general reading room. In some of the newer libraries, often called learning or media centers, there may be no specific reading rooms, but instead comfortable chairs and some tables will be scattered throughout the stacks or wherever the books are located.

3. **Reference Works.** Reference works are almost always kept separate from general books and periodicals. They are likely to be found in the reference room or on shelves in the reading room where they can be easily consulted. They cannot be taken out of the library. On pages 76 and 78 we say something about how to use reference works.

4. **Periodicals.** Periodicals are mainly journals and magazines. They are usually shelved in a periodical room or in a separate section of the reading room. Back issues are usually bound and shelved along with books by subject matter. Occasionally, however, they may be shelved separately, particularly in the smaller branch libraries.

5. **Stacks.** "Stacks" is the term for books arranged on shelves spaced just far enough apart to let you get between them. The stacks in big university libraries may occupy many floors of a large building. Stacks are either *open* or *closed*. Open stacks are available to all users of the library. Closed stacks require a special permit for entry. They are usually restricted to faculty members and graduate students. If your library has open stacks, you may go directly to the shelves to find the books you want. If it has closed stacks, you will have to fill out a card requesting the book you want and wait for a library attendant to get it for you.

6. **Reserve Shelves.** In large libraries there is usually a separate reserve book room where books are shelved according to the courses in which they are used. The idea is to make sure that everybody in the course has access to the required or supplementary reading. These

books usually do not circulate; they may be used only in the library. If they do circulate, it is usually for a short period, perhaps overnight. Penalties for late return of circulating reserve books are steep, so make sure that you know what the time limits are and observe them.

7. *Special Collections and Facilities.* Most libraries, even those with open stacks, have some material, often valuable or rare books, kept in closed stacks or special rooms. To save space, many periodicals and some rare books are placed on microfilm or microfiche to be read with the aid of a microfilm or microfiche reader. The chances are you will sometime have to use microfilm or microfiche, so make sure you know where the collections are and how to use the machines. Your library will also undoubtedly have record and tape collections for foreign languages, music, poetry, and drama. Some libraries have film, videotape, and filmstrip collections.

If a book you need is not in your library, it can usually be obtained for you by loan from another library. Check with a librarian before you decide that you can't get something.

Most large libraries provide daily computer printouts which list the books currently checked out. If the book you want is not on the shelf, you can check the printout to see if someone else is using it. You can ask the librarian to request that it be returned. If the book is neither on the shelf nor circulating, have the librarian put out a search for it.

CLASSIFICATION

All reading matter in a library is classified according to some system. The most widely used systems are the Library of Congress Classification and the Dewey Decimal Classification. The Library of Congress Classification uses letters of the alphabet for its general divisions and numbers for finer distinctions. Within each subject category a letter is used for the author's name and then a serial number to distinguish among the books in this category that might have the same initial. For example, *The Army of the Caesars* by Michael Grant has the number DG 89 .G7 1974b. D is the general letter for history, the G that follows indicates the country or region. The number 89 stands for a particular subject matter of history, and the .G7 the specific number for the book (G is the author's last initial).

The Dewey Decimal Classification is usually to be found in smaller libraries, though there are some fair-sized libraries that use it. It uses numbers rather than letters to indicate the general subject matter. Each general division is subdivided into ten parts, and each of these, in turn, includes ten smaller parts. By use of decimal places, additional subdivisions can be carried out indefinitely.

THE CARD CATALOG

Books are classified three ways: by *author,* by *title,* and by *subject.* Most libraries file all cards in a single alphabetical arrangement, but some libraries, particularly larger ones, use a *divided catalog system.* In such a system one card catalog will contain cards alphabetized by author and title, while the other will contain the subject cards.

How you use the card catalog will depend upon what you already know about the book when you look for it. The subject catalog is particularly useful in the early stages of doing research for a paper. You can look up your subject and thumb through the cards for items that appear to be particularly relevant or interesting. Later, when you know what author or title you are after, you will use the author and title cards to locate particular books.

Here are some general rules you should know in order to make efficient use of the catalog:

1. Cards are alphabetized according to the first word at the top of the card regardless of whether this word is the author, title, or subject. In book titles, articles, such as *the, a,* and *an* are neglected. For example, *The Politics of Jacksonian Finance* by John M. McFaul would be filed under the P's by title, under the M's by author, and under the U's (United States—Politics and Government 1815–1861) by subject.

2. Headings containing abbreviations are alphabetized as if they were spelled out in full, as in:

   MacAdams, Alta
   McAdams, David
   McGuire, J.
   Machado, A.

3. Most libraries alphabetize titles and subjects consisting of more than one word in a word-by-word filing as in the order: New York, Newark. Some libraries, however, use a letter-by-letter system without regard to spacing between words, as in the order: Newark, New York.

4. The titles of books that begin with numbers are alphabetized as if the numbers were spelled out. *20,000 Leagues under the Sea* would be filed by title under the T's.

5. Subdivisions of historical subjects are arranged chronologically as in:

> United States—Politics and Government 1783–1814
> United States—Politics and Government 1815–1861

6. Subdivisions of other subjects are arranged alphabetically as in:

> France—Art
> France—Geography
> France—Government
> France—Music

7. People are listed before places, places before subjects, and subjects before titles as in:

> Jefferson, Thomas   Mineral, Virginia
> Jefferson City,   Mineral
>   Missouri   *Mineral Deposits*, by W.
> *Jefferson*, by A. J.   Lindgren
>   Nock

8. Books by a person are listed before books about a person as in:

> Sinclair, Upton, *World's End*
> Sinclair, Upton. *Upton Sinclair, American Rebel*, by Leon Harris

If you know how to use the card catalog, you can tell a good bit about a book before you see it. Study the sample author, title, and subject cards on page 77 and note what information is available on catalog cards that can help you in research.

PERIODICAL INDEXES

Although the card catalog indexes all volumes and will give you the titles of periodicals in particular subjects, it does not index individual articles in periodicals. Since much of your paper writing, especially in advanced courses, will require you to get information from articles, you will need to consult one of the many indexes to the periodical literature. For current events and news stories, *The Reader's Guide to Periodical Literature* is the most useful index. It lists articles appearing in popular magazines and less-technical journals. For more scholarly articles, particularly in the humanities, arts, and social sciences, *The International Index of Periodicals* is the source to use. Beyond that

are more specialized indexes such as *Engineering Index, Index Medicus* (for medical citations), *Education Index, Business Periodical Index*, and *Art Index*.

ABSTRACTS

Some publications go beyond merely indexing the literature in a field. These are generally called *abstracts*. They summarize the articles so that readers will better know whether or not the articles listed will be useful to them. Wherever these are available, they are most useful for putting the bibliography to a paper together. The best-known examples of such abstracts are *Chemical Abstracts, Biological Abstracts, Psychological Abstracts, Education Abstracts*, and *Sociological Abstracts*. All the abstracts are provided with indexes at annual or semiannual intervals. Hence, to find articles in these fields, first look up the index (if it is the current year, it will be in a separate issue), then jot down the abstract number, and finally look at the abstract to see if the article will be helpful. If it looks promising, copy down the complete citation from the abstract, look up the journal in the card catalog to find its call number, and then request the journal so that you can read the original article.

If you need current newspaper articles, your best bet is *The New York Times Index*, which covers all the important articles published in that newspaper. Despite its name, *The New York Times* is really a national newspaper, so that nearly every college library subscribes to it. Many of these libraries will also subscribe to the index, so the newspaper can be used as a research resource. Even if you wish to search other newspapers, the index is useful, for it serves to date events precisely enough for you to look them up in other newspapers or magazines.

REFERENCE BOOKS

Reference books are helpful not only for digging out materials for research papers but also for answering questions that may interest you. They fall into several categories: encyclopedias, yearbooks, dictionaries, atlases and maps, and books of quotations.

Encyclopedias. If you want to look up some specialized topic such as imperialism, or mathematics in ancient Greece, a general encyclopedia is a good place to start. The best-known American encyclopedia (despite its name) is the *Encyclopaedia Britannica*, but for many purposes other works, such as the *Encyclopedia Americana*, are just as good or better. If your library is a large one, it will contain many encyclopedias from different countries and in different languages. An ar-

CATALOG CARDS BY SUBJECT, AUTHOR, AND TITLE

Subject

```
        Rome -- Politics and Government

DG 89     Grant, Michael, 1914-
 .67         The Army of the Caesars
1974b     New York, Scribner [1974]
             xxxiv, 364 p. illus. 24 cm


  ViU              VA @@ Sc   74-7596
```

```
     McFaul, John M.

 H 62471     The Politics of Jacksonian
  .M3        Finance by John M. McFaul.
             Ithaca, N. Y. Cornell University
             Press [1972]

 H  2471.M3
 IBN 0.8014.078.9     332.1        72-435
                          0973    MARC
```

Author

```
     The Politics of Jacksonian Finance

 HG 2471     McFaul, John M.
                The Politics of Jacksonian
             Finance by John M. McFaul.
             Ithaca, N. Y.  Cornell University
             Press [1972]
             xv, 230 p. 22 cm. $9.95
             Bibliography:  p.217-224
          1. Banks and Banking--United States--History
          2. Currency Question--United States--History
          3. United States--Politics and Government
                                    1815-1861
                                       I.Title
```

Title

ticle in a general encyclopedia can give you a good introduction to a topic. Such articles have well-selected bibliographies which make good starting points for further reading.

There are also specialized encyclopedias. For example, the *McGraw-Hill Encyclopedia of Science and Technology* contains articles on engineering, physics, chemistry, biology, and experimental psychology. The *International Encyclopedia of the Social Sciences* covers psychology, sociology, anthropology, political science, and economics. There are others as well in such special fields as art and music. *Grove's Dictionary of Music and Musicians,* despite its title, is really an encyclopedia about music.

Yearbooks. If you want to find what happened in a particular year, one of the yearbooks is a good reference. The *American Annual* (1923–   ) is the annual supplement to the *Encyclopedia Americana,* and the *Britannica Book of the Year* (1938–   ) is a similar supplement to the *Encyclopaedia Britannica.* Both contain articles covering events or important developments in the year named.

Other yearbooks contain mainly statistical information or brief summaries of events. They give you almost any conceivable kind of statistical fact. Some of them are:

World Almanac and Book of Facts (1868–   ), a compendium of facts, mostly about the United States
Information Please Almanac (1947–   ), a similar compendium with fewer statistics and more articles
Whitaker's Almanac (1869–   ), a British publication similar to the *World Almanac*
The Statesman's Yearbook (1864–   ), information about world governments
United States Statistical Abstracts (1876–   ), a government publication containing statistical information about industrial, social, political, and economic aspects of the United States

Dictionaries. We have already said that some specialized encyclopedias are called dictionaries. In addition, there are two other kinds of dictionaries you will find in the library. One is dictionaries of language, and the other is biographical dictionaries.

Libraries will have the large unabridged dictionaries of the English language that are generally too expensive and unwieldy for home use. Among these are *Webster's New International Dictionary* (sometimes called *Webster's Third*), published by the Merriam-Webster Company; *Funk & Wagnalls' New Stand-*ard Dictionary; and the *Oxford English Dictionary,* or *OED* (also known as the *New English Dictionary,* or *NED*). They contain all words in general use as well as information about the origins and histories of words.

For technical terms not found in these dictionaries, use one of the many specialized dictionaries for such fields as chemistry, psychology, medicine, or biology. In addition, libraries will have bilingual dictionaries giving terms in English and in other languages.

When you want to find information about people, you can use a biographical dictionary. For American statesmen, writers, and other important people who are no longer living, there is the *Dictionary of American Biography.* For important Englishmen, there is a reference series called the *Dictionary of National Biography.* For living people, such as congressmen, judges, writers, and industrial leaders, there are the various publications of *Who's Who. Who's Who* itself contains information mostly about people in Great Britain. *Who's Who in America* is the most general biographical reference for living Americans. Accompanying it in recent years is a volume of *Who Was Who* covering deceased persons who were in *Who's Who in America. Who's Who of American Women* lists women of note, and there are other volumes of *Who's Who* for science, education, and regions of the country. In addition, there are references under a variety of labels other than *Who's Who* listing people in science, state and local government officials, people who are writers, artists, etc.

IN GENERAL

If you have access to a good library, you can hunt down information about the most obscure topic imaginable. The number of books and articles published each year is staggering, but by using reference books, abstracts, indexes, and the like, you can trace down one particular fact out of the whole mass of material you will find in the library. Learning to use these resources puts the whole world of printed matter at your disposal. Being able to locate information is one of the things that a college education can give you.

IMPROVING WRITING SKILLS

Like most skills, the ability to write well comes only through practice. Once you have mastered the rules of composition, grammar, and punctuation, you still need to be concerned enough about the quality of your writing to make improving your use of language a continuing project.

AIDS TO WRITING

Certain things you ought to have on your desk at all times for ready reference. As an absolute minimum you will need a good dictionary and a book on English style. To these, many students will want to add a thesaurus.

The Dictionary. A good dictionary is one that is up to date and complete enough to include all the general, nontechnical words used at the college level. Among the best are *Webster's New World Dictionary, The American College Dictionary,* and *Webster's New Collegiate Dictionary.*

No matter which one you choose, it will not help you unless you get into the habit of consulting it. Of course, you will use it to check the spelling of words that you're not sure about. But you should also use it to look up definitions of words. One of the best ways to educate yourself is to become a definition hunter. By looking up words you don't know or words that seem to be used in unfamiliar ways, you will increase your ability to both read and write.

Style Guides. Besides the dictionary, you should also have handy a reference on grammar, usage, and punctuation. *The Elements of Style* by William Strunk and E. B. White, which we referred to on page 71, is particularly good. This little book, in less than one hundred pages, summarizes the basic rules of usage, the main principles of composition, some rules of form, and ways to improve style. It will answer almost any question you may have about composition, and it describes the common mistakes that college students make in writing.

Other useful handbooks of writing are Perrin's *The Writer's Guide* and the *Harbrace College Handbook.* For a detailed and fascinating account of usage in American English, we suggest Evans' and Evans' *Dictionary of American English Usage.* A more practical book for students is T. H. Bernstein's *The Careful Writer: A Modern Guide to English Usage.*

The Thesaurus. Peter Mark Roget was a nineteenth-century English physician who was also a lover of words. He wrote *A Thesaurus of the English Language* based upon a system that he invented for classifying all human knowledge. Today, there are many versions of Roget's work available, most of them reasonably up to date. One of the sections in the thesaurus, probably the most useful, gives a comprehensive listing of synonyms, words with similar meanings, and antonyms, words with opposite meanings. Referring to it may help you pick just the right word. Many writers

swear by it. A similar work, though built on different principles, is *Webster's Dictionary of Synonyms.*

How far you go in building a personal collection of aids to writing will depend partly on how much money you have to spend and partly on your interests. If you are working in the humanities and social sciences, where you will be required to write more papers than would be the case if you were in the natural sciences, you will probably want more than the basic references. But whatever you have, use them.

DEVELOPING GOOD WRITING

The purpose of writing is to tell people something—to communicate. The main difference between good writing and bad writing is that good writing tells the reader just what the writer intended to communicate. Some writing, of course, has a literary as well as informative purpose, but for most of us, learning to write informative prose clearly, accurately, and simply is enough.

Sentences. Good writing consists of clear sentences arranged in orderly paragraphs. If you are not sure about what a proper sentence is, study the section on sentence structure in a good style handbook. In writing a first draft of something, you don't need to worry too much about the niceties of your sentences (though it is a good idea to get into the habit of *thinking* in good, clear sentences). Most people have enough trouble just getting their ideas on paper. When you do your first revision, however, you will want to look carefully and critically at what you have written. You will want to correct faults and, wherever possible, simplify your expression.

Here are some of the more common sentence faults:

1. The sentence fragment. *High school and college are very different. First, the demands that college makes.* The second "sentence" is not a sentence but a fragment. It has both a subject and a verb, but it is not a complete sentence because it is cast in the form of a subordinate clause. We don't know whether the writer intended "Here are the demands that college makes" or "The demands that college makes are greater." Good writers know how to use sentence fragments effectively. Mark Twain was a master at them. But for most of us, they are to be avoided.

2. The run-on sentence. *The party was a roaring success, beer cans and paper plates were scattered everywhere.* Here, two complete sentences are incorrectly spliced together by

a comma. There are a number of ways to correct this sentence, depending upon what the writer meant. He might have meant, "The party was a roaring success, *but* beer cans and paper plates were scattered everywhere," in which case the separate clauses of a compound sentence are joined by a coordinating conjunction (but). Or possibly the writer simply meant to have two sentences more or less unrelated to one another. In that case he should have written, "The party was a roaring success. Beer cans and paper plates were scattered everywhere." Or he might have converted his run-on sentence into a complex sentence by making one of the clauses subordinate: "*Because* the party was *such* a roaring success, beer cans and paper plates were scattered everywhere."

3. Lack of agreement between subject and verb. *Each of us plan to go.* The simple subject of that sentence, "each," is singular, so the verb should be in the singular form: "Each of us *plans* to go." People commonly commit this error when the subject phrase contains both singular and plural nouns. In that case, you need to find the simple subject of the sentence (what the sentence is really about) and see whether it is singular or plural.

4. Lack of agreement between pronoun and antecedent. *Each person on the team did their best.* The antecedent for the pronoun "their" is "person," which is singular. Therefore, the pronoun should be singular: "Each person on the team did *her* best."

5. Dangling or misplaced modifiers. A typical case of a dangling modifier is one in which the modifier or participle modifies the wrong noun as in, *Having finally found our seats, the game had already started.* The sentence implies that it was the game that found the seats. Clearly the author of this sentence meant something like this: "The game had already started when we finally found our seats."

Another common kind of error is one in which an elliptical construction (an elliptical construction is one with an element implied rather than actually stated in the sentence) results in a dangling modifier: *While still rehearsing, Nancy arrived.* The author meant, "While we were still rehearsing, Nancy arrived." It isn't that elliptical constructions are bad; it is just that you must make your meaning clear.

Most errors of this sort can be detected by paying careful attention to the logic of the sentences you write. But in addition to correcting such errors, you can improve your style by avoiding the passive voice where the active voice would do, by varying the kinds of sentences you write, and by eliminating wordy and awkward constructions.

Paragraphs. A paragraph joins statements that are related but separate. Every paragraph has a *topical sentence.* That sentence contains the main idea of the paragraph. Everything else in that paragraph should develop, explain, or modify that main idea, or be a transitional sentence to the next paragraph. Most of the time the topical sentence comes first. That makes sense, because then the reader knows what the paragraph is about from the beginning. Sometimes, for special effect, a writer will delay the main idea until the end of the paragraph. When you do that you may surprise your readers, for often they may form the wrong idea about what the paragraph says.

Some of the time you will want to pull together everything you have said in a paragraph in a *summary sentence.* You can usually use such a summary statement as a transition to the next paragraph. Thus, by tying together the beginning and end of a paragraph and by relating it to the next paragraph, you can make your writing smooth and easy to follow.

What we have said about paragraphs applies to larger segments of your writing. For example, when you write a paper, you can use the first paragraph as a topical statement of what the paper is about, and the paragraph at the beginning of a section can tell what that section is about.

Writing good paragraphs calls for order and logic. That is why outlining is so useful; it helps you organize your paper into tight, well-constructed units that carry the reader along smoothly and enable him or her to grasp your meaning easily.

If you make writing good paragraphs second nature to you, you can concentrate on the other aspects of writing—grammar, style, and the effective use of vocabulary. To help you appreciate what well-organized paragraphs are like, we have provided an analysis of two sample paragraphs on the next page.

Grammar and Usage. Good writing is based upon a sense for the grammar of the language, and the rules for grammar come from good writing (and speaking). Moreover, grammar is appropriate to the occasion. There are different levels of grammatical usage. A sentence such as "It sure ain't a real friendly dog" is clear and easy to understand. It would not, however, be appropriate in formal standard English. Most edu-

TWO SAMPLE PARAGRAPHS AND THEIR ANALYSIS

(From an essay on Sinclair Lewis)

This mastery of the art of description is evident in *Main Street,* which portrays a small, provincial town in minute detail. Lewis was an acute observer of people and places, with a keen ear for the vernacular of the Middle West. He drew heavily on his own background: Will Kennicott's office in Gopher Prairie was a replica of Dr. E. J. Lewis' office in Sauk Centre, the social work of the Thanatopsis Club—establishing the rest room for farmer's wives, the anti-fly campaign, tree planting—was drawn from the activities of Lewis' stepmother, an active club-woman. The character of Carol and her reaction to Gopher Prairie is in many ways modeled on that of Lewis' first wife, Grace Hegger, and her view of Sauk Centre.

← Transitional sentence
← Topical sentence
Explanation and elaboration

(From an essay on the Missouri Compromise)

If New England opposition to slave representation was the major irritant in the growth of the sectional hostility which broke out in 1819–1821, there were others as well. Over the years there had grown up in the South a distinct anti-Yankee sentiment, in part aggravated by the trading practices of Yankee peddlers in the Southern states. This sentiment was given sharp utterance when the disastrous effects of the Panic of 1819 were felt south of the Potomac. In searching for reasons for their distress it was easy for Southerners to find in such measures as the Tariff of 1816, internal improvement schemes, and the Second Bank of the United States a convenient scapegoat. The exuberant nationalism which had followed the close of the war and had caused the Southerners to support these measures was forgotten, and a sober second thought convinced most of the South that the North was being favored at its expense.

← Topical sentence
Examples and elaboration

---

cated people can use their language at different levels. They can speak colloquially when the occasion demands, and they can speak formally as well. They can also vary their writing, though probably not quite so easily. This ability to move back and forth between the most colloquial style and formal language is one of the chief marks of an educated person.

Standard English varies in level. *Informal English* is more often used in speaking than in writing. It is the way educated people talk in informal situations, where slang, local expressions, and well-controlled deviations from the grammar of standard English are appropriate. *General English* is the kind of language educated people use in more formal conversations, in business letters, and in talks or in articles for general audiences. *Formal English* is more often written than spoken, and it is what you will find in technical writing and academic books.

Most of your writing should be in general English. For the most part, you should avoid a formal style, for it sounds stilted, and it is hard to write clearly and accurately. Be sure you know the main rules of the standard grammar of English and how to use them in a sensible way. If you ignore the basic rules of English, you make your writing illogical and hard to read, and you will appear to be ignorant.

What are these basic rules? We can't take the space here to go over them in detail, but we can present you with some questions which, if you can't answer, tell you that you have a poor grasp of grammar. Can you identify the subject of a sentence? Do you know the difference between the subject phrase and the simple subject? Do you know what a direct object is? Do you know what the term "principal parts of the verb" means, and can you identify them for regular and irregular verbs in English? Can you identify the nominative, objective, and possessive cases of pronouns?

Furthermore, do you know some of the common traps waiting for you in the language? Do you know how to use the verbs "lay" and "lie" correctly? If you were to say, "He laid there for some time," you would be showing your ignorance, for "laid" is the past tense of the verb "to lay," not the past tense of the verb "to lie" (if you don't know the difference between these verbs, look them up in a dictionary or handbook). The past tense of "lie" is "lay," so the sentence should read, "He lay there for some time."

Mistakes such as this one are not terribly important by themselves, and they seldom interfere with your ability to say what you mean. Nevertheless, they show that you do not understand the English language as well as an educated person should. The real purpose of studying grammar is not to avoid trivial mistakes but to help you write good standard English. The trivial errors, however, are often symptomatic of your level of ability in using the language. If you make them, the chances are that you can't identify such important things as the subject of a sentence, the direct object, the object of a preposition, the indirect object, and the verbal auxiliaries. Even more important, the chances are that you do not know how to correct a mistake once you have made one.

Get in the habit of carefully reading what you write so that you correct your own mistakes. When your instructor corrects something on your paper, make sure you know what the correct form is and why you made the error. If you don't know why you made a mistake or why you were corrected, find out. Once more, the little book by Strunk and White, *The Elements of Style*, is invaluable for helping you do this.

Punctuation. Punctuation is essential to clear writing. Anyone can punctuate properly just by learning a few rules and by doing a little thinking. The purpose of periods and commas is to set apart separate ideas. They help readers keep things straight.

The period is the basic punctuation mark, and you use it to show that an idea is complete. A complete idea is expressed by the one-word sentence "Stop." In your writing you would set it off by a period.

How do you know that you have a complete idea? Most of us really know without having people tell us. Think about how you talk. Your intonation changes, and you pause at the end of a sentence. That is just like putting in a period, and yet you don't have to think about it, nor does anyone have to tell you how to do it.

Most of the time a complete idea will relate a subject and a phrase that contains a verb. That's true even in a one-word sentence. The sentence "Stop" implies a subject. It is usually an order, and it is addressed to you, so what it means is, "You stop doing whatever you are doing." Sometimes verb phrases are complicated, and sometimes we modify one idea with another within the same sentence, so that *complex sentences* often contain two or more ideas. But whenever that happens one idea is the main one which the others modify or elaborate.

Commas are used to separate ideas that are related. The following elements are separated by commas:

1. An idea that depends upon another. "If it rains, the picnic will be postponed." The first idea, which is a dependent or subordinate clause, is separated from the main or independent clause by a comma.

2. Two ideas connected by a conjunction. The comma goes before the conjunction, as in "Jerry got a new stereo, but he left it at home."

3. Items listed in a series. "I'm taking economics, psychology, French, and physics."

4. A main clause and parenthetical expressions. "No one, you will be happy to know, flunked the exam."

5. Noun phrases and their appositives. "Bill, my oldest brother, is getting married in June."

6. The parts of dates. For example, "December 25, 1979," or "May to December, 1938," or "Monday, January 20, 1906."

7. Titles in direct address. "I'm calling, Sue, to invite you to a party." "Excuse me, Professor, but I think you are wrong."

8. Nonrestrictive relative clauses. "John, who was the last to leave, got stuck with the bill." Restrictive clauses are not set off by commas, as in, "The person who was the last to leave paid the bill." Notice that in the latter case, the relative clause identifies the person—it is essential to the meaning of the sentence— while in the former case, the relative clause just tells you something incidental about John. The main idea in the first sentence is that John got stuck with the bill, and in the second sentence the main idea says that whoever was the last to leave paid the bill.

This list doesn't exhaust the uses of commas, but it does give you some of the more important and common ones. Furthermore, we have said nothing about colons, semicolons, question marks, and exclamation points. If you think you need some straightening out on these matters, consult one of the handbooks on English usage, or the section on punctuation in a good collegiate dictionary.

Spelling. As a college student, you are expected to spell correctly *all* the words you write. Here are some things you can do to make sure you do so:

1. Be careful. Many misspellings are the result of haste and carelessness.

2. Pay attention to the spelling of new words and names. If you are not the kind of person who can look at a new word and be able to spell it immediately, practice writing new words.

3. Use the dictionary.

4. Familiarize yourself with spelling rules, particularly for the special endings of words. You can find these rules in grammar books and dictionaries.

5. Proofread your work carefully for spelling and typing errors.

Most instructors resent poor spelling. It makes them think that you are either illiterate or that you haven't taken the trouble to be careful with your writing. If you are weak in spelling, invest in one of the programmed textbooks, one that will permit you to test and practice your spelling by yourself. English spelling is a trial: I *choose* a team now, but I *lose* my bet now. And I *chose* a team yesterday, and I carry *loose* change in my pocket. Self-paced programmed instruction is just the thing for learning something, such as spelling, that has a few rules but a lot of exceptions.

Vocabulary. A typical college student "knows" about 160,000 words. These are words that he or she can understand in context (though may not be able to define precisely). Of course, the typical student uses many fewer words. If your vocabulary is too small to allow you to convey your ideas adequately when you write, or if you are often baffled by words you see that you don't understand, you need to improve your vocabulary.

Being in the habit of using the dictionary is a big help. But learning the dictionary definitions, or *denotations*, of words will not necessarily help you understand their *connotations*. The connotation of a word is the meaning it suggests in addition to its literal meaning. For example, using the word "slender" to describe someone connotes approval, whereas "skinny" connotes disapproval, and "scrawny" even more strongly expresses disapproval. "Assertive" is a neutral word, but "pushy" has unpleasant connotations. The more aware you are of the connotations of words, the more precisely you will be able to convey your own attitudes toward things.

One of the most common faults in students' writing is using big words when simple ones would do. Why say, "The methodology employed in this investigation is factor analysis" when "We used the method of factor analysis in this study" would do?

Avoid jargon words such as "finalize"; use "complete" instead. The word "parameters" is often misused (most often to mean "limits"). Avoid it unless you mean it in its precise mathematical sense. Avoid euphemisms such as "passed away" for "died," and "intoxicated" for "drunk."

Another fault is wordiness—using several words where one or two would do. Instead of saying, "In spite of the fact that it snowed, we went ahead with the party," say, "Although it snowed, we went ahead with the party." Or instead of "He did his work in a careless manner," just say, "He worked carelessly." Or, "She is a person who likes everyone," should be, "She likes everyone." When you revise your compositions, simplify wordy constructions when you find them.

Reading a lot is a good way to improve your vocabulary. Make an effort to read things that are well written. Ask yourself why this is good writing and something else bad writing. Try your hand at editing someone else's writing. Many of the things you read could be better written. Textbooks are often written by people who know a great deal about their subject but could learn something about writing. Introductory textbooks by and large are well written (because they are carefully edited, among other reasons), but advanced texts and treatises, particularly in the natural and social sciences, are often full of clumsy writing. Everyone knows how bad government documents often are. See if you can improve the sentences you find in sources such as these. You may never be one of the great stylists of the English language, but if you learn to write a technical report, a stockholder's statement, or a new government regulation so that it can easily be understood by literate people, you will have achieved one of the main purposes of your education.

CHAPTER EIGHT

STUDYING A FOREIGN LANGUAGE

Anybody who has been a moderately good tennis player, or who has been on the high school basketball team, or who has played varsity lacrosse knows how hard you have to work at it to be competitive. You have to work at it every day to be a good athlete. Learning a new language is that way. To become proficient at speaking, reading, and writing a foreign language, you have to put the concentrated effort and practice into it that you would if you wanted to be a professional basketball player.

Nearly everyone has a problem learning a foreign language. If you find reading the language to be easy, you may have trouble understanding the spoken language. A lot of people who read and write well have a tin ear and just can't hear—much less speak—the unfamiliar vowels of French, German, or Swedish. If you get through the hurdle of grammar and drill, you may find that you just can't think in Italian. Or you may be able to understand sentences in Russian but just can't find the right way to put them into English. Find out for yourself just what comes easily to you and what gives you trouble. If you identify those things you can do well, you can use them to get you over the rough spots. Or if you are like a real clod on the athletic field and can't seem to get a hold anywhere in a foreign language, you will have to work extra hard. The purpose of this chapter is to give you some ideas for making your study of foreign languages as efficient and pleasant as possible.

BASIC RULES FOR SUCCESSFUL LANGUAGE LEARNING

KEEP UP WITH THE WORK

Steve runs on the varsity cross-country team. Every day, rain or shine, warm or cold, he runs at least seven miles. He wouldn't think of missing a day's practice. Even a bad cold wouldn't keep him off the course, and once he ran ten miles with an infected splinter in his foot. Steve also takes elementary French. He approaches French with less dedication. Twice he overslept and missed his class. Once he cut class to go to a track meet elsewhere. The week he had a cold, he felt too rotten to go to class. French is his least-favorite subject. So he puts off studying it until the last moment. The result is that he squeaks by with a marginal D. Even if he passes, the chances are he will have to repeat it before he can go on to the next level.

It has never occurred to Steve that the attitudes and habits that make him a good long-distance runner would also make him a good French student. It takes discipline, skill, and endurance. If he kept up with French the way he keeps up with running, he would be an A student.

You can fall behind in economics, history, literature, or even chemistry and catch up—though we don't recommend it. If you fall behind in a foreign language, however, you've had it. Regular attendance, regular daily preparations are not just desirable, they are absolutely necessary in learning a foreign language.

Learning a language is cumulative. Everything you learn later depends upon what you have learned already. You have to know the meanings of words before you can put them together in phrases. You have to know how to pronounce the sounds and hear them accurately before you can talk to and understand a native speaker. You have to know about word order in the new language before you can understand anything but the simplest of sentences. You have to know how verbs are conjugated and nouns and adjectives are declined.

Furthermore, it takes dedicated practice. If you worked out at tennis one day a week, you would never make the tennis team. With a foreign language you must practice regularly, and you must learn the simple things before you can tackle the complicated ones.

SPEND LOTS OF TIME IN RECITATION

Recitation, in class or to yourself, is the basic technique in learning a new language. The easiest way to fail a foreign language course is never to recite. At least 80 percent of your study time, particularly in the early stages of language learning, should be spent in recitation. What is more, you need to recite on a daily basis: every day, not just three days a week.

There are three skills you must master in learning a new language: First, you must learn to read it. Second, you should learn to understand it when you hear it. Third, you should learn to speak it. Americans are notoriously bad about speaking other languages. But we're going to have to learn. We have a large body of French speakers to the north of us growing in importance. And if you are thinking of running for Congress in certain areas of the Southwest, you had better speak Spanish. If the only language you know is English, you are the poorer for it, and learning a foreign language is worth at least as much effort as goes into being a passable golfer, tennis player, or pianist. Even if you only want to learn to read, you have to practice. And practice means recitation and translation as the first and most important step in learning to read.

MASTER THE GRAMMAR

American college courses in foreign languages stress grammar. Language teachers want you to learn the structure of the language you are studying. If you know the rules of grammar in a language, you can construct sentences of your own in that language, and you can understand what people say to you.

One problem with grammar is that many students have either forgotten or never learned the rudiments of English grammar. When they hear about tense, mood, gerunds, participles, and cases in Spanish, French, or Russian, they have no idea what the teacher is talking about. If you find yourself in this spot, try to make up your deficiencies as you go along. You can do this with the help of a handbook of English grammar. Another way is to "translate back" into English. See what the equivalent of the Latin or Russian nominative is in English. In fact, many people report that learning a foreign language this way—mastering the grammar of the language—is the way in which they really came to understand English grammar.

Few students of English grammar, as a matter of fact, will have encountered expressions such as "a noun in the dative case" or "an accusative pronoun." The reason is that among European languages, English is unusual. It depends much more upon word order to express grammatical meaning than upon special word endings. In most other European languages the endings do what word order does in English. In Latin, for example, the word for girl is *puella*. Thus you would say, *puella puerum amat* (the girl loves the boy). But if you wanted to say, "The boy loves the girl," you would change the *-a* ending to *-am*. It would be *puer puellam amat*. You would change the ending because "girl" is now in the accusative case rather than in the nominative. Because of the dependence upon word endings, most Latin sentences can be written in different orders (though typically the verb is last). In English, order is all-important (think about "The boy loves the girl" and "The girl loves the boy").

Whenever you come across a new grammatical term in a foreign language, make sure you understand it. If it has an equivalent in English, or a near equivalent, make sure you know what the comparable English construction would be. You can use the English equivalent to begin to understand the meaning of the grammatical categories in the new language. When you become skilled in the language, you will realize that the grammatical categories in that language have a meaning all their own, and you won't need English as a crutch. If you are studying German you should be able not only to rattle off the declensions of German nouns—nominative, *das Haus;* accusative, *das Haus;* genitive, *des Hauses;* dative, *dem Hause*—but also to understand how they are used in German sentences.

All languages are full of irregularities—exceptions to general rules and bafflingly contrary rules covering only a few words. These have to be learned by brute force. Although grammarians try to discover rules that will apply as broadly as possible, there are always exceptions. If you think French, German, or Russian is maddeningly irregular, consider your blessings— you don't have to learn English as a second language. It is far and away the most irregular of all the familiar European languages.

In all languages the words that are most frequently used tend to be irregular or retain ancient forms. Consider conjugating the verb "to be." The simple present and past tenses of this verb are I am, you are, he/she/it is, we are, you are, they are, I was, you were he/she/it was, we were, you were, they were. Contrast that with I walk, you walk, he/she/it walks, we walk, you walk, they walk, I walked, you walked, he/she/it walked, we walked, you walked, they walked. There are only two rules for walk: Add -s to form the third person singular (she walks), and add -ed to form the past tense. For the most part, the only thing you can do with irregular verbs is to memorize them, recite them, and use them in context in simple sentences. They have to become as second nature as putting one foot before the next in walking.

Language teachers stress grammar because it is the main tool we have for mastering a language when we have a lot of other things to do. You didn't learn to speak English (or whatever your native language is) by learning the rules of grammar. Most people learn the basics of their native tongue between the ages of one and five. But they don't learn it by going to class three or four hours a week and practicing it for another eight or ten. They learn it by being immersed in it for all their waking hours. And even then, a five-year-old still has a long way to go in the use of his or her native language. If you are a college freshman, it took you about eighteen years to achieve the mastery of English you have today. If you don't have all that time to practice, the most efficient way to learn a language is to learn grammatical rules, along with getting as much practice as you can in reading, listening, and speaking.

LEARN TO THINK IN THE LANGUAGE

You know that you have really mastered another language when you can think in that language. To think in a language means not only that you are fluent in it, but also that you don't have to "translate." You don't read English by translating it; that is, you don't turn words into other words in order to understand them. Rather you know directly what the words mean. You don't have to think about it at all. You just know. That is the goal you should work toward in studying another language. Right from the beginning, you should try to associate foreign words not with their English equivalents, but directly with the objects, events, and qualities they name. As you become more skillful in your use of the new language, you will find increasingly that you think in it without having to refer to the English equivalent.

LEARNING TO READ THE LANGUAGE

At first, in order to read in the new language, you will have to translate. Learning to think in a new language is a gradual process which goes by stages. As you progress from one stage to the next, you may find some of the following suggestions useful.

STUDYING BY PHRASES AND SENTENCES

The word-for-word translation that most students do in the very first weeks can get them into difficulty as the material gets more complex. That is especially true in languages such as Latin and German in which the word order is different from that in English. Second-year students in German easily get lost trying to find their way through a sentence word by word, for German word order is so different that it doesn't make sense if it is translated literally in a word-by-word way. You have to get the sense of the main parts of the sentence as a whole before you look up specific words you do not know. And when you look up a new word, you have to keep in mind the relation of that word to the pattern of the sentence as a whole. Those of you who have studied any German at all will know how misleading the word-by-word method sometimes can be in German. German has separable verbs, in which a prefix to the verb can be detached from the verb and moved to the end of the sentence. If you try to translate the stem of the verb without its prefix, you will be translating the wrong word. But even in languages such as French, in which the word order is very much like English, you will find it much better to try to grasp the meaning of a whole sentence. It will seem strange and unnatural at first, but once you get used to it, it will be the only way you will attack new sentences in a foreign language.

If, after a semester or so at a foreign language, you are still translating in a word-by-word way, you need help. You might try discussing the problem with your instructor. It may be that you haven't memorized the basic elements of the vocabulary such as relative pronouns or irregular verbs. These together with verbal auxiliaries and certain other elements (such as prepositions, particularly in German) have to be second nature to you. You have to recognize them instantly when you see them in a sentence, and you have to know immediately what they mean.

Perhaps you don't know the syntax or word order well enough to be able to tell where you are in a sentence. This is particularly difficult for students of German. For example, in the sentence *Haben Sie den Bauer gesehen, der auf dem Wagen sass?* (Have you seen the farmer who sat on the wagon?), a badly confused student may try to translate *der* as a definite article (the) rather than as a relative pronoun (who). This mistake would result from translating the sentence word by word rather than trying to see the pattern that the syntax makes. A parallel problem in French is illustrated by the sentence *Elle a reçu les fleurs que lui ont envoyées des amies* (She received the flowers that friends sent her), where the unobservant student may read the objective pronoun *que* (that) as the nominative pronoun *qui* (who), thus making hash of the sense. If you look over the whole sentence and relate the words one to another, you will not make mistakes such as these.

LOOKING UP WORDS: SOME DOS AND DON'TS

The most common mistake students make in trying to translate something is to look up too many words. There are two things wrong with doing this.

First, you may not have to look up the word if you read on and get the context in which the word is used. Consulting a dictionary is only one way of learning the meaning of a word, and it is both time-consuming and sometimes ineffective, for it isolates the meaning from the context in which the word is used. Most of the words we know in English we learned from context rather than from looking them up in the dictionary or having someone tell us what they mean. Context always limits the kinds of words that can appear in particular places in sentences. Because of this limitation, you can often guess the meaning of a word.

Second, you often find more than one meaning for a word in the dictionary. You will only know which meaning is the correct one by knowing the context in which the word occurs.

Thus, try to guess from context, and even if you do look something up in the dictionary, do so only after you have established the context. Don't just stop when you get to a word you don't know; read the whole sentence before you look it up. Keep to a minimum the number of words you look up. Even if you make a wrong guess, something in the succeeding sentences will tell you that you have made a mistake, and you can then go back and correct it.

If you do have to look up a word, mark it in some way so that you will know that it was a word that was unfamiliar to you. Then make sure you can place the word in the context of the sentence correctly.

Continue on this tack for about half your assignment. At this point a brief rest may be in order anyway. After your break, if you take one, instead of plowing ahead, go back and reread from the beginning the first half of the assignment. This is a way of reciting while the material is still fresh in your mind. This time you should be able to read steadily ahead, and your memory for the words you had to look up the first time will be better for the review.

Even so, you will probably miss a few words. You will have to look them up again. This time, put a dot or check mark in the margin to show which words you had to look up a second time.

There are two important points we are making here: First, *learn the words from context and in context;* second, *always reread a passage soon after you translate it for the first time.* Later on you can concentrate on learning the words that gave you trouble.

DISSECTING WORDS

The time and place for paying attention to individual words is (1) when you have read a sentence and can't get its meaning because you're not sure about one or more words in it, and (2) when you want to build your vocabulary.

While learning a language, you are continuously adding to your store of usable words. You will save yourself a lot of work if you learn how to break words down into their elements. We have already said something about that in connection with building your English vocabulary (page 37), and it is just as appropriate in the study of another language.

Languages are put together in different ways, but most of them are like English in that they have root words to which prefixes and suffixes may be attached. If you learn the general meaning of the prefixes and suffixes (collectively called affixes), you can often figure out a word you have never seen before just by dissecting it. In English, you know that the prefix *pre-* means before. Whenever you see *pre-* at the beginning of a word, you can tell that the word has something to do with going on before, as in premeditation, prelude, or premonition. Other languages work in much the same way, and even though there may seem to be a lot of affixes because of all the combinations they can produce, there are actually relatively few of them to be learned.

Some languages, such as German, have many compound words. These are words in which the elements are not necessarily affixes and roots, but may be two or more whole words glued together. Thus, the German word *Durchgangsgerechtigkeit* means right-of-way or thoroughfare, and it is compounded out of several separate words and affixes. If you study advanced German, you will have to learn how to dissect words, because many of the words you will run across in your reading will not be in the dictionary. The person who wrote them simply made them up by compounding existing words.

USING COGNATES

Many words in other European languages resemble words in English with the same or similar meaning. That is because English has its roots in both the Germanic and Romance (French, Spanish, Italian, etc.) languages. Moreover, many English words were either directly borrowed from Latin and Greek or were coined by using Latin and Greek roots: for example, coaxial, fission, interstellar from the Latin, and economics, drama, biology, cyclotron from the Greek.

As a result, many words in these languages have been carried over into English. Although the original forms often have been modified in the process, there is often a perceptible relation between a word, say, in French and one in English. If you learn to recognize such similar words, called cognates, you will find translation to be easier. To illustrate what we mean, take a pencil and a piece of paper and do the exercise that we have provided on the use of cognates (page 90). You'll find you can guess with fair accuracy the meaning of many of the words in languages you have not ever studied.

You must be careful, however. Cognates can lead you astray, so you cannot rely blindly on similarities between foreign and English words. Sometimes strange things happen in the history of words that are borrowed from one language into another, or words in two different languages that have a common heritage in a third. *Le crayon* does not mean crayon in French; it means pencil. The English word "black" is historically related to the French word *blanc*, which means white! Even when the meanings of cognates are similar, there may be fine shades of difference between them that you can't detect. It is a good rule, therefore, to look up all such words at least once and check their meaning. But do this only after you have attempted a guess based upon their similarity to English. Identifying cognates helps make the study process an active one.

USING CARDS

Studying a language takes a lot of memorizing. A good technique for making memorizing easier is to write a foreign word on one side of a card and its translation on the other. In fact, you can buy such cards already prepared, though it is probably a good idea to make your own, if you have the time. You can test yourself by running through the foreign words while making translations of them. Whenever you're stumped or are not sure, you can flip over the card for the correct answer.

If you make up your own cards, it will help you with foreign spelling as well as provide additional recitation. Keep your working stack of cards small. Make sure you have mastered your initial set before you add new cards to the stack. When you're absolutely sure of a word, take it out of the working stack.

When you begin to translate more difficult passages, it's a good idea to make a card for every word you have to look up. Run over these at set intervals, perhaps once a day. Each time you remember what the word means, put a check mark on the card, and each time you don't, put a zero. When you have five checks in a row without any zeros, you can take the card out of the set.

Another way of using cards is to write down whole phrases, not just single words. These help you think in larger units and to use words in their proper context. Then, too, many phrases are idiomatic and cannot be translated literally on a word-for-word basis. The familiar French phrase *Comment allez-vous?* literally means "How do you go?" but is translated as "How are you?"

Many students write the English equivalent of foreign words in the margins or between the lines of passages they are translating. This is a poor idea. It sounds easier than using cards, but it has two disadvantages. First, it leaves the translation in full view and makes it almost impossible for you to recite without prompting, and second, by focusing your attention on the translation, it keeps you thinking in English rather than in the new language. Since you eventually want to know the meanings of words without connecting them to English, the less you rely on English, the better.

AVOIDING PONIES AND TROTS

If you are in an advanced language class in which you are reading whole books or lengthy excerpts from foreign literature, it is often possible to buy English translations known as "ponies" or "trots." Some trots supply interlinear translations with the English words printed between the lines of the foreign print. Avoid these at all costs. Aside from distracting you, they keep you from figuring out the meaning of words, and they distort the foreign syntax. They deprive you of the opportunity to recite. And they are a real handicap to learning to think in the new language. Finally, the translations may be so free that you may never learn the exact meaning of the words and phrases you are reading. Free translation, which is good when the translator knows precisely what he or she is interpreting, is a poor teacher for the unskilled learner.

Trots which consist of the foreign text on one page and the English equivalent on the opposite page are better. They should be used *very* sparingly, however. They at least permit you to read without looking at the translation. There are times when it is profitable to read an English version of something you are going to translate. And it is fun to read something that is very familiar, such as the Bible, in a foreign language. The best policy, however, is to follow your teacher's advice about such matters.

LEARNING TO SPEAK A FOREIGN LANGUAGE

Much of what we have said about learning to read a new language also applies to learning to speak one. In the early stages of learning, the two go together.

Speaking the language helps you learn to read it. If you wish to gain speaking fluency as rapidly as possible, however, you will need to make use of some special techniques.

You learned to speak English by hearing it spoken and by speaking it yourself. You learned by copying from others, inventing on your own and being corrected, or being aware that you weren't saying things quite the way other people were saying them. By the time you were ready to go to school and long before you could read or write, you had a better mastery of English than a person could acquire by studying it in college for a couple of years. And all this happened without any knowledge of grammar, reading, and writing.

Children are immersed in a world of language. That is how they learn it. Several of the crash programs for teaching people to comprehend and speak a new language in a short period of time—the Berlitz method, for example—make use of total immersion. However, total immersion is seldom possible for most college students. But even if you can't be a part of a total immersion program, you can do everything possible to practice the new language in a variety of situations and use it as much as possible to think with. Seek out native speakers of the language you are studying and get them to talk to you in their native tongue. Read foreign language newspapers and magazines. Go to foreign movies and try to follow the dialogue without relying on the subtitles. Join a foreign language club. Often in cafeterias and dining halls, there will be lunch or dinner tables where only a particular foreign language is spoken. The more you can get yourself into such situations, the better your grasp of the spoken language will be.

IMITATING

To make a language habitual, you must practice it regularly. One aspect of practice is imitation. Most colleges and universities maintain language laboratories where you can listen to prepared tapes or records of native speakers, record your own speech, and correct any errors you may hear yourself making. Extensive listening accustoms your ear to the rhythm of native speech and enables you to understand what you hear. Extensive taping of your own voice gives you practice in making unfamiliar speech sounds.

MEMORIZING

Another aspect of language practice is memorizing. Imitating itself results in a kind of memorizing, but in addition to trying to duplicate what you hear, you must

USE OF COGNATES

Here are two translations of an earlier edition of How to Study, *one in French and one in Spanish. Even if you don't know French or Spanish, read through them and underline any word that resembles a word in English. Most of these words will be cognates; that is to say, they will be related to and will mean the same or similar things as English words. A few will be what the French call "false friends." These are words that resemble English words but mean different things. We have provided a list of words that resemble one another in English and French and in English and Spanish, together with the correct English transla-*

Usage de fiches de vocabulaire

La technique qui suit s'est révélée efficace pour l'acqusition du vocabulaire. Lorsque vous rencontrez un mot moins familier, inscrivez-le au recto d'une fiche avec sa signification au verso; revisez ces fiches chaque jour, pointez-les chaque fois que vous vous souvenez du sens du mot et inscrivez un zéro chaque fois que vous devez regarder au verso pour vous rafraîchir la mémoire. Quand vous aurez pointé la fiche cinq fois sans aucun zéro, vous pourrez considérer que vous connaissez ce mot et vous jetterez la carte, évitant ainsi d'en accumuler un trop grand nombre. (page 74)

French Word	Similar English Word	English Translation
usage	usage	use
technique	technique	technique
suit	suit	follows
révélée	reveal	revealed, shown
efficace	efficacious	efficacious
pour	pour	for
acquisition	acquisition	acquisition
vocabulaire	vocabulary	vocabulary
rencontrez	encounter	meet with
familier	familiar	familiar
inscrivez	inscribe	inscribe, set down
signification	significance	significance
revisez	revise	revise
pointez	point	mark, check
souvenez	souvenir	remember, recall
sens	sense	meaning
zéro	zero	zero
regarder	regard	look at
refraîcher	refresh	refresh
mémoire	memory	memory
considérer	consider	consider
jetterez	jettison	throw away
carte	card	card
accumuler	accumulate	accumulate
grand	grand	large
nombre	number	number

tions. Check the words you underlined against the list, and be sure to note the correct translations. This exercise will show you how helpful hunting for similar words can be in understanding some of the familiar European languages.

The French translation, Comment Étudier, *was adapted from the English by André Roy and published in 1968 by McGraw-Hill Éditeurs, Montreal, Canada. The Spanish translation,* Como Estudiar, *was published in 1967 by Editorial Magisterio Español, S.A., Madrid, Spain.*

Uso de las fichas

Como ya hemos indicado, en el estudio de los idiomas hay que ejercitar mucho la memoria, y los estudiantes han probado un gran número de técnicas para hacerlo más fácil y eficaz. Una técnica muy empleada es escribir una palabra extranjera en la cara de una ficha y su traducción en la otra cara. (Desde luego, puedes comprar tales fichas ya impresas.) Puedes autoexaminarte mirando las palabras extranjeras y viendo las que sabes traducir. Cuando llegues a una cuyo significado no recuerdes, no tienes más que dar la vuelta a la ficha. Esta puede ser una práctica eficaz si se usa juiciosamente. (page 163)

Spanish Word	Similar English Word	English Translation
uso	use	use
indicado	indicate	appropriate, advisable
en	in	at, in, into, by, on
estudio	studio, study	study
idiomas	idioms	language, idiom
mucho	much	much, a lot of
memoria	memory	memory
estudiantes	students	students
probado	prove	test, try, prove
un	one	one, a
gran	grand	big, large, great
numéro	numeral	number
técnicas	technical	technique
empleada	employ	employ, use
escribir	inscribe	write
extranjera	extraneous	foreign
traducción	translation	translation
otra	other	other, another
comprar	compare	buy, purchase
tales	tales	such, such a
impresos	impress	printed
autoexaminarte	self-examination	self-examine
traducir	traduce	translate
significado	significant	meaning
no	no	not, no
eficaz	efficacy	efficacious, efficient
juiciosamente	judicious	judiciously
práctica	practice	method, skill

concentrate on remembering words and phrases. Rehearsing and reciting over and over again seems to be about the best way to do it. The object is to make certain things so habitual that you don't need to think about them. Then you can concentrate on what you want to say and on new combinations of words.

STUDYING OUT LOUD

When you're learning a foreign language, you will want to read aloud as much as possible. As long as you read silently, you are learning the language only visually. Language requries hearing, and it also requires skillful use of the speech muscles. The visual and auditory aspects need to be brought together, and reading out loud will help achieve a synthesis. Be sure to schedule at least some of your study time for a foreign language at a time when speaking out loud will not bother other people.

SPACING STUDY EFFECTIVELY

In learning something that requries repetitive practice—as learning a foreign language does—spacing the practice is essential for efficient learning. Don't make your study periods too long or too short. Divide an assignment into two parts and master each separately. Then allow time for rereading and review. Provide for short rests or breaks. A half-hour is plenty of time if you are reciting out loud. If you break two hours of foreign language study into four half-hour periods separated by rest or by studying other subjects, you will learn more than if you work for two hours uninterruptedly on a foreign language.

IN GENERAL

Some courses emphasize reading the language, others speaking it. Some stress grammar, while others don't. Some require a very precise understanding of words, while others allow rather free translation and

may even encourage it. Larger institutions offer special courses in scientific French or German, so that students in the sciences can learn to read the technical literature in these languages. Whatever the emphasis of the course you are taking, your instructor will stress those techniques that are most suitable for the particular purposes of that course.

Many schools encourage students in foreign languages to study abroad if this is possible. If you have the opportunity to spend a semester or a summer or even an entire year studying in another country, do so. There is no better way to become familiar with the way other people live and think than to live among them yourself for a while.

We have not said anything about the special problems of learning languages that do not use the Roman alphabet—languages such as Greek, Arabic, Hebrew, and Russian—because relatively speaking, few students take such languages, and those who do take them are generally very skilled at learning foreign languages. Even more difficult (and with even fewer students) are languages, such as Chinese, that do not use an alphabet at all. If you have a talent for languages, learning one of those languages, the organization of which is very different from English, can be one of the most valuable experiences of your college years.

Finally, we need to say a word about people who have real difficulties with foreign languages. While there are differences in aptitudes for learning languages, most people who have trouble learning a language do so because either they do not study enough or because they study in the wrong way. Nowhere, except perhaps in studying mathematics, are good work habits more important than in learning foreign languages. Work habits are acquired, not built in, and you must make the effort to develop them if you are going to be successful at a foreign language. If you do have little aptitude for learning languages, you especially need to have good work habits, and you need to allow more time for studying a new language than most students. After all, as Mark Twain remarked, even French babies learn to talk French.

If you have made a career out of avoiding science and mathematics, you have a lot of company. But even if you belong to a big club, it's one you shouldn't be in. In fact, a math or science phobia is one of the worst handicaps you can have in today's world. Not only do such fields as physics, engineering, chemistry, and biology require the tools of scientific thinking and mathematics, but social sciences such as economics, psychology, and sociology and such practical fields as accounting and business administration make use of them. Statistics, finite mathematics, linear algebra, and computer programming are all used in modern business management. Even if you are aiming for a major in literature or drama, you can't claim to be an educated person if you are nearly illiterate in mathematics, as some students are. The sooner you face up to your deficiencies in science and mathematics, the better off you will be.

Skim through this chapter. If what we say is familiar, obvious, or elementary, you don't need to read the chapter in detail. The chances are you are a good student in science. But if you find something that is unfamiliar or that you recognize but need brushing up on, read and read in detail. If you find that you can't understand much of what is in this chapter, you are in serious trouble and need help. But whatever you do, don't give up and decide that you are a basket case. Sometimes deficiencies that prevent a student from understanding mathematics or doing well in science go all the way back to the early grades. If your deficiencies are this deep, you may need special tutoring.

If you think you can get by without understanding basic mathematics, consider the plight of Anne. She graduated with a strong record and a major in English from one of the country's most prestigious colleges. All through her school and college career, she concentrated on avoiding courses in mathematics and science. She barely got through ninth-grade algebra and quit doing any mathematics at all just as soon as she could. In college, she fulfilled her science requirements by taking a "rocks for jocks" course that made almost no demands upon scientific reasoning and none whatever upon mathematics. Two years after graduating from college, as the result of some job experience and other things, she decided that she wanted to take graduate work in psychology. She discovered that while some quite good graduate schools would be willing to take her without an undergraduate major in psychology, not one of them would let her get by without statistics. She had no recourse but to go back and be tutored in the kinds of elementary mathematics and arithmetic operations she had done so much to avoid.

There is no time like the present to begin to correct

CHAPTER NINE

STUDYING MATHEMATICS AND SCIENCE

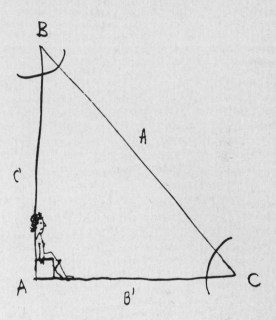

your past mistakes. Use this chapter as a kind of test of how much you know and whether or not you are going about doing science and mathematics the right way. The chances are you can understand basic mathematics, even though you may never get into advanced mathematics or take something such as physics for engineers. If you can't, the sooner you know for sure, the better.

STUDYING MATHEMATICS

Mathematics is a kind of language. Students in the humanities who can understand the most difficult and obscure poetry sometimes throw up their hands in despair when mathematical or arithmetical problems confront them. But they needn't. The main thing about the language of mathematics is that it always means what it says. It contains no ambiguities, no guessing, no possibilities—none of the things that make ordinary languages such as English interesting and tantalizing in themselves. Unlike ordinary language, mathematics means only what its rules say it means. You have to learn to say, "Open sesame!" in just the right way before it will work for you. It requires that you learn how to do a few operations, and you also need some practice, maybe even rote practice.

In mathematics everything proceeds from the simple to the complex. Everything you learn depends upon what you have already learned. That is one of the reasons why so many people stumble with mathematics. If you happen to miss out on something, you may be mystified thereafter because everything else depends upon or makes use of what you missed.

Mathematics is also like a game. You have to play by the rules or you don't play the game. In mathematics, the rules are everything, and once you have violated them, you are out of the game. In a game such as football, you don't have to practice just to learn the rules; the rules come naturally to you as you play the game. But in mathematics, you have to practice so that the rules become second nature to you. Then when you see a problem, you know immediately what to do.

KEEPING UP WITH THE WORK

We have already said many times that keeping up is basic to successful study. In a cumulative subject such as statistics, or business mathematics, it is everything. In psychology or English you could fall behind and catch up without too much trouble, but in mathematics, as in learning a foreign language, once you fall behind, you have a real struggle to get back up to where you ought to be.

And as we pointed out in comparing mathematics

to a game, practice counts. Everyone can understand the principle in factoring, or in solving simultaneous equations, but to be skillful at actually doing it requires practice and a lot of it.

TAKING NOTES IN CLASS

There are some special points about taking notes in mathematics classes. First of all, make sure that everything you write down is accurate. Don't be faced with the fact that you don't understand something because you copied an expression or formula the wrong way. Keep your notes to a minimum, but do make sure that you are able to interpret them later. All you should be trying to do in class is to follow the rigorous chain of thought in solving a problem or deriving an equation. Don't worry so much about what the instructor says as what he or she puts on the blackboard. If you can't understand how the instructor got from one place to another, ask. Even if your instructor seems impatient with questions, ask. If you don't understand something in class, the chances are you will never be able to figure it out on your own. In other subjects, particularly those that are heavily factual, you can take down things you don't really understand with a good chance that with later reflection, you will be able to understand. This will occasionally happen in mathematics if the textbook and the instructor parallel one another very closely, but it doesn't happen nearly as often in mathematics as in other subjects.

PREPARING FOR EXAMINATIONS

Exams in mathematics tap your ability to solve problems, to understand concepts. The main idea is to find out if you can apply what you have presumably learned to some new examples. Sometimes the examples on examinations are not like the ones you have seen before, but even so, practice at solving problems is the most important part of preparation for examinations in mathematics. In reviewing the solution of problems, take advantage of mistakes you made in earlier work. If problem sets and examples have been corrected and handed back to you, note the kinds of mistakes you made and practice more on such problems than on others. If you worked problems from a book and had difficulty finding the answer to some, work more on those problems which gave you the most trouble.

One of the big difficulties for many students, particularly in courses in probability theory or in applied mathematics, is to know how to set up problems when the problem is given in words. If word problems are to be found in your mathematics courses, be sure that you know how to translate them into the correct mathematical operations. Just knowing how to do the operations won't be enough. You have to be able to set up the problem so you can do the operations.

BASIC MATHEMATICAL SKILLS

ARITHMETIC

What is the heading "Arithmetic" doing in a book addressed to college students and students headed for college? Doesn't that belong in elementary school? Perhaps. But a lot of people forget how to do some of the less-familiar arithmetic operations when they don't use them every day, and a few people—otherwise intelligent and educated people—never learn how to do them properly. Fortunately, hand calculators are universally available nowadays, and even the cheapest and most limited of them will do all the ordinary arithmetic operations for you. A few instructors, however, may insist that you do the arithmetic on examination questions by hand. Be sure to find out ahead of time if that is the case so that you can practice doing the kinds of problems that may be required.

One of the things people easily forget because of disuse is how to deal with fractions. In certain courses in mathematics and science you may be forced to deal with fractions without converting them to decimals. If so, you may want a refresher on fractions. We have provided a summary of the rules for working with fractions on page 96.

BUYING A HAND CALCULATOR

Every college student can use a hand calculator, even if for nothing more than balancing a checkbook. For under ten dollars you can buy one that will do all arithmetic operations, extract square roots, and find percentages. For a few dollars more you can buy one that will calculate both natural and decimal logarithms, find trigonometric functions, and carry special codes for going from British to metric units. Because calculators vary so much in what they do, some people own several.

If you are to buy only one and if it is to be a fairly expensive one, shop around carefully for it. Many of the more expensive calculators are specialized, and you should make sure that the one you buy will do the particular things you need. Some are meant for engineering work, others are specialized for statistical calculations, and still others are designed for typical business problems. After you have bought one, take the time to read the manual carefully, and work through some sample problems. Some calculators are so complicated that you must practice using them. Most of the more expensive ones have dual function keys. These make it possible to increase the number of operations without increasing the number of keys. Knowing how to move back and forth between the two functions may require a little practice. Even more important, the more sophisticated calculators have memory registers. These enable you to store the solution to part of a problem while you work on the remainder. You will need practice in putting results into memory storage and then retrieving them when you need them for further calculation.

The most expensive calculators are programmable; that is to say, they are really miniature computers. You can work out your own problem-solving methods that can be used over and over again. Students in the physical and social sciences sometimes buy such programmable calculators specialized for their kind of work. However, such calculators may cost several hundred dollars and are really meant only for advanced students.

No matter if your calculator is of the simplest kind. Learn how to use it properly. Keep the instruction manual with it, so that you will never be caught not knowing how to do something.

SETTING UP PROBLEMS

One of the hardest things the ordinary student faces in dealing with subjects that demand arithmetic and mathematics is knowing how to set up problems. For example, how would you set up this problem? Your college accepts 60 percent of all its applicants. You know that 360 students were accepted the year you came in. How large was the applicant pool from which your class was selected? To answer this problem you must first set it up properly. To do this, you will either mentally or on paper write out an equation. Usually in writing an equation we let x or y stand for the answer we are seeking—in this case the total number of applicants. You must write the equation so that it corresponds exactly to the wording of the problem. Here is the equation for this problem:

$$0.6 \times x = 360$$

The quantity 0.6 stands for 60 percent. Why? Because 60 percent means 60 out of 100, which as a decimal fraction is written as 60/100 or 0.6. Then 0.6 $\times x$ stands for 60 percent of the total applicant pool. The total applicant pool is the unknown quantity, and so we represent it by x. We say 0.6 *times* x because whenever we say that something is a percentage of something else, we are implicitly multiplying. Thus, 70 percent of 200 is 140 (0.7 $\times$ 200).

SOME RULES FOR COMPUTING FRACTIONS

Definitions

1. A fraction is one or more of the equal parts into which something can be divided. Examples are:

$$\frac{1}{2} \quad \frac{1}{3} \quad \frac{3}{4}$$

2. Fractions are written $\frac{1}{2}$ or ½.
3. The lower number is the *denominator*.
4. The upper number is the *numerator*.
5. *Mixed numbers* are whole numbers and fractions. Examples are:

$$3\frac{1}{2} \quad 2\frac{2}{3}$$

Adding fractions

1. To add fractions, the denominators must all be the same. Thus $\frac{1}{2}$ and $\frac{1}{3}$ cannot be added until the 2 and 3 are changed.
2. To make the denominators the same, find the *smallest* number (the lowest common denominator) that can be divided evenly by all the denominators. Examples are:

> For 2 and 3, it is 6.
> For 7 and 13, it is 91 (7 × 13 = 91).
> For 2, 8, and 9, it is 72.

Note: For many cases, you will have difficulty finding the smallest number by inspection. Find the smallest number into which you can divide as many of the numbers as possible. Then multiply that number by the number you *cannot* divide into it. This will be the lowest common denominator. Take, for example, 2, 3, 6, 7, 8, 9. All but 7 can be evenly divided into 72. The lowest common denominator is therefore 72 × 7 = 504.

3. Multiply the numerator by the number of times the original denominator goes into the lowest common denominator. An example is:

$$\frac{1}{2} + \frac{1}{3} = \frac{1 \times 3}{6} + \frac{1 \times 2}{6} = \frac{3}{6} + \frac{2}{6}$$

4. Add the numerators and place the lowest common denominator as the denominator of the sum. An example is:

$$\frac{3}{7} + \frac{1}{13} = \frac{3 \times 13}{91} + \frac{1 \times 7}{91} = \frac{39}{91} + \frac{7}{91} = \frac{46}{91}$$

5. If the numerator is larger than the denominator, change to a mixed number. An example is:

$$\frac{23}{7} = 3\frac{2}{7}$$

Subtracting fractions

1. All the rules are the same as for addition except rule 4.
2. For rule 4, subtract instead of adding the numerators. An example is:

$$\frac{3}{7} - \frac{1}{13} = \frac{39}{91} - \frac{7}{91} = \frac{32}{91}$$

Multiplying fractions

1. To multiply fractions, multiply the numerators together and the denominators together. Write the result as a fraction. An example is:

$$\frac{3}{4} \times \frac{5}{7} = \frac{15}{28} \text{ or } \frac{5}{6} \times \frac{2}{5} = \frac{10}{30} = \frac{1}{3}$$

2. To multiply a whole number and a fraction, multiply the whole number by the numerator and place the result over the denominator. An example is:

$$5 \times \frac{2}{3} = \frac{10}{3} = 3\frac{1}{3}$$

Dividing fractions

1. Turn the divisor upside down and multiply. An example is:

$$\frac{4}{9} \div \frac{1}{3} = \frac{4}{9} \times \frac{3}{1} = \frac{12}{9} = 1\frac{3}{9} = 1\frac{1}{3}$$

2. Whole numbers can be written in the form of a fraction with 1 as the denominator. An example is:

$$3 = \frac{3}{1}$$

3. Therefore, to divide a fraction by a whole number, write the whole number as a fraction and invert. An example is:

$$\frac{4}{9} \div 3 = \frac{4}{9} \div \frac{3}{1} = \frac{4}{9} \times \frac{1}{3} = \frac{4}{27}$$

But we cannot solve the problem the way it is now set up. That is because the unknown quantity, x, must always be isolated on one side of the equation. Therefore, we rearrange the equation this way:

$$x = \frac{360}{0.6}$$

If you don't know how we did this or why we *divided* 360 by 0.6, you have forgotten algebra. You will find a brief account of some elementary rules of algebra in the next section. If this account doesn't ring a bell right away, the chances are that you need some special remedial work before you can do even the elementary college courses that require some mathematics.

The answer to our problem is 600 (360 divided by 0.6).

A LITTLE ALGEBRA

Most college students have had some algebra, but because the basic operations were often poorly learned or easily forgotten, many students have to refresh themselves when they take a course in elementary statistics or some other course that demands a little algebra. Some students, like Anne, have to be tutored in the basics before they can tackle courses in statistics or business mathematics. In this section we have brought together a few of the most basic principles of algebra.

First of all, numbers in algebra have signs; they are either positive or negative. If a number has a minus sign in front of it, it is negative. Thus, -8 is negative eight. If a number has no sign or a plus sign in front of it, it is positive. Thus 8 or $+8$ is positive eight. Sometimes students are confused, for the plus and minus signs are also used in algebra and arithmetic to indicate the operations of addition and subtraction. But if you will keep in mind that the operations, addition and subtraction, and the signs of numbers are different, you won't be confused.

Everyone is acquainted with positive and negative numbers because that is the way we scale temperature. When we read that the temperature in Chicago yesterday was -2, we know that it means that it was 2 degrees below zero. There are a lot of uses for negative numbers that are not quite so obvious. For example, if I owe \$15 more than I have, I might say that my assets are $-\$15$.

You can think of negative and positive numbers as numbers that keep increasing from zero in opposite directions like this:

$$-5 \quad -4 \quad -3 \quad -2 \quad -1 \quad 0 \quad +1 \quad +2 \quad +3 \quad +4 \quad +5$$

Rules for Addition and Subtraction of Algebraic Numbers. The rules for algebraic addition and subtraction, or the addition and subtraction of negative *and* positive numbers, are simple, and they should cause you no trouble, if you are careful. Here they are:

1. If all the numbers are either positive or negative, to add find the sum of the numbers and give the sum the sign of the numbers. Thus -2 plus -4 is -6.

2. If two numbers have opposite signs, then the sum is the difference between them with the sign of the sum being the sign of the larger number. Thus 4 plus -7 is -3, and -4 plus 7 is 3.

3. If you have to add a series of numbers which have different signs, find the sum of the positive numbers and the sum of the negative numbers separately and then find the *algebraic* sum of the two. To add -5, 3, -1, 6, -2, -7, and 8, find the sum of -5, -1, -2, and -7, which is -15, and the sum of 3, 6, and 8, which is 17. The sum of -15 and 17 is 2. If you use a hand calculator, you don't need to find the separate simple sums; you can just add the numbers together. But you must be sure to press the right keys. Thus, in doing the above sum you would press the minus key, then 5, then the *plus* key, then 3, then the minus key, then 1, etc. When you have entered all the numbers, you press the equal ($=$) key.

4. For algebraic subtraction, you change the sign of the number to be subtracted and then add. Thus, the difference between 8 and -3 is 11. When you subtract numbers opposite in sign, you are finding out how far apart the numbers are. For example, if the temperature this morning is 8 degrees in Cleveland and -3 degrees in Minneapolis, the difference in temperature is 11 degrees.

Algebraic addition and subtraction are easy, but you have to be alert to know which operation to apply to a particular problem. Watch out for problems in which numbers are both positive and negative. Make sure you set such a problem up in the right way.

Some Basic Rules of Algebra. If you are going to take a course that makes some mathematical demands—say physics for liberal arts students—you had better brush up on a few fundamental rules of algebra. If you don't feel confident about the matter, you should get hold of a book that reviews basic mathematics and assure yourself that you can do such things as add and subtract polynomials, that you can solve equations for numerical values, and that you know how to simplify, factor, and rearrange terms. An excellent book for this purpose is *Basic Mathematics* by H. Kruglak and J. T. Moore, in Schaum's Outline Series.

There are a couple of aspects of rearranging terms that are so important that you will run into them even if you never take a course in the physical sciences. They are (1) how to change signs when you move simple terms from one side of an equation to another, and (2) how to move part of a fraction or a product from one side of an equation to another. It was this latter operation we had to employ in order to set up the equation $x = 360/0.6$.

1. In order to move a single number (for example, 253 or 4 or a single term such as x or a or y) from one side of the equation to the other, you change the sign. Thus, to solve the equation

$$x - 5 = 30$$

you move $- 5$ to the other side and make it $+ 5$ (remember that a number with no sign in front of it is always considered to be positive):

$$x - 5 = 30$$
$$x = 30 + 5$$
$$x = 35$$

2. In order to move the denominator of a fraction to the other side, multiply the term on the other side, and in order to move one term of a product to the other side, you divide it into the term on the other side. Thus,

$$\frac{x}{5} = 4$$
$$x = 4 \times 5$$
$$x = 20$$

and

$$4 \times x = 20$$
$$x = \frac{20}{4}$$
$$x = 5$$

These simple rules won't tell you what to do with complicated expressions, but if you understand them, you should have no trouble learning to deal with the rules that tell you how to decompose complicated expressions and treat the simple terms the way we did the ones above.

POWERS, ROOTS, AND LOGARITHMS

As recently as ten years ago, every serious student of the physical sciences or engineering had to have two things: (1) a slide rule and (2) a book of mathematical tables. He or she needed the book of mathematical tables for many purposes, for example, to look up powers, roots, and logarithms. The slide rule also served a lot of purposes—most commonly, to do multiplication and division. In doing multiplication and division, the slide rule made use of the principle of logarithms.

The slide rule is now an antique, and the book of mathematical tables is much less often used than formerly. The reason is the development of the hand calculator. A good calculator will enable you to calculate any power, any root, any logarithm, either to the natural or decimal base, and lots besides. But even if you don't have to learn how to use a slide rule or a book of tables, you still must know what the concepts mentioned above are to be able to understand quantitative ideas in science. Many of the quantitative results in modern science are written in something called the *scientific notation*, and that is based upon powers and logarithms.

The power of a number results from multiplying the number by itself. Thus 3×3, or 9, is a power of 3. It happens to be the second power of 3 because there are *two* numbers, 3 and 3, that are multiplied together. Usually we call the second power of a number its square. So 3×3, or 9, is the square of 3. We can write it this way: 3^2. The number on the right, called the exponent, tells the number of terms multiplied. Thus, in addition to 3^2 we can have 3^3. That number, 3^3, tells us that there are three numbers multiplied together—$3 \times 3 \times 3$. The result of 3^3 is 27 (3×3 is 9, and 9×3 is 27). The third power of a number is called the cube. Higher powers don't have special names. Thus, 3^5 is just that, $3 \times 3 \times 3 \times 3 \times 3$, or 243. Powers very quickly become big numbers. The tenth power of 2, 2^{10}, is 1,024, and just two powers higher, 2^{12}, is 4,096. Scientific notation is useful with very big numbers. Instead of writing out 120,000,000,000, we can say it is 1.2×10^{11}, or $1.2 \times 100,000,000,000$. Your astronomy professor might say, "The sun is on the order of magnitude of 9.3×10^7 miles from earth." You would know that the sun is 93 million miles away.

Roots, in a sense, are the opposite of powers. The square root of 9 is 3. So a root is the number you need to multiply by itself to get the number you started with ($3 \times 3 = 9$). The square root of a number is most often written as $\sqrt{9} = 3$. You can also have cube and higher roots. Thus, the cube root of 27, written as $\sqrt[3]{27}$, is 3. Calculating roots is not so easy as it sounds, and most of us older folks learned to calculate them by clumsy approximation methods. Nowadays, however, all but the very cheapest hand calculators have a square root button, and the more expensive calculators have a button for computing any root (it is generally identified by $\sqrt[x]{y}$.

What are logarithms? Logarithms are special kinds of powers. There are two kinds, decimal logarithms and natural logarithms. Natural logarithms are important mathematically, but students who are not going to be mathematics or science majors are not likely to encounter them. Almost any student, however, is likely to encounter decimal logarithms. Decimal logarithms are basically powers of the number 10. Thus, the second power of 10 (10^2) is 100, and in logarithmic terms it is called log 2. The third power of 10 is log 3, and it is 1,000. If you think about it a bit, you will see that the logarithm, or power of 10, is simply the number of zeros when the number is written in ordinary notation. Thus, 100,000,000,000 is log 11.

To write the number 314,000,000,000 in the scientific notation, you separate it into two parts: first, you write 3.14, and second, you multiply it by 10^{11}. Thus 314,000,000,000 equals 3.14×10^{11}, or $3.14 \times$ log 11. But logarithms have other uses than just to represent very large numbers that we might want to express as orders of magnitude without being very precise. They can be used to represent and do calculations with more complicated large numbers, such as 5,011,872. That number can be represented as $10^{6.7}$. To put it another way, 5,011,872 equals log 6.7.

Now when you see a number like $10^{3.2}$ or log 3.2, you will know that it is simply another way of writing an ordinary number, in this case, 1,584.89. How do we get from $10^{3.2}$ to 1,584.89 or from $10^{6.7}$ to 5,011,872? Until recently, we had to rely on published tables of logarithms to do that. But nowadays, all scientific hand calculators have keys for doing the necessary calculation. The key for going from log notation to ordinary notation is simply marked 10^x, while the key for going from ordinary notation to logarithms is marked log.

In any event, you should not simply panic when you see something like log 3.476 or an expression like $10^{3.476}$. You now know that it is another way of writing the kind of numbers you have been used to dealing with all along.

Other Mathematical Functions. We have only scratched the surface of the kinds of mathematical problems you will encounter if you take anything but the most elementary kind of mathematics or science course. There is, for example, a whole family of important mathematical functions called the trigonometric functions. We haven't described these because they are more likely to be found in engineering and science courses than in the kind of courses you are probably taking if you need to read this section carefully. But they're not difficult to understand. They are just like most things in mathematics, a matter of careful study.

WATCHING NOTATION

All mathematics, in principle, consists of simple, easy steps. A lot of knowing how to deal with it consists of learning how to decompose complicated operations into those easy steps. That is why learning how to set up problems properly is so important.

Another aspect of learning how to get those operations into the proper steps is to master the notation. A basic rule in dealing with mathematics in particular and the sciences in general is, *Know exactly what each symbol stands for.* If you're not sure, you are in trouble. Any time you have the least doubt, check the textbook or ask. Also, while mathematics itself is precise and unambiguous, the notation or system of symbols used in it is not. You can be pretty sure what π means, but a symbol such as σ or λ has several different meanings, which will vary from use to use. Also, different mathematical symbols may be used for the same thing by different authorities. Make sure you know how a symbol is being used in the context of the particular course you are taking or the particular book you are reading.

TALKING TO COMPUTERS

Closely allied to mathematics and, in fact, a special branch of it, is computer science. Like all mathematics, computer science is based upon exact and unbending logic. And thereby lies the trouble some people have with computers. They expect a computer to understand them even when they are not being precise and logical. After all, other people do so, so why shouldn't computers? But computers only understand things that are said in just the right way to them, and they can only perform by rigidly logical operations.

More and more often, students find that certain courses in sciences, even elementary courses, require that problems be done on a computer. Students sometimes try to skip these assignments because getting access to the computer terminal is hard, because they are afraid of the special language they must use to talk to computers, or even because they are afraid of punching the wrong keys on the terminal.

But computer languages are not all that difficult. They are really simplified versions of English, simplified in such a way that all the ambiguities and illogical aspects of ordinary English are removed. You have to be precise and efficient when communicating with computers, and in the main, that is what computer languages are designed for. Some of them, it is true, have special purposes, but the more common ones— the ones most students are likely to encounter—are simply designed for efficiency and precision in programming computers. Furthermore, it is not that hard to deal with mistakes in punching keys on the terminal. If you know how, it is easy to erase them and start over.

The easiest computer language is called BASIC. It is easiest because it is most like English. The most widely used language is FORTRAN (FORmula TRANslator). It is designed for the greatest flexibility. Learning one or more of these languages is not especially difficult, and learning how to use them in programming problems for computers does not demand extraordinary mathematical skills or abilities. People with quite modest backgrounds in mathematics often become skilled computer programmers. Whether you yourself learn how to program or not, you should learn enough about computers and how to deal with them to enable you to use canned or predesigned programs.

As you probably know, computers are used to deal with many situations not traditionally associated with mathematics and science. Their use in business is almost endless. They keep track of payroll, of personnel files, of inventories, of orders, and they do accounting, economic forecasting, and budgeting. They design traffic systems, run assembly lines, and monitor the flow of electric power over vast reaches of the country.

If you have a talent for planning things in small, logical steps, and for designing orderly routines, you might like working with computers. If you are to be a serious student of computer science in all its reaches, you must master quite a bit of mathematics and in particular a branch of mathematical logic called Boolean algebra. Most computers work by having the flow of tiny amounts of electric current obey the laws of Boolean algebra. But you needn't understand how computers work in detail in order to make use of them. In the modern world, a phobia about computers is just as crippling as a phobia about mathematics itself.

STUDYING THE SCIENCES

As most of you know, there are natural and social sciences. The natural sciences study nature (e.g., physics, astronomy, chemistry, geology, biology), and the social sciences study humanity and its relation to nature (e.g., sociology, economics, political science, anthropology). Psychology is both a natural and a social science. In its biological aspects it is a natural science, and in other aspects it is a social science.

Science is basically a matter of solving problems in order to increase knowledge. Sometimes it begins with the collection of facts and then goes from there to the building of theories which summarize and interrelate those facts. At other times it begins with theories and then goes to the collection of facts in order to find out whether the theories are right or not.

All stages of science depend upon problem solving. Collecting facts requires us to be clever in devising methods for so doing. Thinking up theories, refining them and finding ways to test them also requires problem solving. And solving practical problems by applying science is, by definition, problem solving.

Different sciences go about solving problems in different ways. Physics and certain branches of engineering rely most heavily upon mathematics. Chemistry, while increasingly mathematical, still relies more upon models or pictures of atomic and molecular relations. And almost all the natural sciences tend to make more use of mathematics than do the social sciences, though once again there are important exceptions.

It should be apparent by now that many of the things we said about the study of mathematics also apply to the study of the sciences. In both mathematics and science *understanding* is more important than the learning of particular facts or the memorizing of particular formulas. In many of your science courses you will be given sets of problems that are very much like the sets of problems you get in courses in mathematics. But there are, nevertheless, a few things that are unique to sciences.

SCIENTIFIC LANGUAGE

All sciences make use of technical language. Sometimes it is a matter of giving a highly restricted and particular definition to a common word. For example, in introductory physics you learn to define the word *force* by an equation: Force = mass × acceleration. All the other meanings of force that you use in your daily life are irrelevant, and you must learn to forget them when you go into physics class. At other times, sciences invent special terms to describe theories, facts, and principles. For example, if you take a course in atomic physics, you will learn about things such as quarks and mesons.

Scientific language is meant to be more precise than ordinary language. That is why so many strange terms are invented—to avoid confusion with ordinary meanings. Unlike learning ordinary words, scientific words cannot be easily learned from context. You will be required to read and understand precise definitions of terms. Usually in textbooks on science, technical terms are defined the first time they are introduced. If you somehow miss such a definition and find yourself lost, look in the index for the first reference to the term. The chances are overwhelming that a definition will accompany it. If it doesn't occur there, look up the other references to the term. Occasionally the writer of a scientific text will not define some particular term because he or she assumes that you will have learned it in a more elementary course.

Despite the fact that you can rarely determine scientific meanings accurately from context, you can use devices such as 3×5 cards to improve your scientific vocabulary.

A special word about words in psychology and the social sciences is in order. Many of the terms you will encounter in these subjects will be like the word "force" in physics, familiar to you already. But beware. In physics you are likely to be aware that ordinary words are used in special senses. But in psychology or economics, you may assume that you know about the word already, for you already know a lot about people and money. But you will find that the psychologist or economist will use a familiar word, just as will the physicist, in a highly restricted way, and he or she will expect you to use the word that way too.

LABORATORY WORK

Most elementary science courses have laboratories, and many colleges and universities require students to take at least one laboratory course. Laboratory courses are all designed to show you how to go about doing science, but different ones emphasize one or more special features. Physics labs, for example, often stress precise measurement, chemistry labs traditionally emphasize careful procedures, and old-fashioned biology labs require detailed observation. All, however, are designed to demonstrate the scientific method and illustrate how to draw inferences from observation and experimentation.

Because the kinds of experiments and observations you will do in lab have been done by thousands, indeed millions, of students before, there is a tendency to regard them as mechanical chores to be gotten through as painlessly as possible. Try to avoid that view. Many of the experiments you will do are repetitions of fundamental discoveries in science. Try to put yourself in the position of the person who first made those observations.

Needless to say, you should be careful and accurate in making measurements and recording data. Check all your calculations for accuracy. Keep a full record of everything you do. If you have a workbook, keep it neat. By and large scientists are neat, at least about

their science, and a sloppy workbook is going to be looked down upon by a laboratory instructor. You will usually be given a set organization by which to report the results of your experiments. Hold to it strictly. Scientists set great store by orderly procedures, and if you follow the rules both in the conduct of laboratory experiments and the reporting of them, you will be getting into the habitual ways of doing things in that particular science.

READING SCIENCE TEXTS

In Chapter 4 we said that different subjects require different strategies in reading. In this section we will say a few things about reading from scientific texts.

Problems. One of the characteristics of scientific texts is that examples and problems are worked out for you in the text itself. Don't just read these. Even if you think you understand, if you only read you may skip over some crucial step that you really don't follow. Work the problem out yourself just as it is presented in the text. That way you will really know if you know how to do each step. If you can get the same answer at each step as that given in the textbook, the chances are you know how to do all the operations. Occasionally in introductory texts in science and engineering the obvious steps in some mathematical derivation are skipped. But when you do the problem, don't skip. Make sure you know all the intervening steps that the author did not bother to include, particularly if you are new to the field.

Graphs and Diagrams. Another characteristic of scientific texts is that they are full of diagrams and graphs. These aren't just decorative devices used to break up pages of solid print. They are usually essential to an understanding of the text. Be sure to read them and to make sure that you understand every aspect of them.

Graphs are among the most common kinds of illustrations found in scientific texts. Graphs are found in books in economics, psychology, physics, engineering, chemistry, biology—in fact, in all the natural and social sciences. Most graphs show the relation between two variables. These are represented by numbers on the vertical axis and the horizontal axis of the graph respectively. The vertical axis is sometimes called the y-axis and the horizontal axis the x-axis. A line or curve on the graph shows you each value of y that corresponds to a particular value of x. The line works exactly like an equation. It will give you the same result as substituting for x or y in an equation. For example, the straight line in the illustration labeled "Reading a

Graph" (below) corresponds to the equation $y = 0 + 0.5x$. If you substitute 4 for x, then $y = 2$.

In scientific graphs the x-axis is customarily the independent variable and the y-axis the dependent variable. The independent variable is usually the known, the quantity that the experimenter varies, while the dependent variable is the unknown, the quantity that depends upon the independent variable.

One of the most elementary experiments in physics is to measure the time it takes a steel ball to pass successive distances when it rolls down an inclined plane. The successive distances are the independent variable, and the time that it takes the ball to get from one distance to the next is the dependent variable. This experiment, which is done in thousands of high school and college physics labs each year, is like the original observations Galileo made on the effects of gravity. If you do the experiment, you will find that time increases as the square of the distance already traveled. If you were to make a graph of the result it would look like the line for the equation $y = 2 + 0.5x^2$ in "Reading a Graph."

Not all diagrams are graphs. Instead, some illustrate spatial relations or such abstract relations as the direction in space of a force applied to a body. If you have studied physics, you will recognize such diagrams as illustrating vectors and vector addition.

The term "vector" scares a lot of students, but it shouldn't. It is just a way of saying that forces differ in magnitude and direction. If you give a book a light shove toward the center of your desk, it will travel a short distance. You would represent that by a short line pointing to the middle of the desk. If you give the same book a hard shove, it may travel to the edge of the desk. You would represent that by a longer line reaching from where you shoved the book to the edge of the desk. These lines would be vectors.

Diagrams that illustrate how things work are probably even more common in the natural sciences. Examine these in every detail. Be sure to compare the labels with the information in the caption or legend for the illustration. Even photographs can be important in scientific texts. Whatever you do, treat all the material in a scientific text as worthy of study. It is

READING A GRAPH

Each line represents an equation. For any given equation, you can find the value of y that corresponds to any given value of x. The straight line represents the equation y = 0 + 0.5x, and the curved line represents the equation y = 2 + 0.5x².

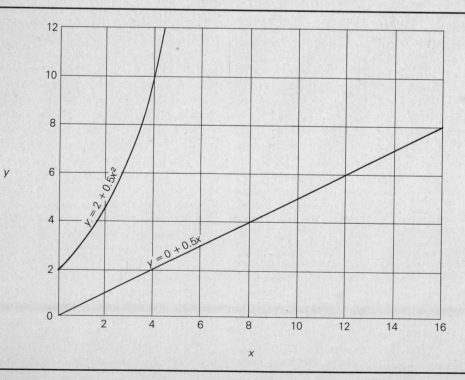

READING A TABLE

Value of y for different values of x in different equations.

| x | $y = a + bx$ | | $y = x^2$ | $y = \log x$ |
	$a = 2; b = 1/2$	$a = 3; b = 1/3$		
0.00	2.00	3.00	0.00	$-\infty$
1.00	2.50	3.33	1.00	0.000
2.00	3.00	3.67	4.00	0.301
3.00	3.50	4.00	9.00	0.477
4.00	4.00	4.33	16.00	0.602
5.00	4.50	4.67	25.00	0.699
6.00	5.00	5.00	36.00	0.778
7.00	5.50	5.33	49.00	0.845
8.00	6.00	5.67	64.00	0.903
9.00	6.50	6.00	81.00	0.954
10.00	7.00	6.33	100.00	1.000
11.00	7.50	6.67	121.00	1.041
12.00	8.00	7.00	144.00	1.079
13.00	8.50	7.33	169.00	1.114
14.00	9.00	7.67	196.00	1.146
15.00	9.50	8.00	225.00	1.176
16.00	10.00	8.33	256.00	1.204

often a good idea to sketch out diagrams yourself, just to make sure you haven't missed something.

Tables. Students sometimes want to skip tables because they are dull and often hard to read. Don't. The information that is in a table is important. Very often a table will say much the same thing a graph says. Instead of the x- and the y-axis, you will find numbers listed in parallel columns corresponding to the x and y variables. Each x value corresponds to the y value opposite it. On this page, you will find an exercise in reading simple numerical tables. Make sure that you understand how to read this table. If you can't follow it, you will have trouble with almost any scientific course.

Sometimes it helps to translate part or all of a table into a graph. Usually the equation relating the various parts of a table will not be given. You can see, however, what the relation looks like at a glance by plotting on graph paper a point for every pair of x and y values in the table and then connecting the points together. Often you will be required to do just that with the results from your laboratory experiments. Your results will consist of pairs of x and y values, which you will first list in a table and then use to construct a graph. You will sometimes be asked to draw a smooth curve through the points. A smooth curve doesn't exactly

cross through every point, but it expresses the mathematical relation among the points.

Special Sections in Science Texts. Nowadays science texts, particularly elementary texts, will be more than solid pages of type broken up by headings and containing illustrations and graphs. In addition there will be special sections of text set off in boxes. Some parts of the text may even be set in a different size or style of type, or even printed in a different color. The purpose is to segregate special material or material illustrating and amplifying rather than explaining. Be sure to read these. Do so even if the material is not likely to turn up on the examination. You will have a better understanding of the acceleration of motion in falling bodies, for example, if you read a historical account of just how Galileo did and reported his experiments. Even if Galileo is never mentioned in the examination, reading that account will serve to impress the experiment upon your mind, and it will add a little human interest.

THE METRIC SYSTEM

If you take any course in the sciences, you will have to forget about feet, yards, quarts, and gallons and begin to think about centimeters, liters, and grams.

The United States is one of the few places left in the world that does not use the metric system. Science, however, is an international enterprise, and American scientists, like all others, always have presented their results in metric measures.

Even though the metric system may be unfamiliar to you, once you work with it, you will see its advantages. If you have a board that is two feet and seven inches and another one that is three feet and nine inches and you want to know how long they would be together, you would have to add the feet and inches separately and then convert the sixteen inches to one additional foot with four inches left over.

The trouble is that we do our arithmetic in a decimal system and feet come in units of twelve inches (while yards come in units of three feet). Pounds come in units of sixteen ounces and gallons in units of four quarts. So there is no order to the system at all. The metric system is entirely in decimal units. One hundred centimeters make a meter, and there are ten millimeters to a centimeter. A kilometer is 1,000 meters. The result is that you can convert from meters to kilometers, or meters to millimeters just by moving a decimal point.

Your only problem is to learn to think in these units rather than in the familiar feet, yards, ounces, and pounds. Taking a course in science will help you do this, and since the United States is committed to making the metric system official in the near future, you will have to learn to think metric eventually anyway. Just having the experience of expressing results in the metric system will make it easier for you. Initially, you may want some help from the British system (as our system is generally called). It is like learning to think in a foreign language. You have to go through an initial period of translating. We have provided a conversion table for you below, and this will help you in the translation process. But as soon as you can, get to the point at which you think directly in the metric system.

A CONCLUDING WORD

What we have said here touches only the most elementary aspects of science. In fact, except for the tips on how to read texts and how to study for exams, there is nothing here than an average tenth grader who has had a little science and math does not know. Yet some of you will be puzzled by what you read here. If you don't understand, don't let it go by. Don't put it down to being "dumb in math" or "having no head for science." The chances are that you missed learning something that is essential—just being home sick a couple of weeks while in the seventh grade could have done it.

Some of you, for example, may have been puzzled by the discussion of graphs a few pages back. That may be because no one ever showed you how to relate the numbers on the axes (you may not even know what axes are) to the points and lines on the graph. Don't take it lying down. You don't *need to be* illiterate in science and math. If necessary, get someone to help you. Many institutions run special remedial programs in math. If you are deficient, and your institution has such a program, the sooner you get into it the better off you will be.

Many students get anxious about math because it seems to go so fast and so much over their heads. Once again, being anxious about math is not necessary. It is something you can get over if you go about it in the right way. Once again, many colleges run "math anxiety clinics," the purpose of which is not so much to cram a lot of mathematics into you as it is to get you to think about mathematics in such a way that you can be relaxed about it. Math anxiety is something that is curable, and given the importance of mathematics, it is something you ought to work at to get over.

CONVERTING TO THE METRIC SYSTEM

Here are the metric equivalents of some of the more common British units.

1 inch	= 2.5400 centimeters	1 centimeter	= 0.3937 inch
1 foot	= 0.3048 meter	1 meter	= 3.2808 feet
1 yard	= 0.9144 meter	1 meter	= 1.0936 yards
1 mile	= 1.6093 kilometers	1 kilometer	= 0.6214 mile
1 quart	= 0.9464 liter	1 liter	= 1.0567 quarts
1 gallon	= 3.7854 liters	1 liter	= 0.2642 gallon
1 ounce	= 28.3495 grams	1 gram	= 0.0353 ounce
1 pound	= 0.4536 kilogram	1 kilogram	= 2.2046 pounds

We have tried to show you how to become a better student by improving your classroom skills and learning how to study textbooks and write papers more effectively. There are other resources available to you, some of which may be recommended by your instructors and some of which you will have to seek out for yourself. Furthermore, there are some things you can do to improve the quality of your life in college.

USING STUDY AIDS EFFECTIVELY

WORKBOOKS AND OUTLINES

Workbooks sometimes accompany textbooks assigned in college courses. These typically include special projects and exercises which illustrate and explain the textbook, review questions, and self-test items that provide practice for examinations. The authors of workbooks try to present material in a way that will interest you and help you to study effectively.

Sometimes instructors require the workbook; in other cases they will recommend it but not require it. Even if your instructor doesn't mention a workbook at all, you would do well to find out if one does accompany the textbook. Usually, the preface to the text will tell you whether or not there is a workbook or manual. If you can, look at the workbook to see if you think it will be useful to you. Almost all workbooks are of some value, and some will help you enormously.

Subject outlines are also sometimes useful. In most college bookstores you will find some paperback books with titles like *Outline of Chemistry, Outline of European History,* etc. One or more outlines are published for each introductory course and some for more advanced courses. These outlines are just what their name implies. They give the bare essentials without extended explanations, illustrations, and details.

Because not all courses with a given title are the same, an outline may not correspond to the content of your particular course. You should check before buying one. Perhaps the best use for an outline is to review a more elementary subject. Sometime you may want to take a course for which you have not had the proper prerequisite. In that case, an outline provides you with a very efficient way of correcting your deficiency.

OUTSIDE READINGS

Textbooks and workbooks usually make up most of the reading for introductory courses. In advanced courses and in a few introductory courses, instructors assign outside readings or recommend them.

Many students don't bother with these outside

CHAPTER TEN

GETTING HELP

readings unless they are required. That is too bad, because it is things like outside reading that give depth to your education. Outside readings help you better to understand your textbook, and they give you a different perspective on the subject. In the humanities, outside readings provide the real essentials. To read about Plato in a textbook on the history of philosophy is only an introduction to Plato himself. Finally, outside readings can make study more satisfying and arouse your curiosity. They help you to decide what things you want to study on your own.

Journals and periodicals of all kinds provide another perspective for your courses. For courses in commerce and management, the *Wall Street Journal* and *Business Week* provide background. For students of science, *Scientific American* and the *American Scientist* are interesting. If you are studying literature, one of several quarterly reviews will offer you current criticism as well as fiction and poetry.

FILMS

Motion pictures and videotapes are often used as teaching aids. They combine the best features of a teacher's explanation with the visual presentation of things that cannot be brought into the classroom in any other way.

Instructional films are often entertaining, and thereby lies the problem. Students sit back and relax when a film is being shown. But if the film is a good and useful one, it must be studied as carefully as a textbook or class notes. Pay attention to what your instructor says about the film. Take notes if you can. Repeat new technical terms to yourself as they occur. Recite the important points the film makes. Look for the main ideas. Because a film moves fast, it is important that you jot down all the main points as soon as the film is over, or you will forget them.

TV INSTRUCTION

At many colleges and universities segments of courses and sometimes entire courses are videotaped and shown on closed-circuit TV. You may not like the idea, because TV is an impersonal teacher. But the kinds of things taught on TV would be impersonally taught in a big lecture anyway. And compared with the conventional lecture, TV has some advantages. Demonstrations can be seen much more clearly than they could be seen in the lecture hall. TV tapes are usually very well prepared. The presentation is usually much better than in the typical lecture. Finally, an instructor is usually present in the classroom when TV teaching is done, and since the tapes are typically shown to small groups, you can ask questions.

There is little difference between what you do in a course taught by TV and a conventional one. You do need to remember that TV courses, like films, generally move faster than conventional lectures. Be especially careful to take notes rapidly and carefully. Because TV lessons are generally well organized, it will probably be easier to take notes in outline form or something close to it.

PROGRAMMED TEXTS AND SELF-PACED COURSES

Programmed learning was developed in connection with teaching machines. Although teaching machines still are not widely used, programmed instruction has been adapted to textbooks, and it is widely employed. Programmed texts are available for nearly all the basic courses in college.

Programmed texts are a way of getting you to teach yourself in small, carefully planned steps. Often they consist of sets of questions and answers with varying amounts of illustrative material. In all cases, their format provides some way of keeping the answer to a question or the word that completes a phrase out of sight while the student thinks of an answer. But the answer is immediately available so that a mistake can be corrected. In some institutions whole courses are programmed and self-paced. In such a course, by working intensively, a student can do a whole semester's work in a couple of weeks. Where teaching machines are available and linked to a computer, the student can interact with the program—ask it questions and try different alternatives.

The advantages of programmed instruction are (1) it provides you with immediate testing and the opportunity for correction, and (2) it allows you to go at a pace suited to your own temperament, intelligence, and level of preparation. Some programs are designed to be "error-free"; that is to say, the material is broken down into such small steps that you almost never get a question wrong.

The disadvantage of programmed learning is that many students, particularly bright ones, find programmed texts to be boring and frustrating. Their standard format of having questions or statements presented over and over in the simplest possible way makes learning seem to be repetitive. If you have this reaction to programmed texts, we suggest that to combat it you distribute your study time as much as possible. Spend twenty or thirty minutes on a fair-sized segment of the program, rest briefly, review the segment, take another rest, and then turn to something else. After you have studied another subject, come back to the programmed text and tackle another segment.

Although programmed texts have been constructed

to teach all sorts of subjects, they are best at teaching facts and skills rather than things you have to think about. If you are poor at things such as spelling, arithmetic, grammar, etc., you should look for a programmed book on the subject. Because it corrects your specific mistakes and makes you respond to everything, you will get more out of it than working from a standard book. One of the best ways to learn a computer language and how to program a computer is to use a programmed text.

Often programmed texts are used to supplement conventional textbooks and lectures, In fact, many workbooks that accompany textbooks are in the format of a program. If you are assigned a programmed text in a course, use it as an aid to recitation, not as a substitute for the methods of study we have described in earlier chapters. Continue to take notes in class and from your reading. However, much of the time you would have spent in recitation with your notes can be spent with the programmed text.

TEST FILES

All sorts of student organizations maintain test files. Sororities, fraternities, dormitories, and student cooperatives all keep files that contain old examinations and often old course outlines, notes, and even term papers. Some colleges and individual instructors arrange for files of old exams to be placed on reserve in the library so that they will be available to all students.

How useful are these files? Not as much as students think, especially if they are used as a crutch and substitute for good work habits. Old tests may give you an idea of what some professor's exam will be like. Or you can see how someone else organized the course, and you can see what some other student thought important enough to write down. Old term papers can help you get ideas for papers and tell you how they should be written.

Beyond these uses, however, files are of little value. Most professors change their courses, the reading assignments, and their lectures every year. Instructors who use objective questions usually draw these from a large pool of questions so that only a small percentage will be the same for any two exams. To use files of old exams to predict what will happen on an exam is risky. It can mislead you into not studying something which you may need to know.

To use old course notes and outlines as a substitute for class attendance is also risky. You will never know what has changed. And old notes vary in quality. You don't really know how good the material is.

The worst thing about old files is that they encourage poor study habits. They tempt some students into dishonesty by turning in someone else's work as their own. Plagiarism is a serious offense in college, and you could easily be dismissed if you are caught using someone else's work.

That brings us to the subject of commercially sold term papers. Aside from the dishonesty of passing off someone else's work as your own, there can be unfortunate consequences to buying term papers. It is illegal in some states, and commercial term papers are generally easy to detect. But most of all, you are cheating mainly yourself by using them. The things you came to college for—to learn to think, to critically analyze ideas, and to learn how to express your own ideas—are lost if you let someone else do your work.

GETTING HELP FROM SPECIAL SOURCES

There are times when every student needs help from other people. Some of it is routine for all students—academic advising, for example. Some of it is needed by students who have particular difficulties. Every college and university is able to provide you with some help if you need it. The various services that exist for your benefit can often mean the difference between academic success and failure, not to mention the difference between personal satisfaction and unhappiness.

ACADEMIC ADVISING

Every school has its own system for helping students to choose courses, to decide on a major, to understand what they may and may not do under college rules. In many colleges, every student is assigned a faculty advisor. The advisor's duty is to help the student in all matters academic. How the relationship works out in practice depends upon both the student and the advisor.

First of all, you should do for yourself all that you can do. Read the catalog, consult the schedule, do the arithmetic to determine how many credits you will need to take each semester. When you have worked out a tentative schedule and thought about any questions you have, see your advisor. Remember that an advisor's job is to advise, not to make your decisions for you. Your advisor can give you information you can't get yourself and he or she can give you opinions, usually based on a lot of experience. But the choices are yours.

If you don't seem to get on well with your advisor, or he or she can't give you the advice you need, consult the academic dean. In most colleges and universities, the dean's office coordinates faculty advising, and in some institutions the dean's office itself bears the sole responsibility for advising. In that case, there will be a staff to do it.

Many students hesitate to see the dean about their academic problems. But in most institutions, the office of the dean exists to serve students and welcomes them. At some small colleges, you will probably get to know the dean personally. At large universities, there is usually a staff of associate and assistant deans whose primary job is to be completely accessible to students. So don't be bashful. Sometimes a problem that seems unsolvable can be quickly untangled by a visit to the dean's office.

This office is the best source for information about college rules and regulations. If you are uncertain about such things as the number of credits required for graduation, the number of pass/fail courses you can take, distributional requirements, and other such matters, go to the dean's office. Don't rely on the student grapevine for answers to questions about policy; as often as not, it's wrong.

Suppose you are working hard in one of your courses, but you just can't seem to master the material. What do you do?

The first step is to recognize your problem as soon as possible. Don't drift along hoping that things will take care of themselves. Don't wait for an F on the midterm to tell you what you knew well enough all along. As soon as you sense difficulties ask yourself the following questions: Am I adequately prepared for this course? Do other students seem to have the background for it that I lack? Is there some one thing that gives me trouble? Do I have difficulty with the terminology? With calculations, problems, or lab work? Do I have trouble getting all the reading done?

Your next step is to decide whether you can do something about your problem or whether you must think about dropping the course. At this point you should confer with the instructor. If you can say what your problem is, he or she may be able to tell you what you are doing wrong or locate some background material to remedy your deficiency. On the other hand, it may be that you have gotten yourself into a course that is too difficult for you. This can happen, for example, if you continue in a foreign language you started in high school or in another institution. Or you may have signed up for an advanced course without realizing that you lacked the background.

If you seek help early enough, you can either improve your work or you can drop the course and rearrange your program. It is not a good idea, however, to drop a course impulsively and without seeking the advice of your instructor and your faculty advisor. This is particularly true if the course is a required one for you. Most colleges ask that a student get approval from both the instructor and the advisor in order to drop a course, just to ensure that the student is taking a wise action.

Suppose that you have waited too long to drop the course without some kind of penalty. It is still not too late to confer with the instructor to see what you can do to retrieve the situation. If you're really interested in improving, instructors are almost always willing to show you what you have done wrong on an exam or a paper and what you should have done. Of course, you may not be able to do enough to avoid failing the course. Even so, you may have learned something about how to avoid similar difficulties in the future. A grade of F does not mean that you are a failure as a student. But you do have to learn something from your experience to avoid drifting into failing out of college.

COUNSELING SERVICES

Personal problems often get in the way of academic work. If you have personal worries or difficulties that make it hard for you to work, you ought to be able to tell these problems to your advisor or academic dean and look for help and guidance. Often, just stating your problem to someone helps, because doing so points the way to a solution. Or your advisor may be able to give you a word of wisdom. If, however, you have long-standing problems or problems that are too personal, the chances are that your faculty advisor or dean will have neither the time nor background to deal with them. In that case, he or she would probably refer you

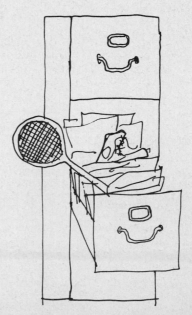

to the counseling center or to a qualified professional counselor in the community.

Most counseling centers are especially prepared to deal with the problems of young adults. Conflict with parents, development of a sense of identity, feelings of insecurity, interpersonal problems, sexual problems, and an inability to concentrate are examples of the sort of things counselors deal with every day.

If one of these problems or one like it bothers you, you are fairly typical. Almost everyone faces difficulties like these sometime between the ages of seventeen and twenty-five. And many people need the help of someone else to get through a difficult period.

In the long run, of course, you are the only one who can solve your own problems. A counselor cannot press a button and make them go away. But it does help to discuss them with an experienced counselor, who can often supply a different perspective that shows you how to solve them. It makes no sense to be miserable. If you feel depressed, anxious, or in some personal difficulty, by all means seek help without delay.

MEDICAL SERVICES

The college years tend not to be the healthiest years of a person's life. Poor eating habits, insufficient sleep, crowded and badly ventilated classrooms all contribute to a lowered resistance to infection. Minor respiratory diseases, stomach complaints, and mononucleosis are endemic on college campuses.

All residential colleges and many commuter colleges maintain some kind of student health service. These are usually prepared to deal with acute and not too serious illnesses. Any complaint that requires extensive diagnostic testing or hospitalization is likely to be referred to a local physician or hospital.

One of the most common student ailments is infectious mononucleosis, which often makes itself known with no more dramatic symptoms than chronic tiredness and lack of energy. Sometimes it is accompanied by a sore throat, elevated temperature, and swollen glands. If you find that you are tired all the time, consult one of the college physicians. It will probably turn out to be something that can best be cured by proper rest and a better diet, but it may be "mono" or one of the related virus diseases that will require bed rest and treatment.

Most student health services provide information about birth control, venereal disease, pregnancy, and abortion and make referrals when they are needed. College students who are sexually active should take the responsibility for not being faced with unwanted pregnancies and/or the possibility of abortion. The latter is a poor method of birth control, because it is expensive and emotionally and physically demanding. If you suspect that you have been exposed to or have contracted a venereal disease, get medical attention immediately. Without treatment, these diseases become harder to cure and may produce permanent damage.

TUTORIAL AND REMEDIAL SERVICES

If you are having trouble with a particular course, you can usually find someone to tutor you. Many colleges and universities maintain special tutorial services staffed by advanced undergraduates and/or graduate students. Typically tutoring will be available in basic subjects such as chemistry, biology, physics, mathematics, and foreign languages.

Some instructors schedule extra problem sessions for students who are having trouble with something in their courses. These sessions are usually held in the evening or late afternoon. Too often, the students who need the help most ignore it when it is offered. If you're finding the work in some course difficult, be sure to go to every extra-help session that is offered, even if you have to give up something else to do it.

Studying with other students for an examination is useful if done properly. Before you go into a review session with other students, you should have studied the material thoroughly by yourself. When the group first meets, it should plan what to do and set up an agenda. Each student can take a turn at summarizing important points. Don't get bogged down arguing about trivial points. Anything new that a student says ought to be checked for accuracy. Group studying can provide a good opportunity for oral recitation, and it allows students to correct one another's misunderstandings.

If you don't understand something in a course and you know another student who does understand that point, ask him or her to explain it to you. If, on the other hand, someone asks you for help on a point, take the time to go over it with her or him. Besides being a friendly thing to do, it will help you because it gives you a chance to recite what you know. There is no better way to learn a subject than to teach it to someone else.

Open enrollment is common at most community colleges, and there are a fair number of city and state universities that admit students who are capable of doing college work but who lack skill in reading, writing, and mathematics. Most of these schools provide a full range of remedial services, sometimes offered through noncredit courses in basic mathematics and English, sometimes through remedial centers where students can get personal tutoring.

Joe was a student who grew up as one of seven children in a poor family. His father, who had been an unskilled worker, died when Joe was ten. Although Joe liked school and did well, when he reached the eighth grade, he was advised by the school counselor to enter a vocational program in high school. A college preparatory program wasn't even a possibility. Joe did make it through high school, and he got a job as a mechanic in a neighborhood garage after he graduated. He was good at his work, and one day one of his customers said, "Joe, you're smart; you ought to be an engineer or something."

This casual remark set him thinking. He went to the public library and, with the help of the librarian, found some books and pamphlets about various careers in engineering. He discovered things that he had never even heard of before. The librarian suggested that Joe talk to someone at the local community college. The upshot was that two years after his high school graduation, Joe entered the college as a part-time student.

He was insecure and anxious, and the work was so much harder and more theoretical than he had imagined it would be that he was sure he would never make it. Fortunately, his college was prepared to meet his needs. He took three remedial courses during his first year: one in mathematics, one in reading, and one in composition. During his second year he made an A and B in chemistry and calculus, and he got enough financial aid to enable him to go full time. At the end of his third year at the community college, he applied for admission to the school of engineering at the state university. He was accepted.

Then he really had an adjustment to make. He was away from home for the first time, and he had to borrow money to make it. He was in a far more cosmopolitan environment than he had ever been in before. He had lived his entire life in a tight community in which all the parents were either immigrants or first-generation Americans and in which nearly all the people his age went into blue-collar jobs when they got out of school. What is more, he was taking professional courses for the first time, and he found them difficult.

He brought his problems to his advisor, who suggested that Joe take advantage of a new tutorial program that the school of engineering had set up. The result was that his first-semester grades were adequate, and his second-semester grades were good. Two years later, he received his bachelor's degree in electrical engineering.

A surprisingly large number of students have histories like Joe's. Where there is a willingness to supply remedial help, many people who otherwise could not make it manage to correct the deficiencies of their early education.

CAREER COUNSELING

If, like Joe, you are in a school of engineering, you have already made a tentative decision about your career. Students in liberal arts, on the other hand, may only have some vague idea about what they want to do. Failure of motivation is one of the things that is often a consequence of this uncertainty. Or it may produce a feeling of anxiety.

Even students who enter college thinking they know what they want to do, change their minds. Premedical students discover that medicine is not really for them. A student who enters college with some vague plan to apply to law school may discover that he or she really likes sociology or psychology. Such uncertainty and change are natural and to be expected. Students are learning new things about the world, and it is not surprising that they change or discover new interests.

Most colleges and universities maintain an office concerned with career planning and placement. Freshmen who have no idea how to focus their interests in order to choose a major are just as much the concern of such an office as seniors who know what they want to do and need to find a job to do it. The former need to assess their abilities, interests, values, priorities, and goals; the latter need to know how to prepare résumés and how to be interviewed. Students who intend to go on to graduate or professional school need to know what the admission requirements are and how to apply.

The typical career planning and placement office will help students deal with these questions; moreover, such offices usually keep permanent files for students who want to place letters of recommendation there from professors and deans for prospective employers.

If you don't know what you want to do and feel as though you ought to know, seek career counseling. Go as early in your college career as possible, because it will help you determine how far and in what direction your abilities and interests will permit you to go. Of all the students who enter college, only little more than half will finish with a bachelor's degree. Although many careers are open to people without college degrees, there are more available to college graduates. If you really want to enter an occupation requiring a degree and you are doing only marginal work, you will need to do something. You will have to improve your study habits. Failing that, you should seriously entertain the idea of a leave of absence.

If you decide on a college program that doesn't prepare you for what you eventually find out you want to do, you can always get yourself qualified if your original college record is a good one. Jill's case illustrates that.

An able student, Jill entered her state university with some vague idea of studying medicine. She took the premed chemistry course in her freshman year, and although she did reasonably well in it, she didn't really like it. She discovered the intellectual excitement of studying philosophy, and she enjoyed her literature and history courses. She finally decided to leave the sciences and concentrate on the humanities with a major in history.

Jill assumed that after graduation she would probably go to law school because she had heard that law schools had no specific course requirements other than a background in the liberal arts, high grades, and good LSAT scores. When she reached her senior year, however, she knew that she really didn't want to study law. She graduated with high honors, took a civil service exam, and got a job in the planning office of the suburban county where she had grown up. The job took hold, and after two years, she applied for graduate work in architecture. She had a talent for it, and in the summers she works in a prestigious firm of city planners. When she gets through her schooling in architecture, she will have a job in the firm and, what is more important, an occupation she genuinely likes.

Karen is a magna cum laude graduate of one of New England's best colleges with a major in English. Unsure of what she wanted to do, she worked for three years and came to the conclusion that she wanted a stable career that would provide her with a good income. She enrolled in an accounting course at night at a local university. She completed the program in accounting, passed the CPA exam, and is currently a member of the largest accounting firm in her hometown. She enjoys her job because it is challenging, provides opportunities for professional advancement, and provides her with the level of income that ensures the style of living she likes.

From medicine to architecture and city planning, from literature to accounting. People do find themselves. Cases like these of students who didn't discover until after graduation from college what they really wanted to be are fairly common. Equally common are instances of students who make poor beginnings but good endings. Ken was a mediocre high school student. He spent a year and a half at a local community college with his work going from bad to worse. Finally, he flunked out. He was drafted and sent to Vietnam. During the three years Ken spent in the army, much of it in combat service, his attitude toward things changed and his goals became clearer. As soon as he was discharged he enrolled once again in the community college. He did honors work in the liberal arts transfer program and transferred to a local university as a mathematics major. He is now a second-year law student at one of the country's best law schools.

The point we're making is if you don't yet know what you want to do or if you think that your past performance blew your chances of ever doing what you want to do, there is no need to be discouraged. Many people can and do make choices later, change their minds, and somehow find something they like.

TRANSFER STUDENT SERVICES

Today's college students are much more likely than students of even a decade ago to take their degree from a different institution than the one they entered. The existence of large numbers of community colleges providing only two years of study, the wish of many students to start their college careers in small places and then go on to large universities, and increased mobility generally have all acted to increase the frequency of transfers.

Students transfer for a variety of reasons. Sometimes it is a personal matter, and sometimes they just want a different kind of institution. The student who is in a two-year college and who wants a bachelor's degree has no choice.

If for some reason you are dissatisfied in your present situation or are in a community college and thinking about going on, be sure you plan your transfer very carefully. You will want advice on the pros and cons. Be very well acquainted with the institution to which you wish to transfer. You don't want to have to make another move.

Students who know why they are transferring and who know what to expect at the new institution do well. Few of them, however, are prepared for the magnitude of the adjustment they have to make. Very often transferring means facing severer academic demands in a more competitive atmosphere. It is not at all unusual for transfer students to see their grade point averages drop a full point in their first semester at the new institution. The student who transfers from a small college to a large university has to face bigger classes and a more impersonal atmosphere. Transfer students have to make new friends and establish new associations. This is not always easy to do at large universities, especially if the student doesn't live in a dormitory or residence hall. The problem of overcoming social isolation is one of the biggest problems transfer students face.

Most colleges and universities that expect transfer students in any numbers recognize the potential for difficulties and provide support services for transfer students. There is usually a special orientation program for new transfers. The orientation program includes social gatherings along with academic orientation. Transfer students can get to know one another and become acquainted with student government officers.

Some schools arrange for student volunteers to meet individually with transfer students and to be available on a friend-to-friend basis to answer questions and provide introductions.

If you are or will be a new transfer student, take advantage of all the programs designed to make your adjustment easier and more rapid. Don't, however, expect everything to be done for you. Take the initiative yourself. Be sure you confer with your faculty advisor. Look into special-interest groups and organizations. If you're having problems, the worst thing you can do is sit alone in your room and feel sorry for yourself. Get help. And remember that although many transfer students do experience some difficulties, these are usually temporary. An overwhelming majority turn out to be happy about their decision to transfer, and by the time they graduate they feel as much a part of the school as any student who entered as a freshman.

OLDER STUDENTS IN COLLEGE

There was a time when nearly everybody in college was between seventeen and twenty-two years of age. Beginning with the college generation after World War II when older veterans returned to their studies, the number of older people entering college for the first time and returning to complete a degree after many years has increased steadily.

If you are an older student, you have one big advantage over your younger fellow students—maturity. You know who you are and where you are going. The kinds of problems that are common to young adults you have already solved. This leaves you free to apply your energy to intellectual pursuits. It makes it possible for you to enjoy learning in a way that young people cannot always manage.

Some older people hesitate to return to school because they think that they have forgotten their academic skills, and they are afraid that they will not be able to compete with active, alert young minds. The large number of highly successful older students testifies that it just isn't so. Rusty skills are soon polished; quick minds that seem to be dull from disuse revive rapidly when they meet interesting and challenging ideas. And wisdom brings tremendous assets to the classroom.

Flora Wilson had two years at a posh women's college thirty years ago. She married at the end of her second year, and she settled into being a full-time homemaker, caring for four children. Through PTA activities she got interested in community affairs. By the time her last child had left home, she was a respected civic leader with an important role in local and state politics. Despite all this, she felt the lack of a college degree. After a lot of thought and a good deal of uncertainty and with plenty of encouragement from her family and friends, she returned to college. Although she was well into her fifties, she was accepted by a very strong local university, and she was able to get nearly all her earlier credits transferred. Perhaps she worked a little harder at first than she needed to, but she enjoyed it, and she got to know a lot of young people, some of whom came to visit her house on a regular basis. When she graduated two years later, she promptly got a job on the staff of an important local politician, and she is thoroughly engrossed in her interesting work.

When John Kovacks attended college for two years in the 1950s, he hadn't been terribly interested in academic work, and his grades were only mediocre. He dropped out and went to work in a bank. A renewed religious commitment led him to question what he was doing. He wanted to be a social worker, an occupation that he thought would let him be of service to people who needed help. He was married and had two teenage sons to support. Nevertheless, by relying on his wife's income as a teacher, by cutting out luxuries, and by taking out a second mortgage, Mr. Kovacks got through two years of college and two years in a master's program for social workers. He is now doing family counseling for a social agency, and he feels happier and more useful than he has ever felt before.

You don't have to want to change occupations to go back. Frank Seidman had two years in the local university—one with a strong national reputation. After the war he entered the brokerage business and was both prosperous and happy. But he wanted his college degree. He went back to the evening division of the university and got his degree in the same year that his daughter went off to college. An acquaintance of his, a Harvard graduate, president of a bank, and a member of the university's board of trustees, went back at the same time to get a master's degree in the evening division.

Betty Little got married before she even finished high school. She and her husband had three children. Somehow, she managed to work part-time and take care of the children while her husband finished his education. When he got his bachelor's degree he said, "Betty, now it's your turn." She made up her high school deficiencies and enrolled in a nearby university as a freshman. She was twenty-eight years old with three children under ten. It wasn't easy for her; the demands on her time were horrendous. But she was well organized and energetic, and above all, she was delighted with her courses. As soon as she gets her degree, her husband will start work on a Ph.D. in education. And the longer she stays in school, the more convinced she is that she too would like to go on to graduate work eventually.

These instances are typical of the experience of older students. Problems? Yes. Insurmountable problems? Sometimes, but not often. Most colleges and universities recognize the needs of older students. One or two private colleges have decided to specialize in providing educational opportunities for people in their middle years, particularly for women who want to return to the job market. Institutions are recognizing that it is necessary to be more flexible with older students. The scheduling needs of older students are often complex. The result is that they need more help in problem solving than younger students, though they don't need the advice and counseling so much. If you are an older student returning to college, be sure you find someone who can help you solve problems and bend the bureaucratic rules.

MAKING A GOOD PERSONAL ADJUSTMENT

The college years are one of the major transitional periods in a person's life. On top of new academic and personal adjustments, students are aware that in a very short time, they will be on their own. The world outside of the academic walls can seem threatening. Jobs for college graduates are no longer as plentiful as they once were. Professions are becoming overcrowded. Statisticians tell us that in the near future, not every college graduate will be able to find employment geared to his or her education. And in the background are all those problems of inflation, recession, chronic international crises, energy shortages, and the many stubborn social problems over which people feel they have little control.

Though students love their college years and look back on them with warm memories, they also find the period to be one of the most difficult of their lives. There is no simple formula for getting you through the adjustment problems you may have, but there are some good principles, most of them common sense, that may help you.

1. *Be Realistic.* One of the most obvious characteristics of well-adjusted persons is that they are realistic about most things. They understand their own motives, they set reasonable goals for themselves, and they know how to avoid unnecessary trouble. Find out what you can reasonably expect to achieve and adjust your efforts and goals to what you know. Don't underestimate yourself. If you make mediocre grades, determine whether it is because you

have a real struggle understanding, because you haven't had the right background, or because you just can't get into things academic. But don't overestimate either. Don't set a goal of becoming a doctor if you are a mediocre student with average work habits and limited financial resources. You might make it if you have excellent work habits, even though your abilities are limited, and sufficient money, or you might make it if you have great ability, good work habits, and no money. The point is, be realistic and know yourself and your circumstances.

Face your personal problems as objectively as you can. Sometimes your friends can be more objective about you than you can be yourself, but you may put them on the spot. They may not want to hurt your feelings. But it is better to talk to your friends about something that is bothering you than to keep it to yourself. Your advisor, or a professional counselor, may help. Beyond that, most campuses abound with groups that offer peer counseling about special problems, such as sexuality or drugs. A peer counselor is a responsible fellow student who can be more objective about your problems than you or your friends.

2. *Accept Anxiety.* Anxiety is a natural outcome of experience with fear-provoking situations and can never be completely eliminated. Most things we fear don't turn out to be as bad as we imagined them to be. The difference between courage and cowardice is that a courageous person accepts fear and goes ahead in spite of it, while the coward lets himself be overcome by it. Remember Franklin Roosevelt's words: "We have nothing to fear but fear itself." It is reasonable and natural to feel fearful in the face of unpredictable, difficult, or threatening situations.

It is only when anxiety gets to become unreasonable that you should be concerned. If you experience *free-floating anxiety,* that is to say, a feeling of fear or dread that doesn't attach to any one particular thing but which seems to invade the whole of your life, then you need to do something about it. And a refuge in drugs, alcohol, inaction, or aimlessly watching TV all day won't help.

3. *Minimize Use of Defense Mechanisms.* All of us have conscious or unconscious ways of coping with anxiety. Many of these ways are realistic.

If you are anxious about an examination, you study for it. If you are prepared, you feel less anxious. And if you do well, you won't be so anxious the next time. Suppose you do badly. You are now more anxious than ever, and you seem to have no realistic way of doing anything about it.

When we are anxious and we have no obvious way to do something about it, we are inclined to try to fool ourselves in various ways. You might convince yourself, for example, that the exam was unfair or that you were poorly prepared in high school for work at this level. This takes the blame away from you and externalizes it.

Adjustments of this sort are called *defense mechanisms*. They mainly defend against anxiety, but also against feelings of inferiority and worthlessness. We all use them to a certain degree, but if you come to depend upon them to the exclusion of realistic solutions of problems, you are in trouble.

Rationalization is the most obvious defense mechanism. Failing an exam because you didn't study and accepting the blame for it makes you anxious or uncomfortable. But if you can put it down to the incompetence of the grading assistant, you feel better about it. And you are relieved of the responsibility of doing something about it. You don't have to study harder, because if it is the grading assistant, there is nothing you can do about it.

Projection is imputing to others the motives or faults that lie in ourselves. If, for example, you have a strong desire to cheat on an exam but are unwilling to admit it to yourself, you may be unduly suspicious of others and accuse them of cheating even when there is no evidence for it. Or if you are angry at someone but cannot admit your anger because you have been taught that you shouldn't feel angry, you may project your anger on to someone else and accuse that person of being hostile to you.

Displacement is directing our feelings toward something or someone else other than the true cause of them. If you are angry at someone you are not supposed to be angry at, you may displace your feelings toward something or someone it is safe to be angry at. If you are mad at your instructor because he humiliated you with severe criticism, you may pick a fight with your roommate.

Fantasy is what we engage in when we daydream. It is a common defense against anxiety, especially among adolescents. Because it can be enormously satisfying in its own right, it often becomes an obsession. Because the hard work of studying may make you anxious, you may substitute daydreaming, thinking of satisfactions that you do not have in the real world. Almost every college student spends some appreciable time daydreaming. If daydreaming is used as a substitute for problem solving and if the inadequacies of the real world are replaced by the ideals of daydreams, it can be dangerous.

Identification occurs when we substitute someone else's achievements and goals for our own. We do that when we identify with groups which we belong to or are associated with. Take, for example, our college's basketball team. When the team wins, we feel more worthwhile. We also identify with other persons. This is a natural and useful kind of adjustment until it becomes a complete substitute for taking pleasure in our own achievements and working toward our own unique set of goals.

These and other defense mechanisms are often harmless and convenient ways of reducing life's stress and making our lives richer and more interesting. But if they become a substitute for working to eliminate the source of our stresses and are used to sidestep persistent and severe problems, they can be a source of real trouble. They attack the symptom—anxiety—rather than the cause. Hence, resorting to them to deal with a chronic problem not only postpones but probably increases the severity of the problem. Finally, they have a way of breaking down under severe stress, with the result that a person is suddenly flooded with feelings of anxiety or depression. These *anxiety attacks*, as they are often called, can be very uncomfortable, and they sometimes totally incapacitate a person.

4. *Understand Motives.* Defenses are sometimes ways of fooling yourself about your own motives. You would be better off recognizing them as such and trying to understand your own motives. When your grades are poor, it is easy to blame everyone but yourself—your instructor, a bad cold, family problems, etc. But you need to ask yourself, What do I really want? An honest answer might be that you

want good grades all right, but without having to work for them. If you admit this to yourself, you can see that some combination of goals is usually unattainable. You cannot be the sparkling center of the social life of your fraternity or sorority and at the same time suppose that you can achieve grades good enough to get you into the Harvard Law School. You have to decide what you are willing to compromise to achieve some particular goal. It is a general rule of life that we cannot have everything we want, and rather than let circumstances decide what you get, it would be better to decide yourself.

5. **Alter Goals Appropriately.** One of the reasons for trying to understand your own motives is so that you can alter them appropriately. Often our goals come not from ourselves but from other people, and when we recognize that we may want to change them. Fred, for example, came to college with the idea of being a doctor, only to be frustrated by his lack of interest in premedical courses. In the middle of his sophomore year, his anxiety, under the difficulties he experienced in organic chemistry, reached the acute stage. He sought help at the counseling center, where after a few sessions, he became aware that medicine was a goal his parents set for him and that being a doctor was not what he wanted for himself. He was able to see that his poor performance in premed courses was in part an unconscious rebellion against his parents' goal. Though he had to face a row with his parents, he set his career goals toward things that were closer to his own interests and abilities.

6. **Learn to Postpone Satisfactions.** When two motives conflict, one way to resolve the conflict is to postpone the satisfaction of one of them. This is another way of taking control over your own life rather than letting circumstances and other people control it for you. Most college students are used to postponing satisfactions in large ways, because, in a sense, the price of being in college for most students is that they must postpone some material rewards. But we have to do that on a daily basis too. If you're going to take the time to participate in student government, or work on the paper, you have to postpone something to make the time. Or maybe it is the other way around. You may want to drop out of working on the school paper because it is taking too much

time. The point is, examine your options and choose one. If you don't, circumstances will do it for you.

7. **Build up Frustration Tolerance.** If you postpone something you want, it frustrates you. Therefore, you have to learn to tolerate frustration. Tolerating frustration, like the acceptance of anxiety, is the mark of a mature, well-adjusted person. We can't always get what we want when we want it, and we're usually happier if we stop fretting about it.

Frustration tolerance, like habits and attitudes, is acquired by experience. It is easiest to train ourselves to it with the little things—failing to find a parking space, or waiting for a late friend. When you can accept and experience frustration with reasonable grace, you will find your life to be pleasanter. Once frustration is accepted for what it is, it is not nearly so unpleasant.

8. **Learn to Express Emotions.** Some personal problems arise because people try to hold down their emotions, especially hostile ones. Many people learn through early training to become fearful of acting assertively and expressing their feelings. Well-adjusted people, on the other hand, express their feelings openly where appropriate. They achieve a balance between excessive and inconsiderate display of feelings and complete restraint. The best way of achieving this balance is to develop socially acceptable ways of showing your feelings. It is possible to say what displeases you without losing your temper, and it is better to do that than to go around feeling put upon and martyred.

9. **Keep Busy.** Keeping occupied with useful work or other activities is another mark of the well-adjusted person. This doesn't mean that you are forever running around frantically doing things. But it does mean doing things so that you have some sense of satisfaction from accomplishment. And it means that you have enough to do to keep you from ruminating on your troubles or spending the whole day in idle daydreaming. Work by itself is not a cure for emotional problems, but it often does keep us from making those problems worse, and it provides deep satisfaction in its own right.

All these dos and don'ts sound a little old-fashioned in an age in which we are supposed to be free to do what we want to. But the idea that we are completely free to do whatever is in our power is a delusion. The minute we do one thing, we make it impossible to do something else. If you are going to study organic chemistry, you can't spend the evening getting mellow on alcohol or high on marijuana. And if you don't recognize your own real self—your goals, aspirations, prejudices, sexual feelings, emotions, abilities—you will end up being victimized by your ignorance.

If you are really at sea about yourself, insecure and unable to determine what it is you want, reading this or any other book won't help very much. You need to explore your problems with the kind of give-and-take that occurs in a personal or group counseling situation. It doesn't matter so much what the setting is—health services, a psychological clinic, your physician's office, or a church—as it does that you recognize you have a problem you can't solve on your own.

College isn't training for life; it is life. This book has been about coping with the intellectual demands of college because these are the central purposes of college. You can't meet those demands unless you have both the skills to apply to them and the personal adjustment to free you to do so.

INDEX

PROVISIONAL WORKING SCHEDULE

Time \ Day	Monday	Tuesday	Wednesday	Thursday	Friday	Saturday	Sunday
7:00							
8:00							
8:30							
9:00							
9:30							
10:00							
10:30							
11:00							
11:30							
12:00							
12:30							
1:00							
1:30							
2:00							
2:30							
3:00							
3:30							
4:00							
4:30							
5:00							
5:30							
6:00							
6:30							
7:00							
7:30							
8:00							
8:30							
9:00							
9:30							
10:00							
10:30							
11:00							

PROVISIONAL WORKING SCHEDULE

Time \ Day	Monday	Tuesday	Wednesday	Thursday	Friday	Saturday	Sunday
7:00							
8:00							
8:30							
9:00							
9:30							
10:00							
10:30							
11:00							
11:30							
12:00							
12:30							
1:00							
1:30							
2:00							
2:30							
3:00							
3:30							
4:00							
4:30							
5:00							
5:30							
6:00							
6:30							
7:00							
7:30							
8:00							
8:30							
9:00							
9:30							
10:00							
10:30							
11:00							

FINAL WORKING SCHEDULE

Time \ Day	Monday	Tuesday	Wednesday	Thursday	Friday	Saturday	Sunday
7:00							
8:00							
8:30							
9:00							
9:30							
10:00							
10:30							
11:00							
11:30							
12:00							
12:30							
1:00							
1:30							
2:00							
2:30							
3:00							
3:30							
4:00							
4:30							
5:00							
5:30							
6:00							
6:30							
7:00							
7:30							
8:00							
8:30							
9:00							
9:30							
10:00							
10:30							
11:00							

122788

FINAL WORKING SCHEDULE

Time \ Day	Monday	Tuesday	Wednesday	Thursday	Friday	Saturday	Sunday
7:00							
8:00							
8:30							
9:00							
9:30							
10:00							
10:30							
11:00							
11:30							
12:00							
12:30							
1:00							
1:30							
2:00							
2:30							
3:00							
3:30							
4:00							
4:30							
5:00							
5:30							
6:00							
6:30							
7:00							
7:30							
8:00							
8:30							
9:00							
9:30							
10:00							
10:30							
11:00							